FIRST YEAR OUT

A Transition Story

By Sabrina Symington

Jessica Kingsley Publishers
London and Philadelphia

For my mom and dad, who have supported me through every single thing I have ever done.

And for my Adam, who made me whole, and who taught me to see myself as I truly am.

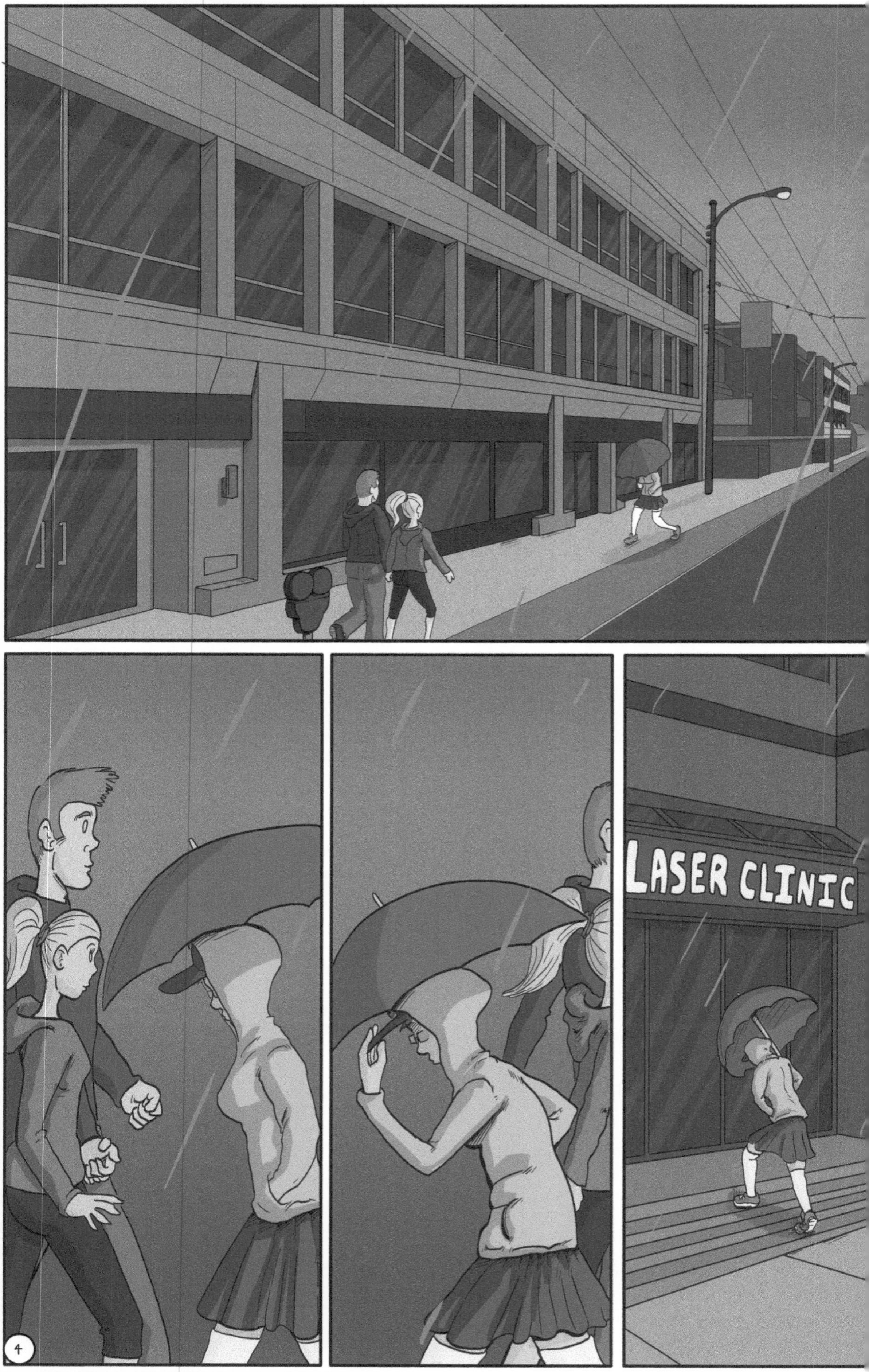
LASER CLINIC

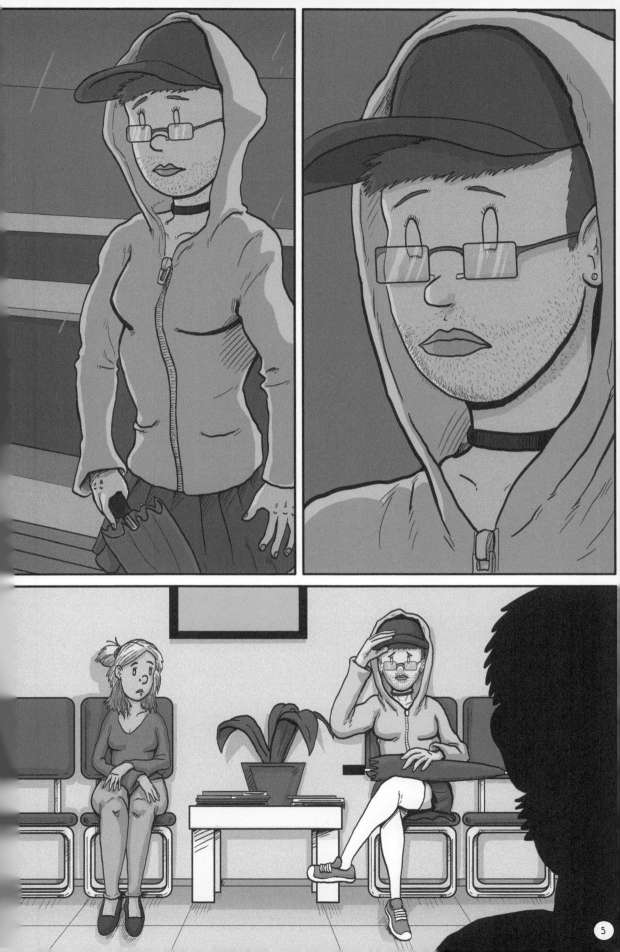

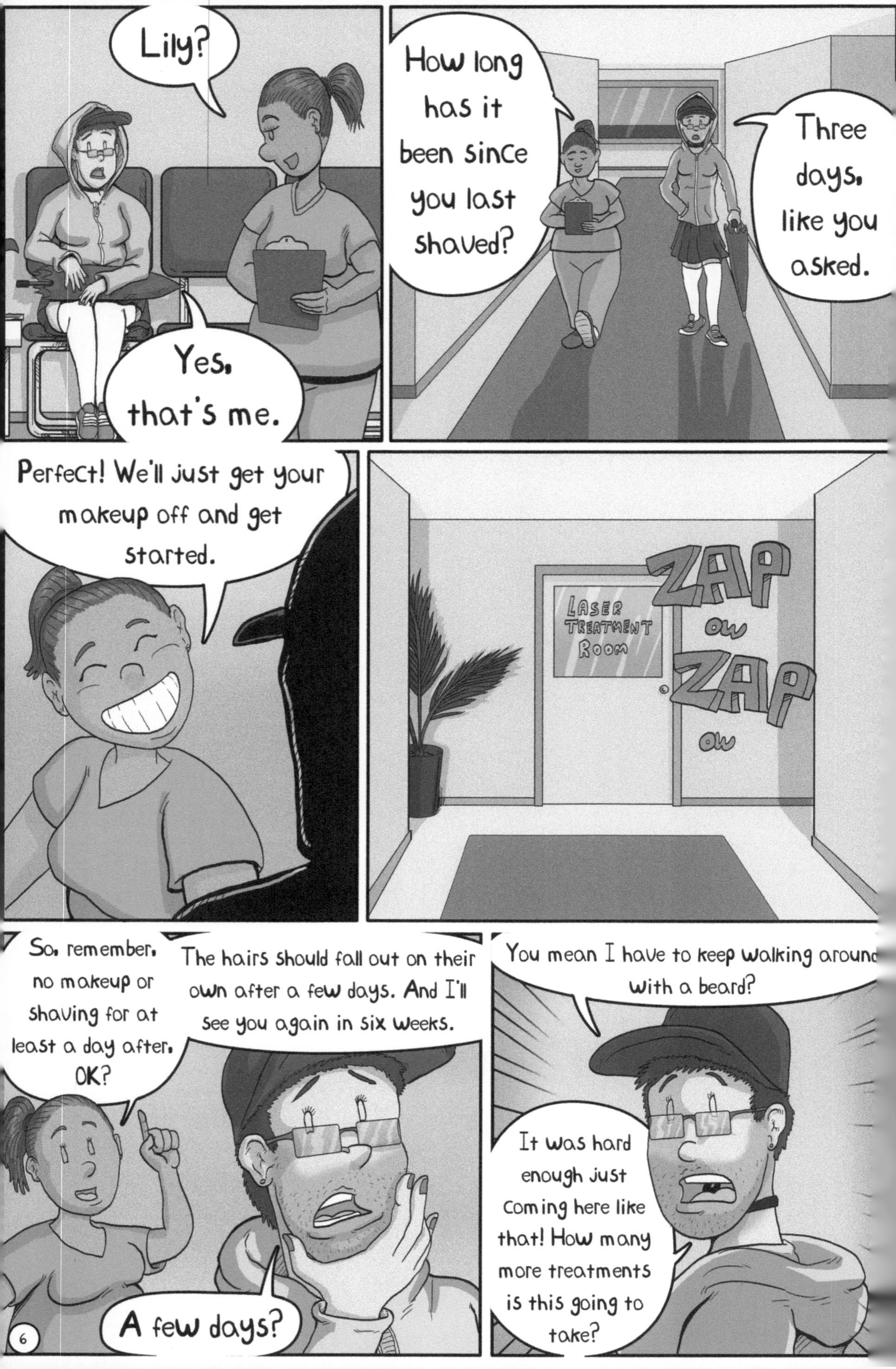

Lily?
Yes, that's me.
How long has it been since you last shaved?
Three days, like you asked.
Perfect! We'll just get your makeup off and get started.
LASER TREATMENT ROOM
ZAP
ow
ZAP
ow
So, remember, no makeup or shaving for at least a day after, OK?
The hairs should fall out on their own after a few days. And I'll see you again in six weeks.
A few days?
You mean I have to keep walking around with a beard?
It was hard enough just coming here like that! How many more treatments is this going to take?

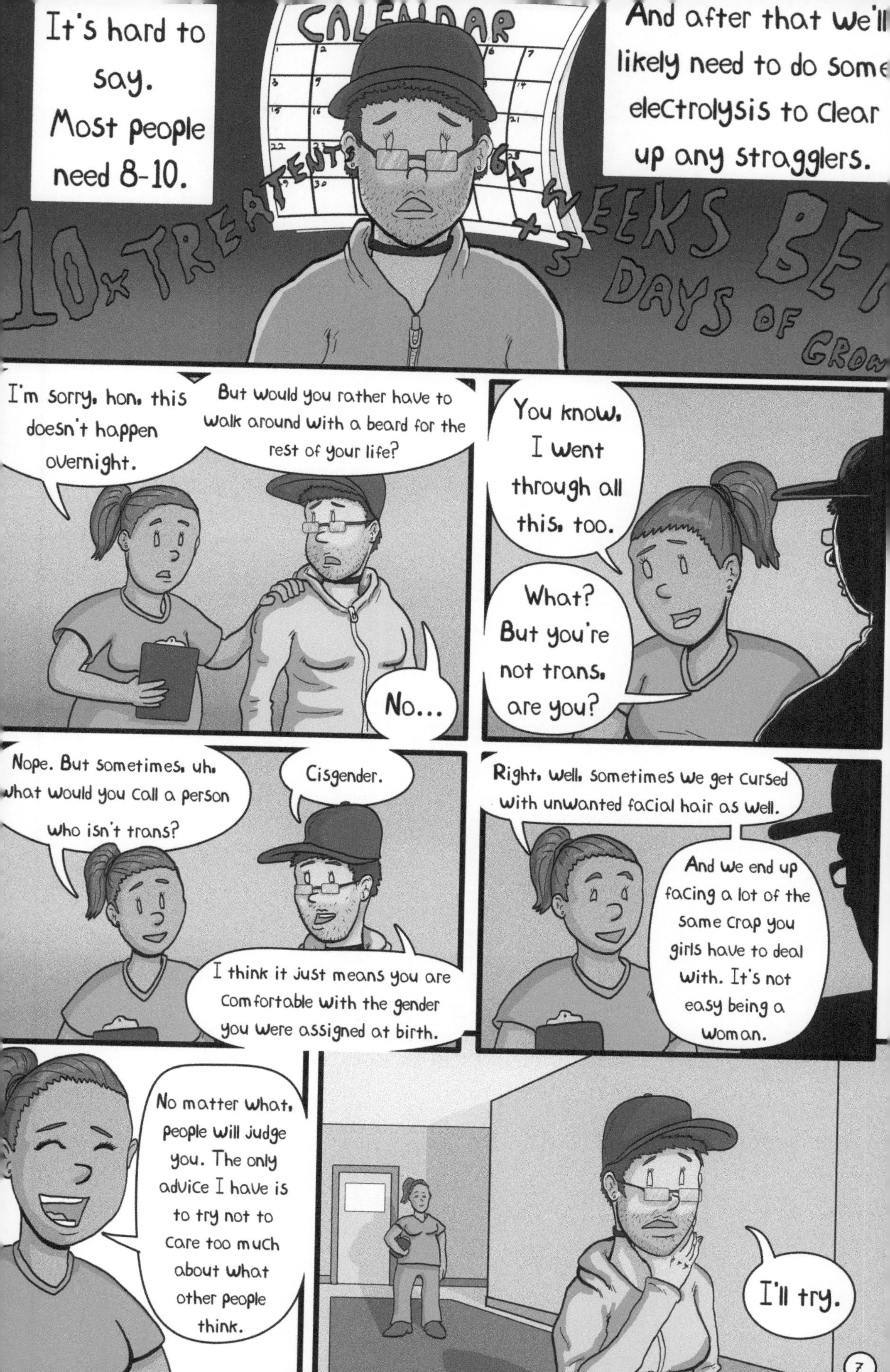
It's hard to say. Most people need 8-10.
CALENDAR
10x TREATENTS
6x WEEKS
+3 DAYS OF GROW
And after that we'll likely need to do some electrolysis to clear up any stragglers.
I'm sorry, hon, this doesn't happen overnight.
But would you rather have to walk around with a beard for the rest of your life?
No...
You know, I went through all this, too.
What? But you're not trans, are you?
Nope. But sometimes, uh, what would you call a person who isn't trans?
Cisgender.
I think it just means you are comfortable with the gender you were assigned at birth.
Right, well, sometimes we get cursed with unwanted facial hair as well.
And we end up facing a lot of the same crap you girls have to deal with. It's not easy being a woman.
No matter what, people will judge you. The only advice I have is to try not to care too much about what other people think.
I'll try.

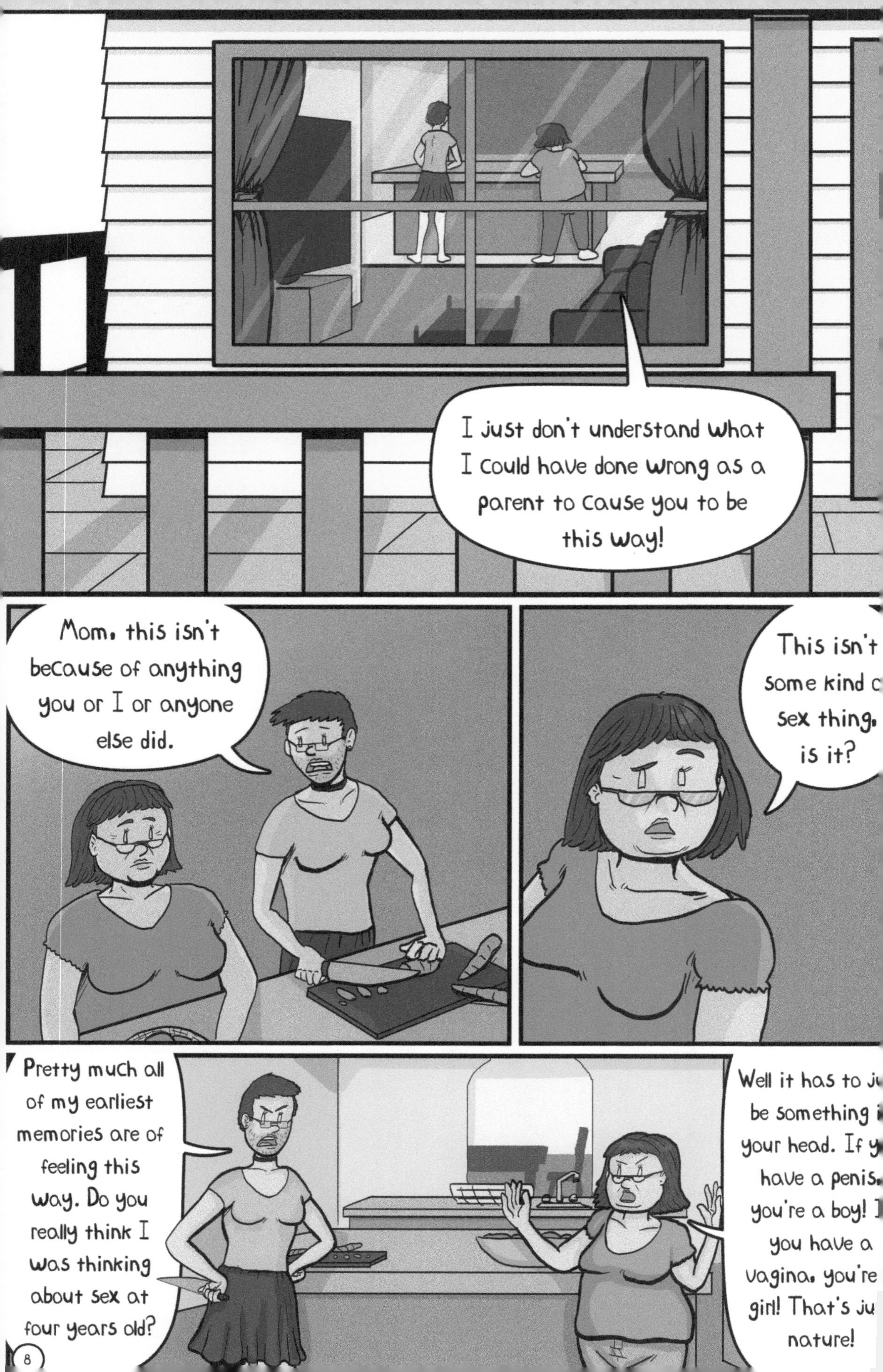
I just don't understand what I could have done wrong as a parent to cause you to be this way!
Mom, this isn't because of anything you or I or anyone else did.
This isn't some kind c sex thing, is it?
Pretty much all of my earliest memories are of feeling this way. Do you really think I was thinking about sex at four years old?
Well it has to ju be something i your head. If y have a penis, you're a boy! I you have a vagina, you're girl! That's ju nature!

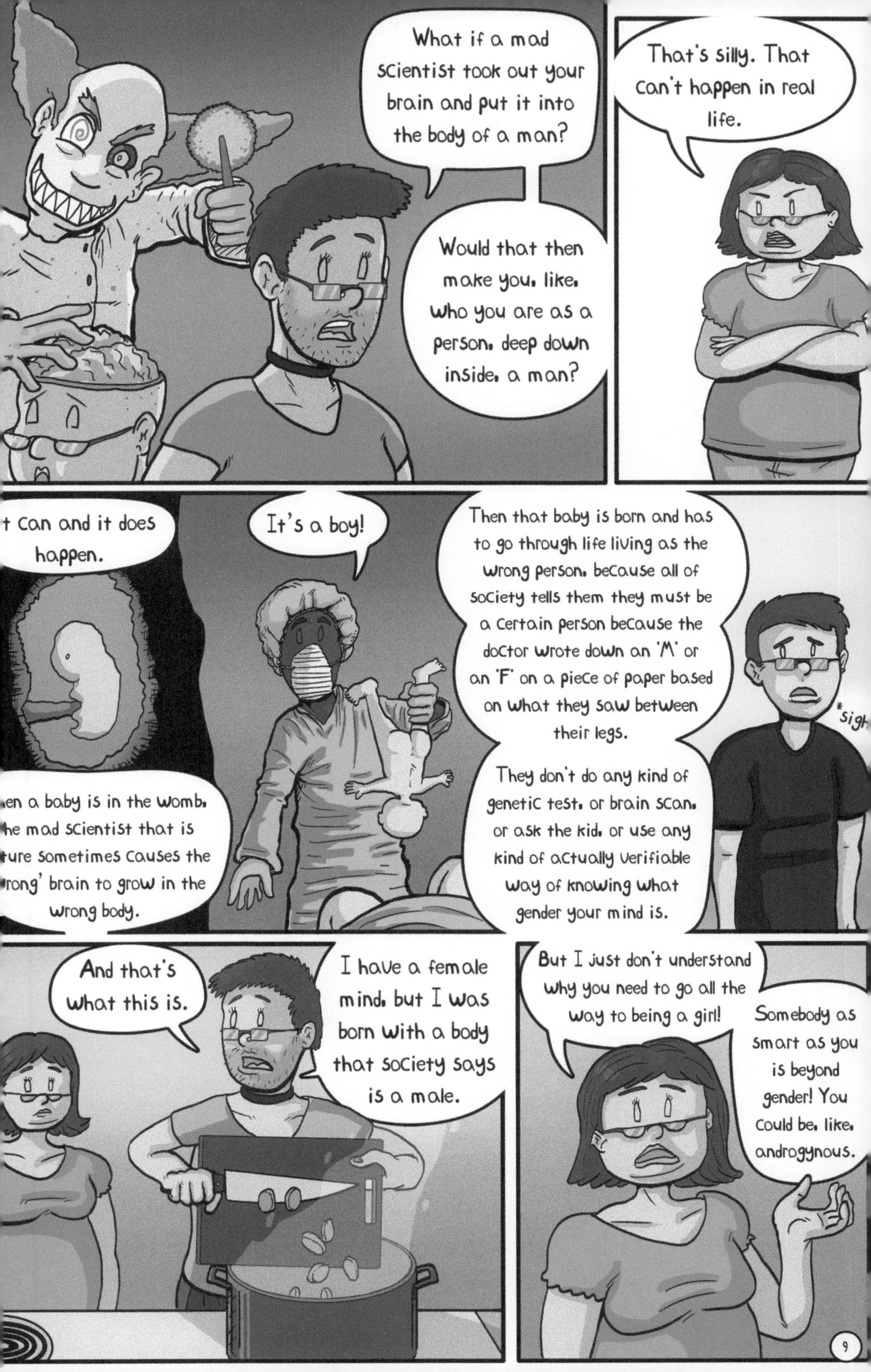

What if a mad scientist took out your brain and put it into the body of a man?
Would that then make you, like, who you are as a person, deep down inside, a man?
That's silly. That can't happen in real life.
t can and it does happen.
en a baby is in the womb, he mad scientist that is ture sometimes causes the rong' brain to grow in the wrong body.
It's a boy!
Then that baby is born and has to go through life living as the wrong person, because all of society tells them they must be a certain person because the doctor wrote down an 'M' or an 'F' on a piece of paper based on what they saw between their legs.
They don't do any kind of genetic test, or brain scan, or ask the kid, or use any kind of actually verifiable way of knowing what gender your mind is.
*sigh
And that's what this is.
I have a female mind, but I was born with a body that society says is a male.
But I just don't understand why you need to go all the way to being a girl!
Somebody as smart as you is beyond gender! You could be, like, androgynous.

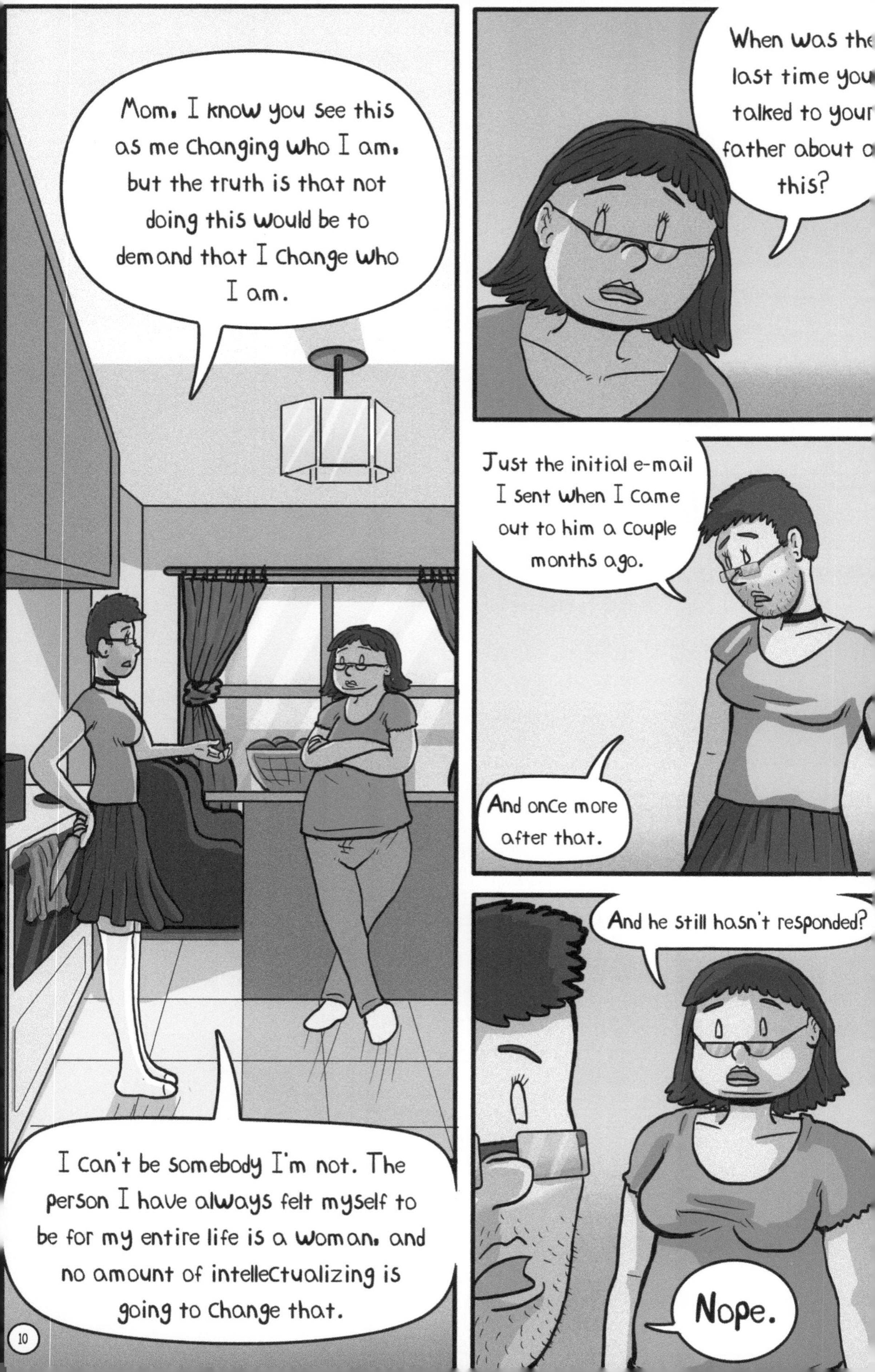
Mom, I know you see this as me changing who I am, but the truth is that not doing this would be to demand that I change who I am.
I can't be somebody I'm not. The person I have always felt myself to be for my entire life is a woman, and no amount of intellectualizing is going to change that.
When was the last time you talked to your father about all this?
Just the initial e-mail I sent when I came out to him a couple months ago.
And once more after that.
And he still hasn't responded?
Nope.

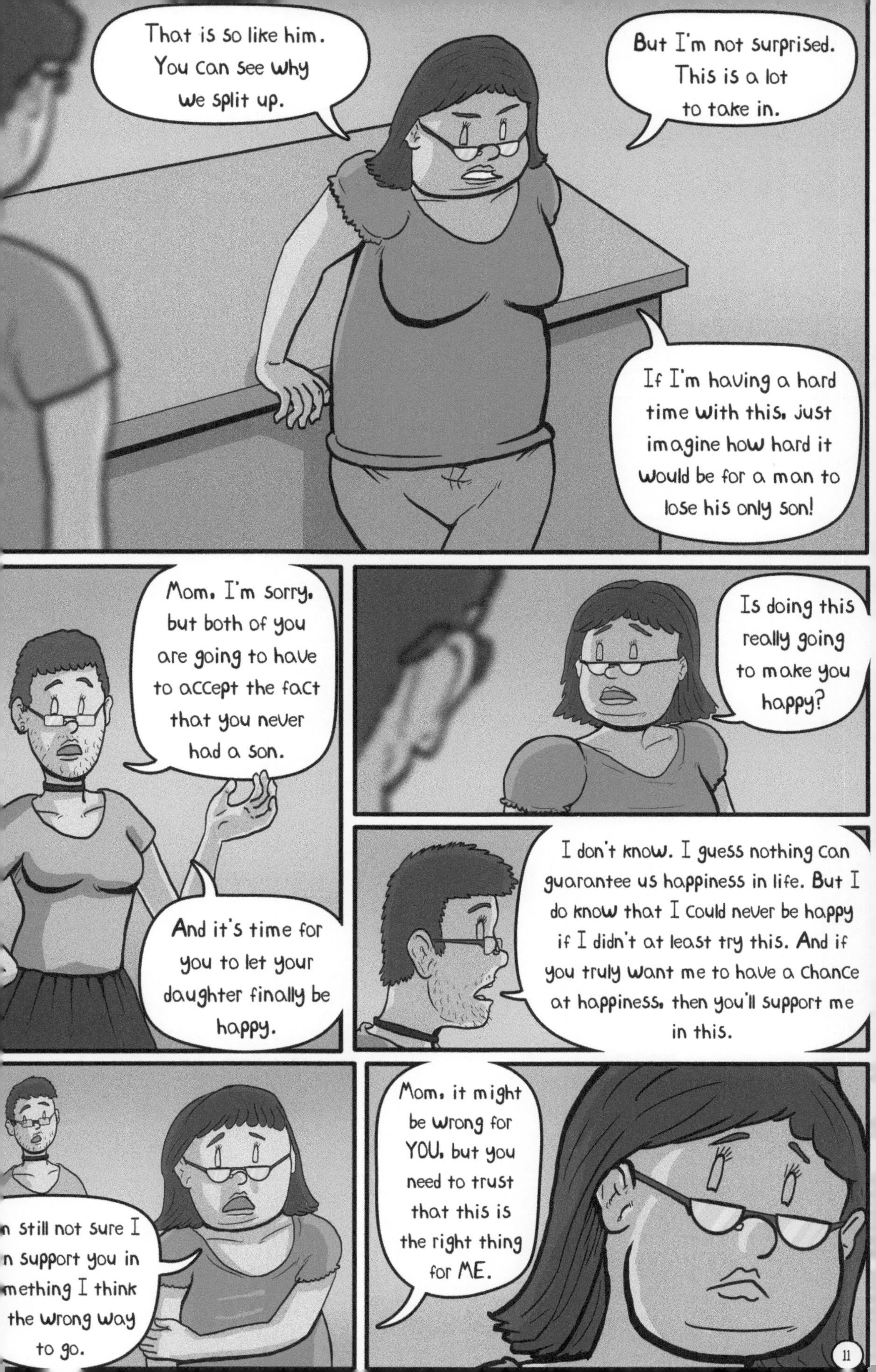
That is so like him. You can see why we split up.
But I'm not surprised. This is a lot to take in.
If I'm having a hard time with this, just imagine how hard it would be for a man to lose his only son!
Mom, I'm sorry, but both of you are going to have to accept the fact that you never had a son.
And it's time for you to let your daughter finally be happy.
Is doing this really going to make you happy?
I don't know. I guess nothing can guarantee us happiness in life. But I do know that I could never be happy if I didn't at least try this. And if you truly want me to have a chance at happiness, then you'll support me in this.
n still not sure I n support you in mething I think the wrong way to go.
Mom, it might be wrong for YOU, but you need to trust that this is the right thing for ME.

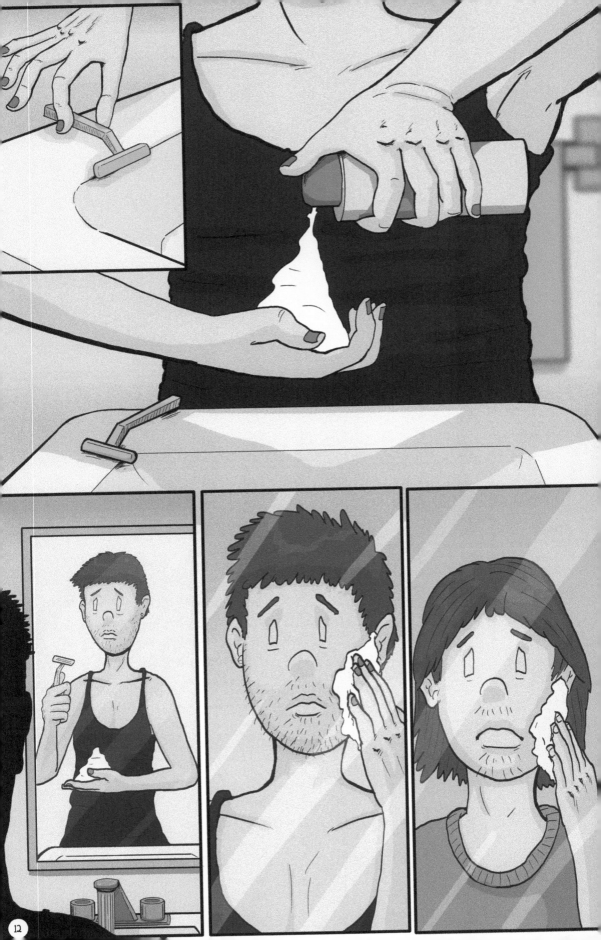

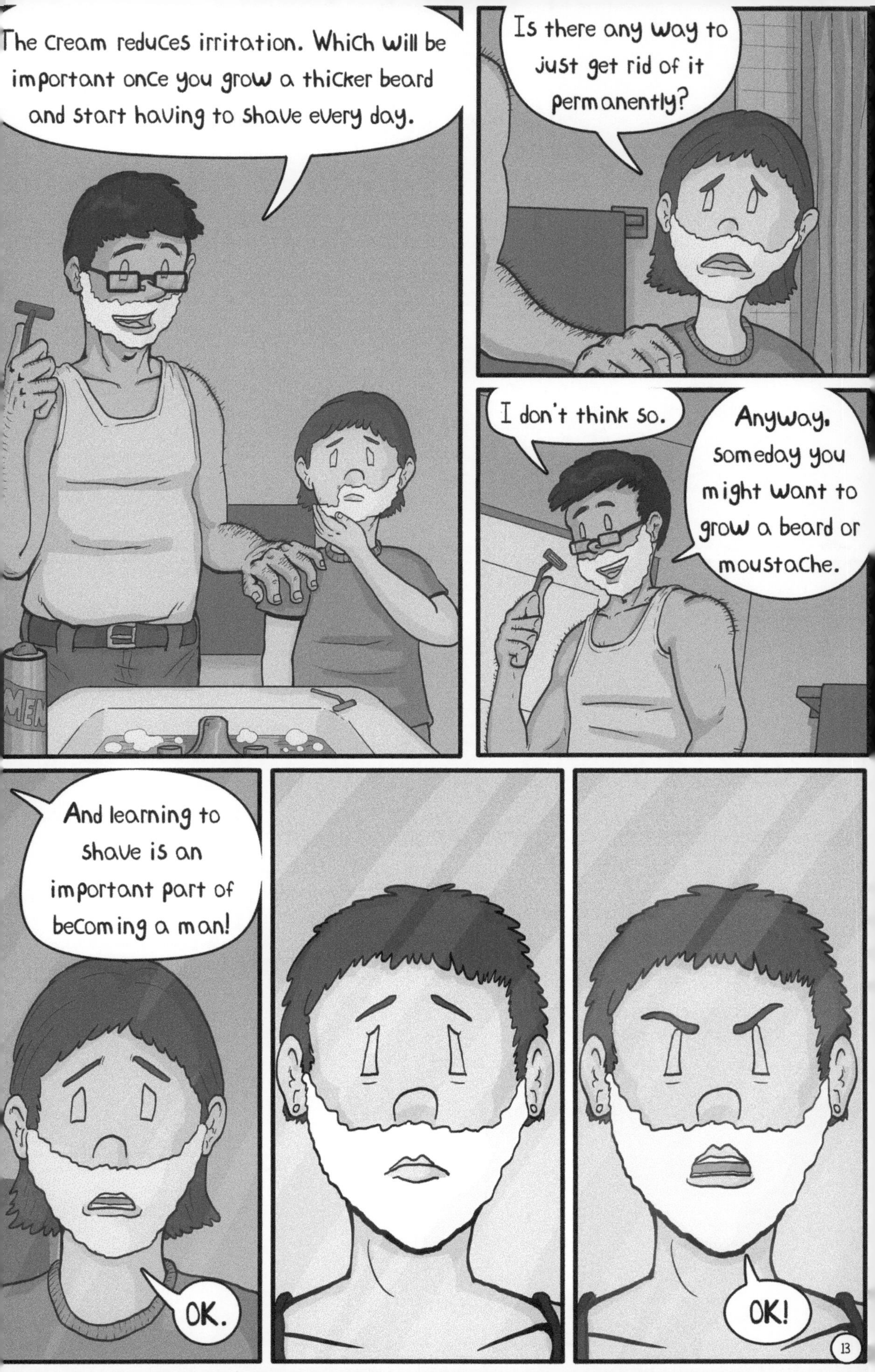
The cream reduces irritation. Which will be important once you grow a thicker beard and start having to shave every day.
MEN
Is there any way to just get rid of it permanently?
I don't think so.
Anyway, someday you might want to grow a beard or moustache.
And learning to shave is an important part of becoming a man!
OK.
OK!

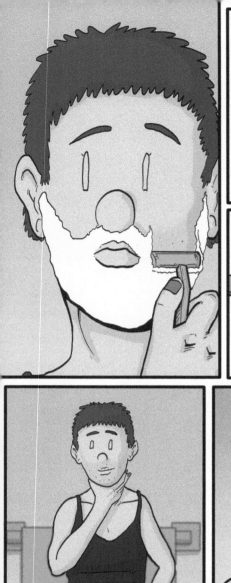

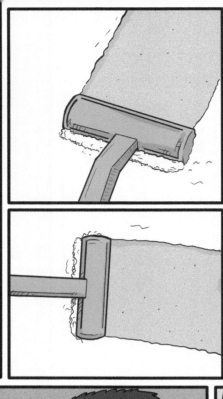

Red lipstick helps neutralize the blue of the beard stubble.

Next, concealer is used t● mask it.

Foundation is used to even everything out.

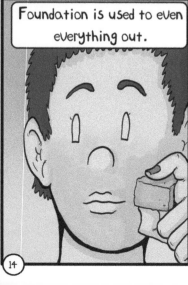

After that it's eyes.

Contouring.

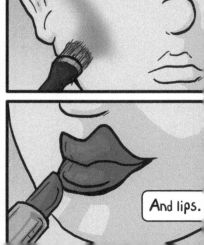

And lips.

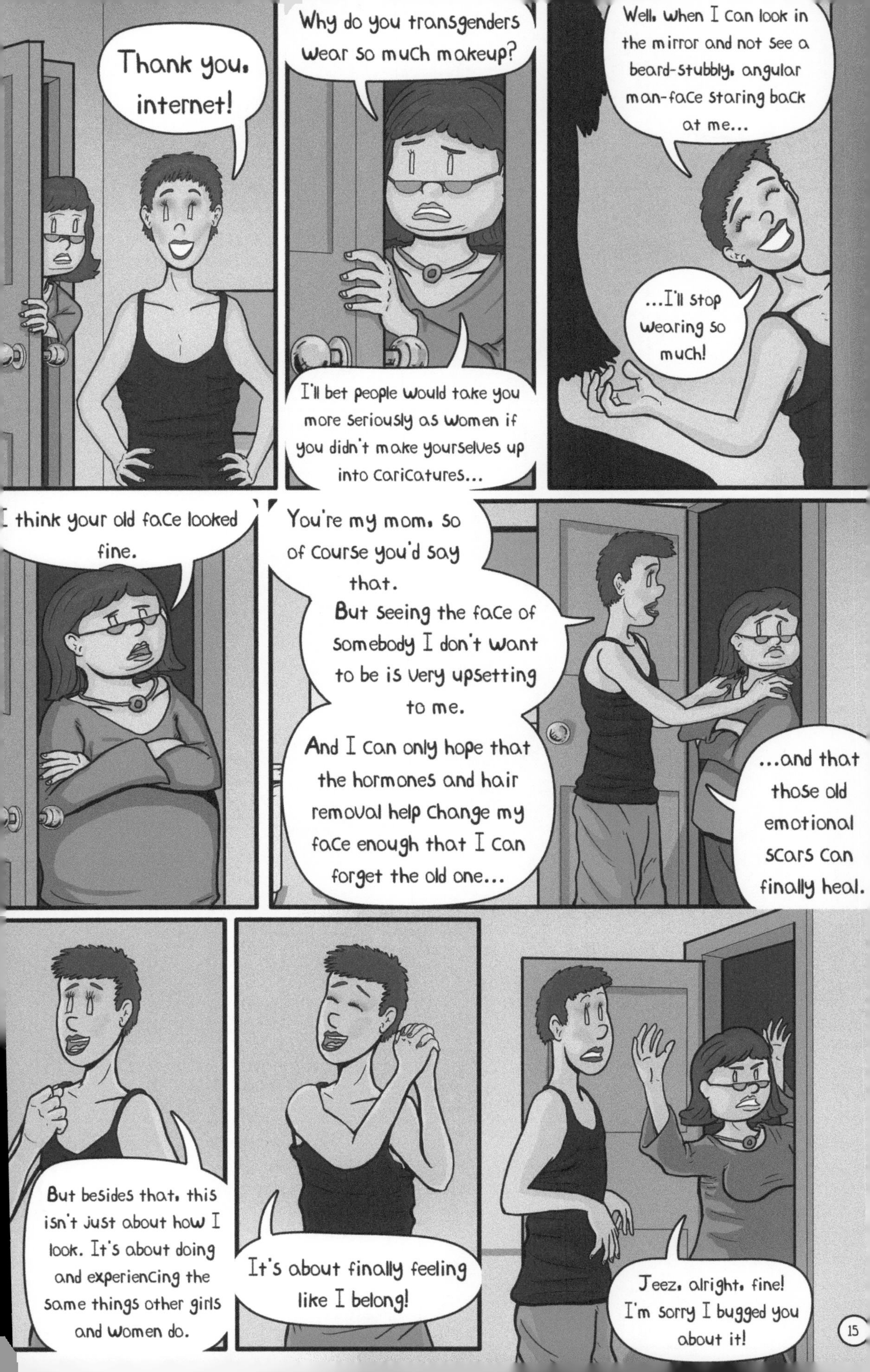

Thank you, internet!
Why do you transgenders wear so much makeup?
I'll bet people would take you more seriously as women if you didn't make yourselves up into caricatures...
Well, when I can look in the mirror and not see a beard-stubbly, angular man-face staring back at me...
...I'll stop wearing so much!
I think your old face looked fine.
You're my mom, so of course you'd say that.
But seeing the face of somebody I don't want to be is very upsetting to me.
And I can only hope that the hormones and hair removal help change my face enough that I can forget the old one...
...and that those old emotional scars can finally heal.
But besides that, this isn't just about how I look. It's about doing and experiencing the same things other girls and women do.
It's about finally feeling like I belong!
Jeez, alright, fine! I'm sorry I bugged you about it!

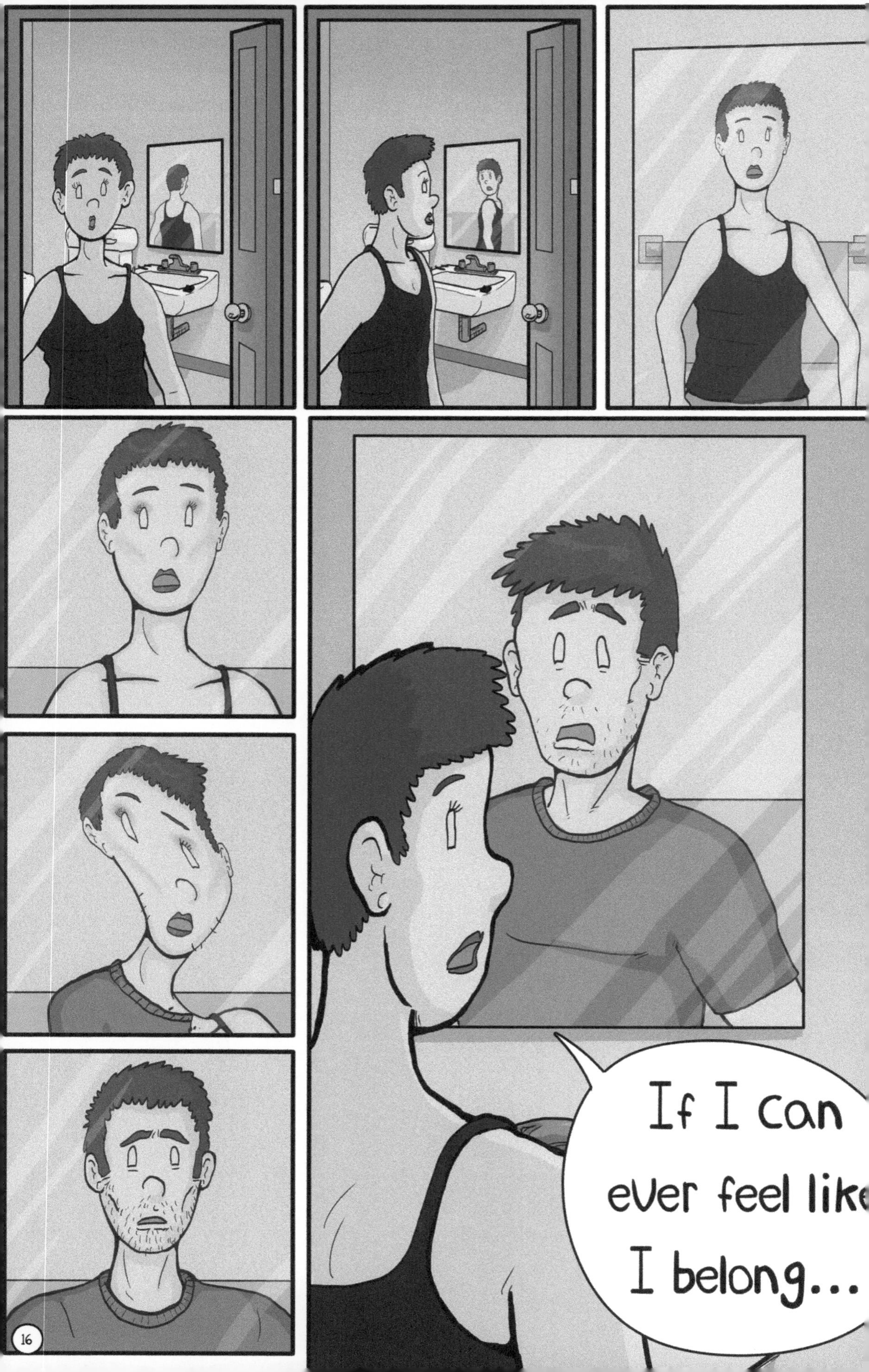
If I can ever feel like I belong...

'Tucking' is the act of pressing one's genitals down to create a smooth, flat presentation of the crotch, like that of a female.

First, the testicles are pressed up inside the body cavity.

Next, the penis is laid flat tightly against the crotch.

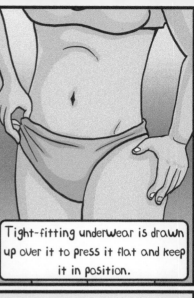

Tight-fitting underwear is drawn up over it to press it flat and keep it in position.

Pulling the back end of the underwear upwards across the buttocks helps keep everything pressed down.

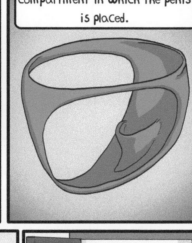

Special underwear can also be purchased which has a small compartment in which the penis is placed.

Tucking not only aids in the public presentation of being female...

...but also reduces the uncomfortable, and often distressing, sensations felt by preoperative transgender women of the penis hanging freely and moving around.

Well, she does look quite good in those pants...

17

Hormone Replacement Therapy is frequently prescribed for transgender individuals to change their body chemistry to match their correct gender.

Estrogen, testosterone blockers, and, occasionally, progesterone, are the drugs typically prescribed to those transitioning to present as female.

Finasteride

Estradi

Spironolactone

Progestero

Softening of Skin and Facial Features

Fat Redistributed to Breasts and Hips

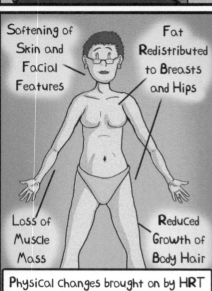

Loss of Muscle Mass

Reduced Growth of Body Hair

Physical changes brought on by HRT can take several years to fully occur, and are mainly limited to soft tissues such as body fat and muscle mass distribution.

Hard structures like adult bones and cartilage cannot be changed by HRT.

Nose and 'Adam's Apple'

Face and Skeletal Structure

Feet a Hand.

But more important than the physical changes are the changes to one's emotional state. Having the incorrect body chemistry for one's brain is extremely stressful, and most transgender patients on HRT report immediate improvements in their mental well-being once HRT has commenced.

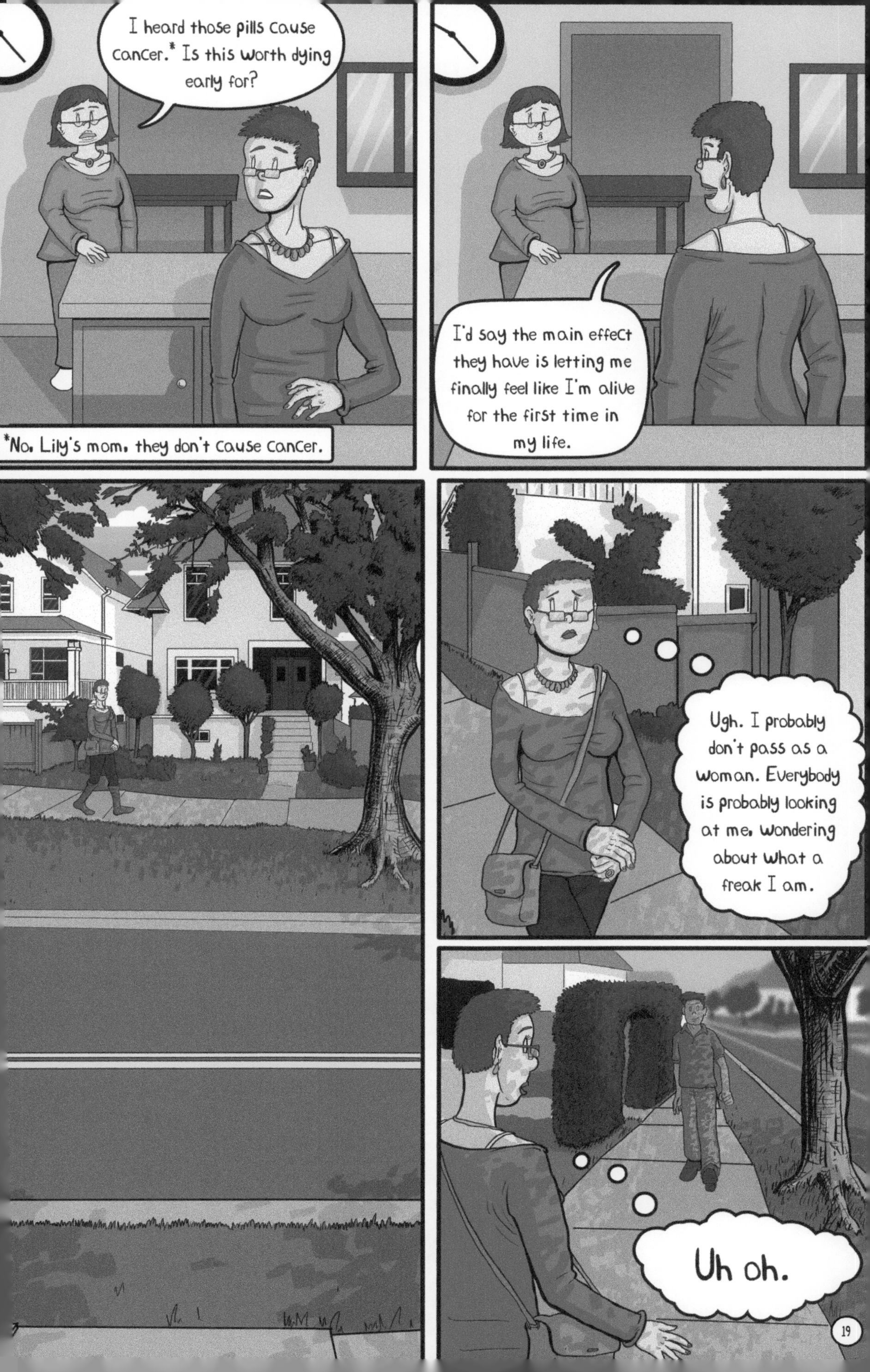

I heard those pills cause cancer.* Is this worth dying early for?
*No, Lily's mom, they don't cause cancer.
I'd say the main effect they have is letting me finally feel like I'm alive for the first time in my life.
Ugh. I probably don't pass as a woman. Everybody is probably looking at me, wondering about what a freak I am.
Uh oh.

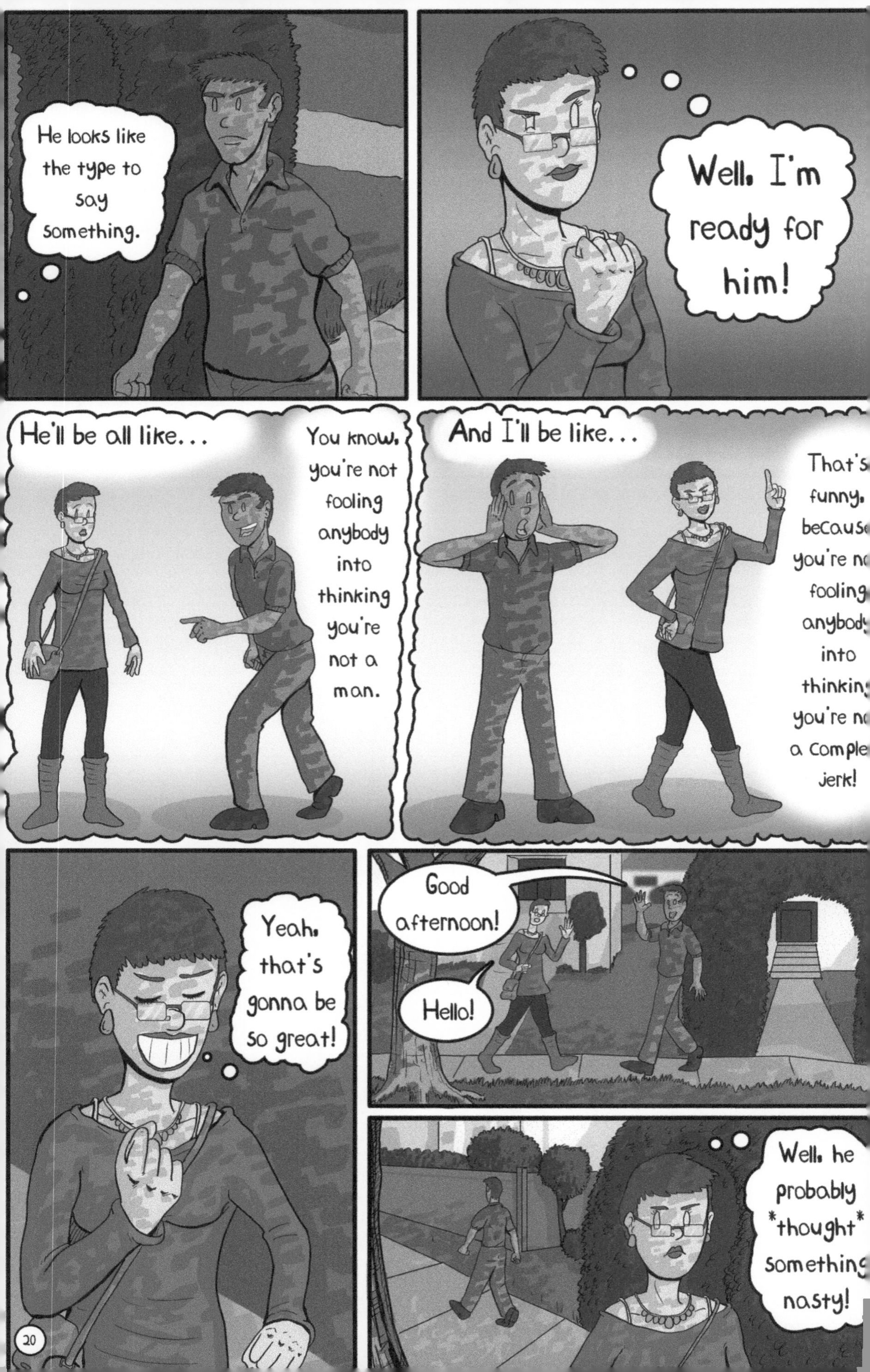
He looks like the type to say something.
Well, I'm ready for him!
He'll be all like...
You know, you're not fooling anybody into thinking you're not a man.
And I'll be like...
That's funny, because you're no fooling anybody into thinking you're no a comple jerk!
Yeah, that's gonna be so great!
Good afternoon!
Hello!
Well, he probably *thought* something nasty!

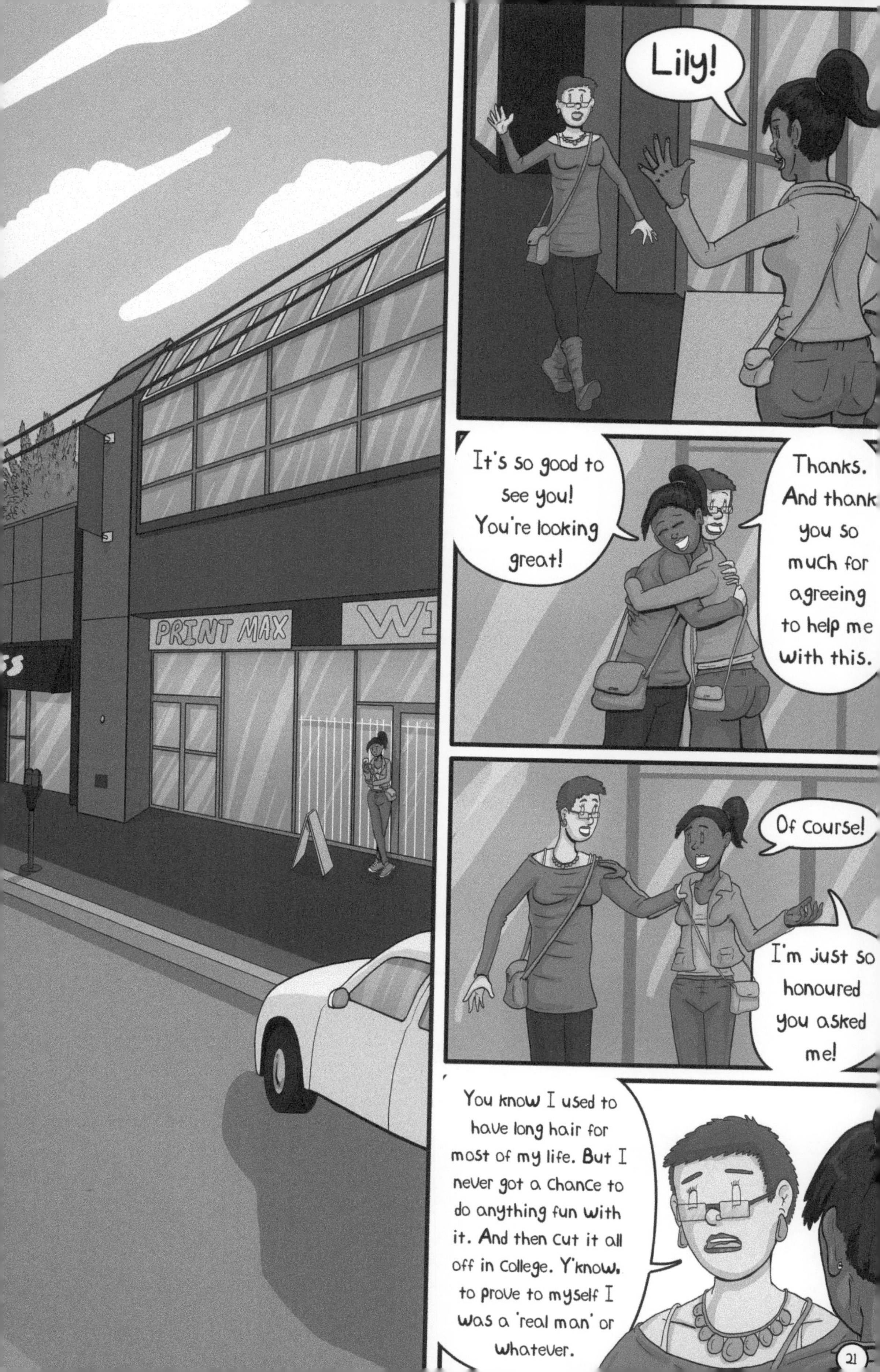
PRINT MAX
Lily!
It's so good to see you! You're looking great!
Thanks. And thank you so much for agreeing to help me with this.
Of course!
I'm just so honoured you asked me!
You know I used to have long hair for most of my life. But I never got a chance to do anything fun with it. And then cut it all off in college. Y'know, to prove to myself I was a 'real man' or whatever.

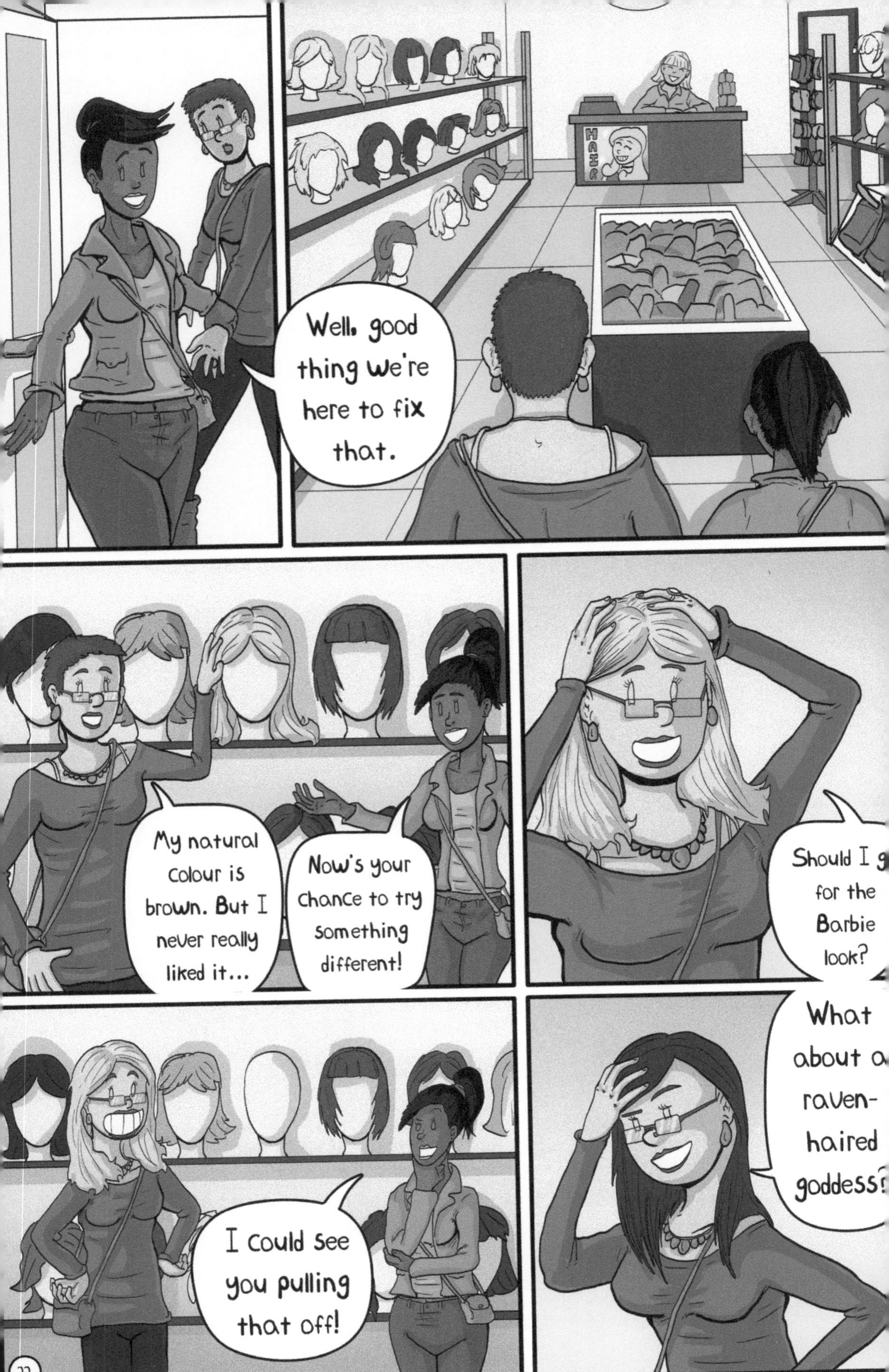
Well, good thing we're here to fix that.
My natural colour is brown. But I never really liked it...
Now's your chance to try something different!
Should I g for the Barbie look?
What about a raven-haired goddess?
I could see you pulling that off!

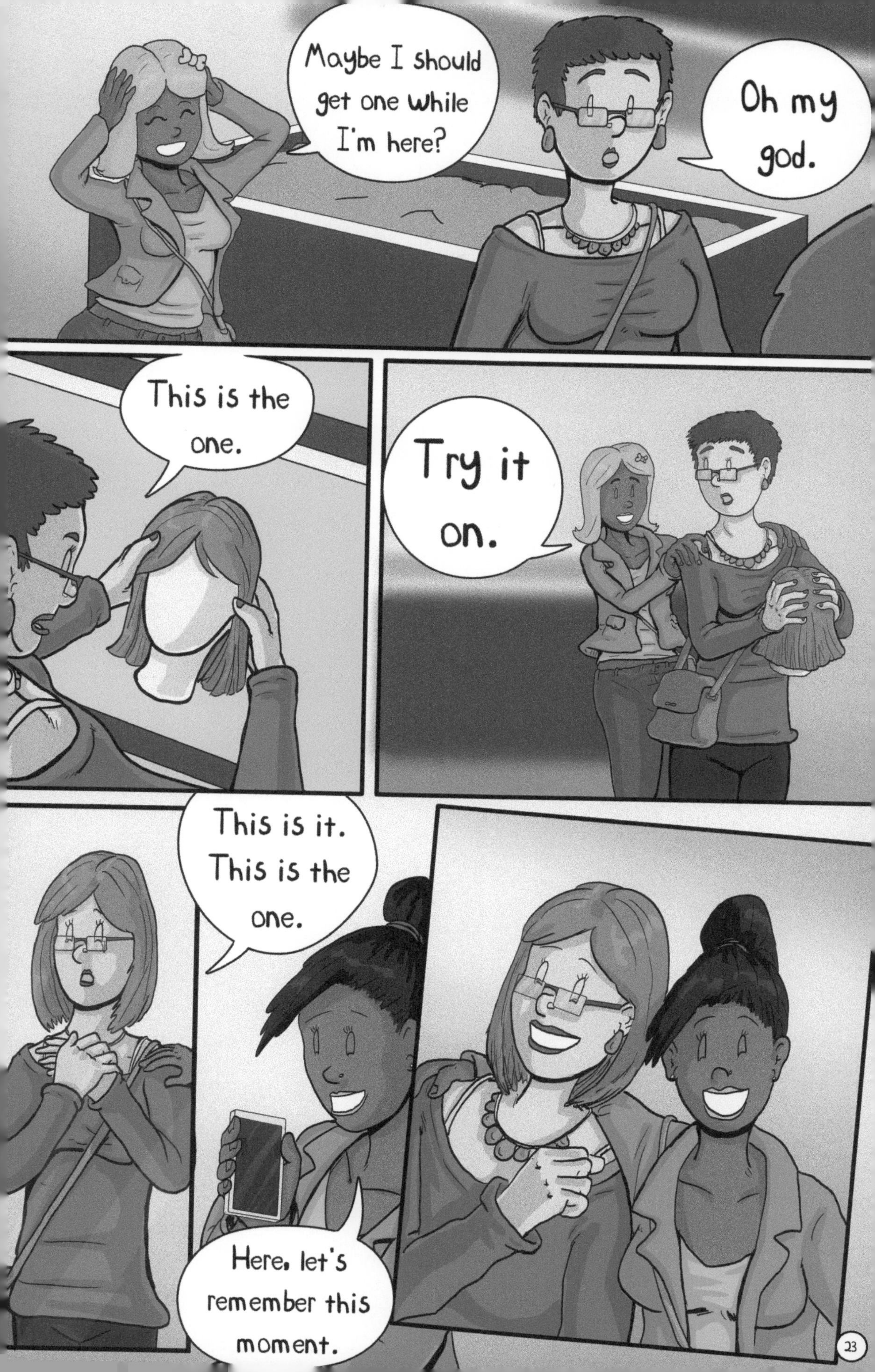
Maybe I should get one while I'm here?
Oh my god.
This is the one.
Try it on.
This is it. This is the one.
Here, let's remember this moment.

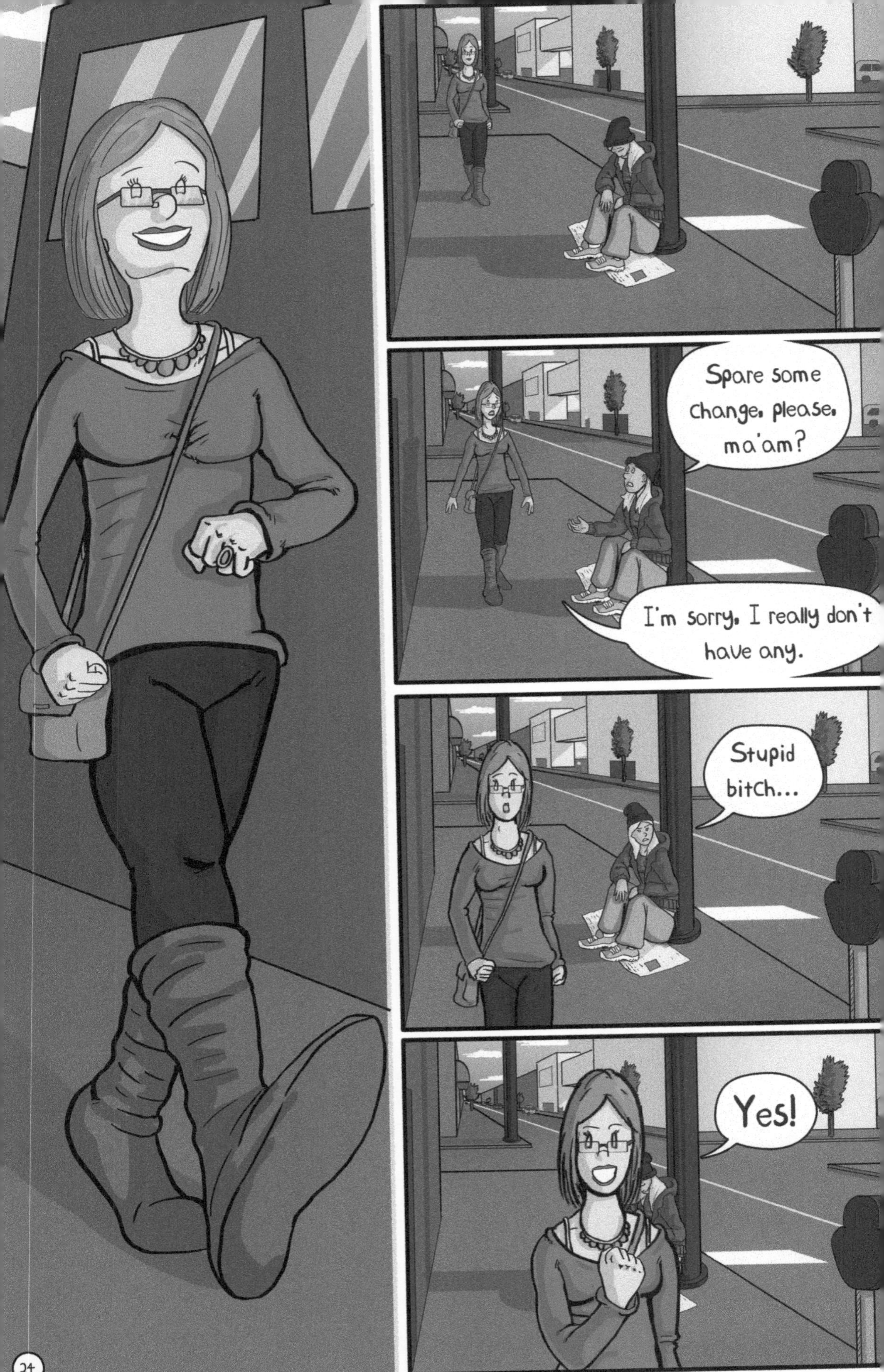
Spare some change, please, ma'am?
I'm sorry, I really don't have any.
Stupid bitch...
Yes!

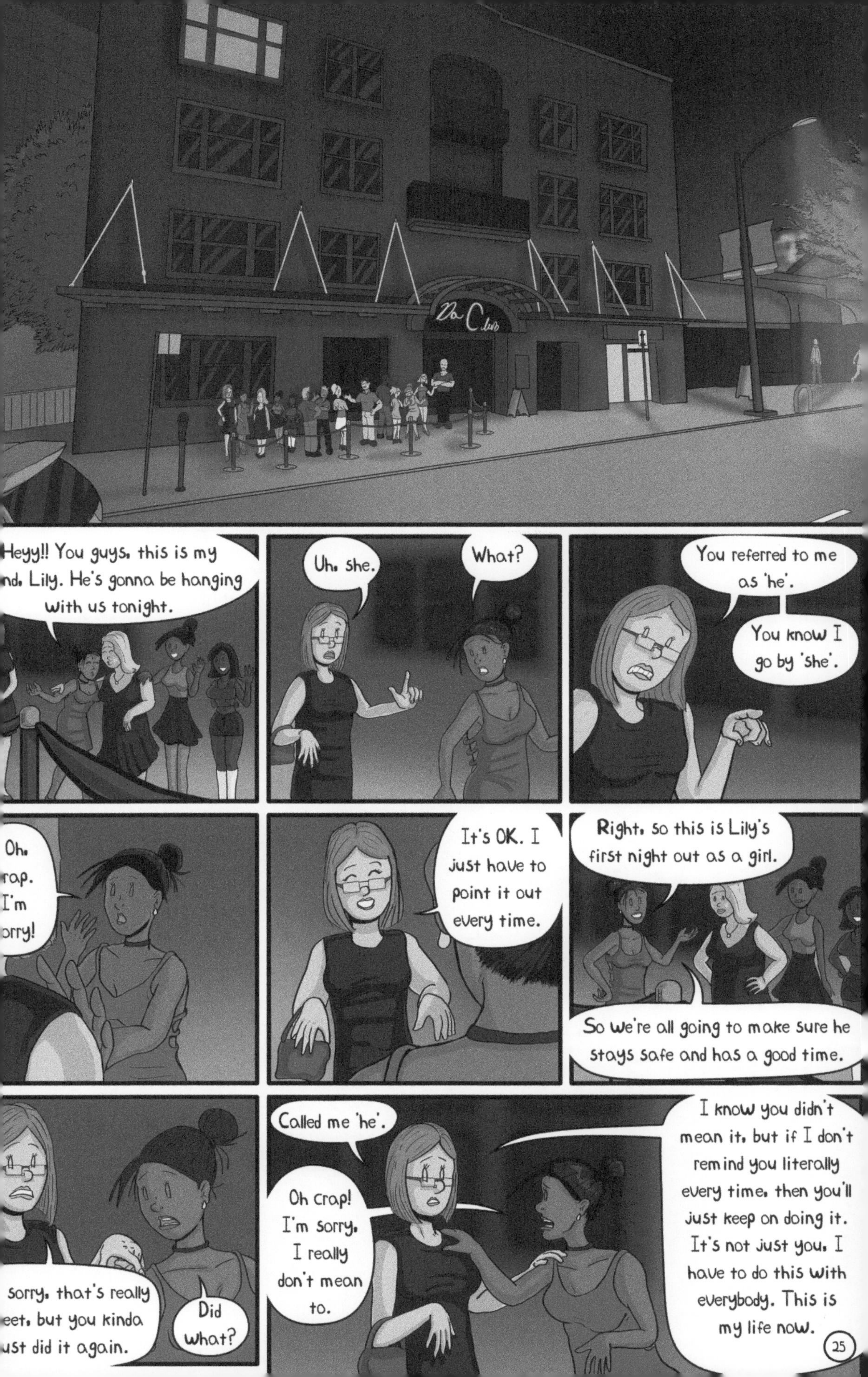
Da Club
Heyy!! You guys, this is my
nd, Lily. He's gonna be hanging with us tonight.
Uh, she.
What?
You referred to me as 'he'.
You know I go by 'she'.
Oh,
rap. I'm
orry!
It's OK. I just have to point it out every time.
Right, so this is Lily's first night out as a girl.
So we're all going to make sure he stays safe and has a good time.
sorry, that's really
eet, but you kinda
ust did it again.
Did what?
Called me 'he'.
Oh crap! I'm sorry. I really don't mean to.
I know you didn't mean it, but if I don't remind you literally every time, then you'll just keep on doing it. It's not just you. I have to do this with everybody. This is my life now.

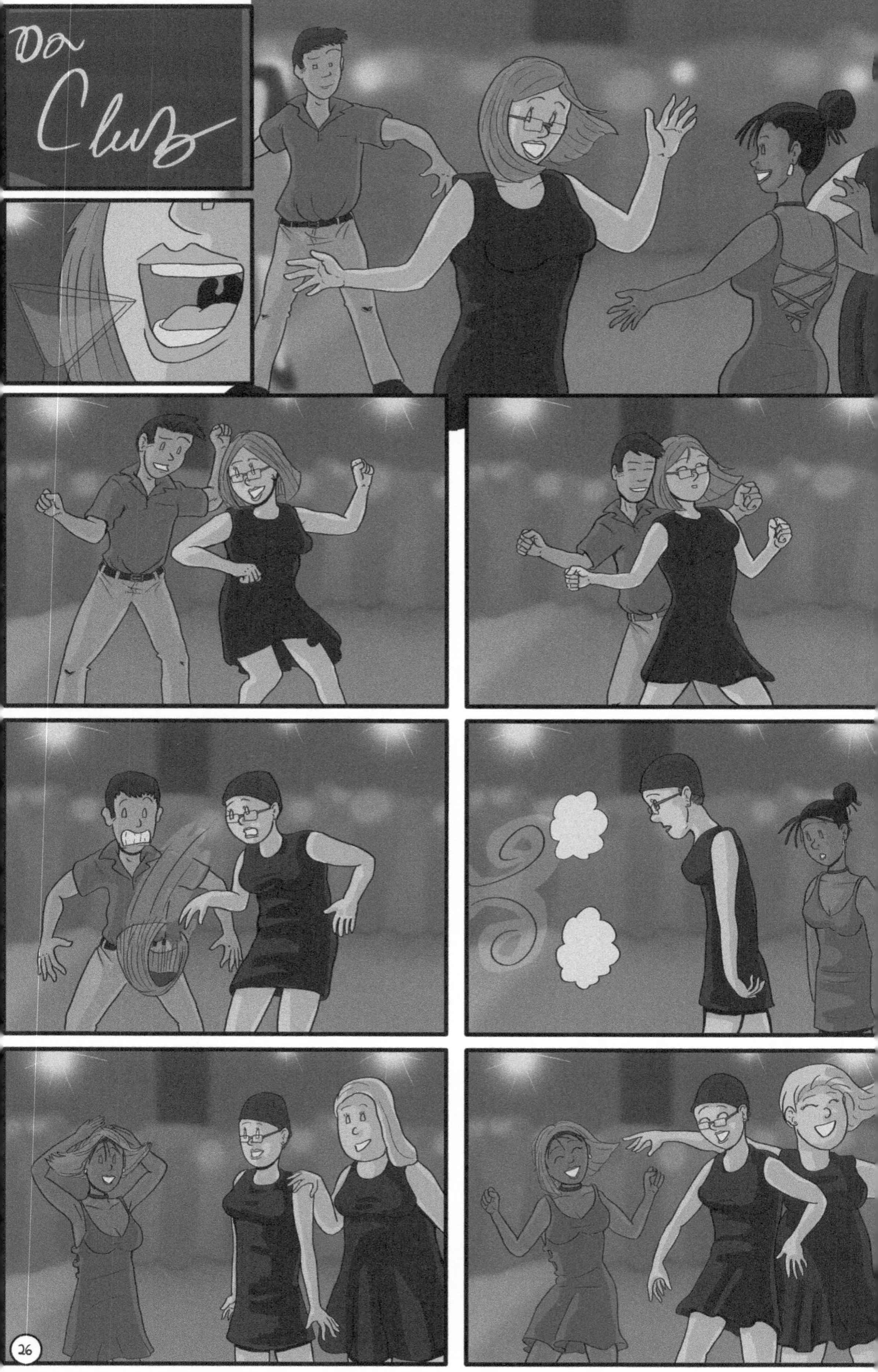
Da Club

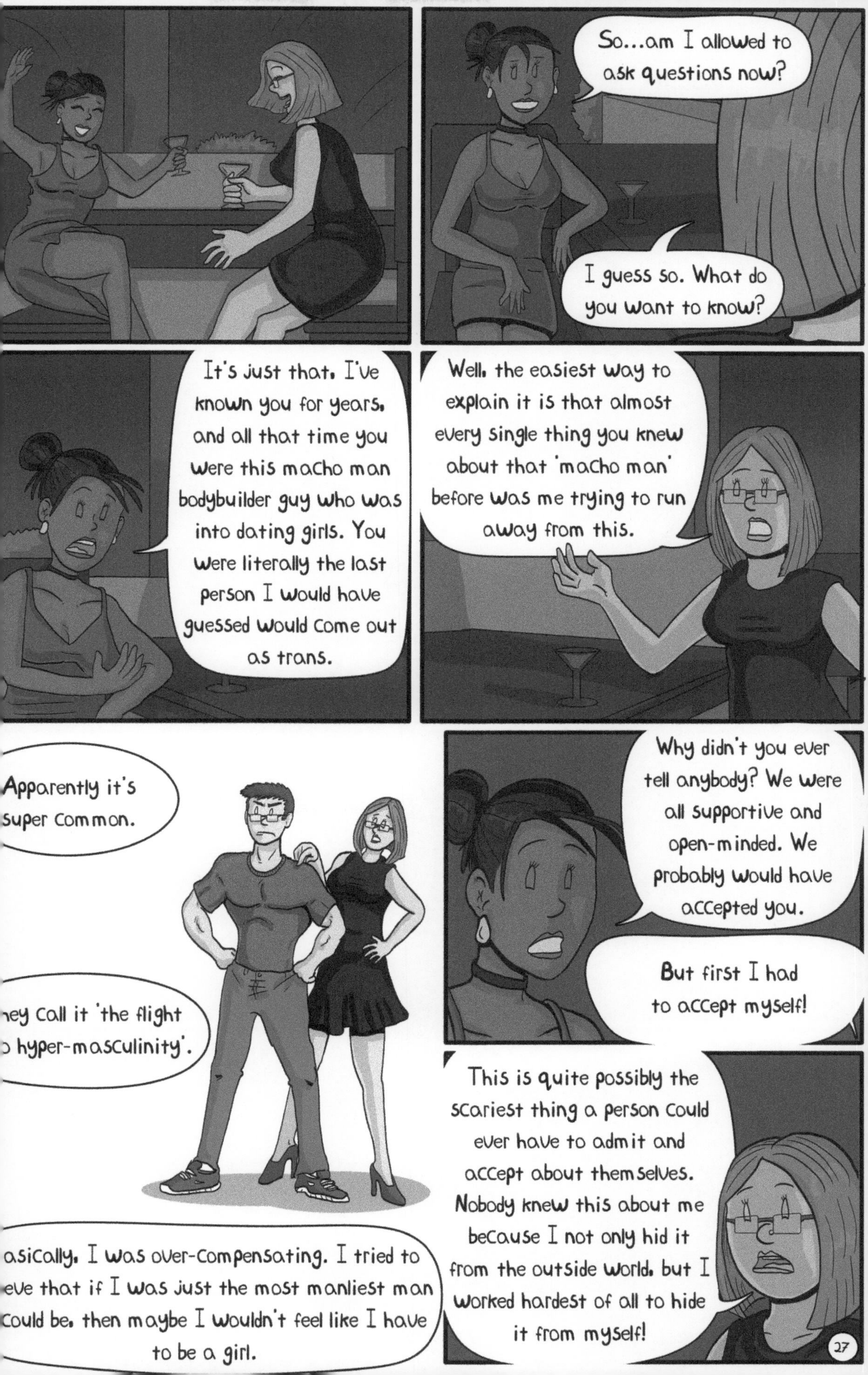
So...am I allowed to ask questions now?
I guess so. What do you want to know?
It's just that. I've known you for years. and all that time you were this macho man bodybuilder guy who was into dating girls. You were literally the last person I would have guessed would come out as trans.
Well. the easiest way to explain it is that almost every single thing you knew about that 'macho man' before was me trying to run away from this.
Apparently it's super common.
hey call it 'the flight o hyper-masculinity'.
asically. I was over-compensating. I tried to eve that if I was just the most manliest man could be. then maybe I wouldn't feel like I have to be a girl.
Why didn't you ever tell anybody? We were all supportive and open-minded. We probably would have accepted you.
But first I had to accept myself!
This is quite possibly the scariest thing a person could ever have to admit and accept about themselves. Nobody knew this about me because I not only hid it from the outside world. but I worked hardest of all to hide it from myself!

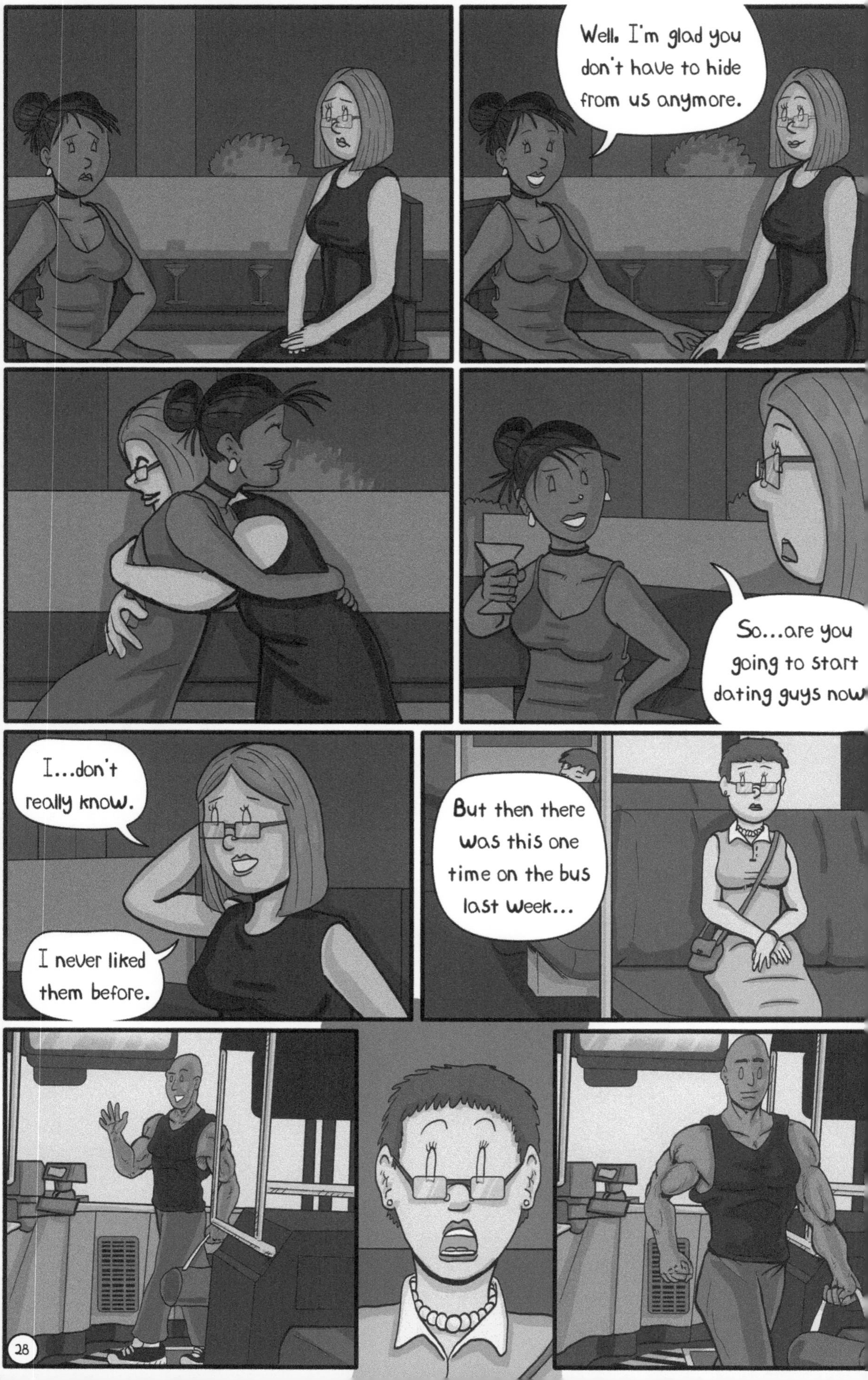
Well, I'm glad you don't have to hide from us anymore.
So...are you going to start dating guys now
I...don't really know.
I never liked them before.
But then there was this one time on the bus last week...

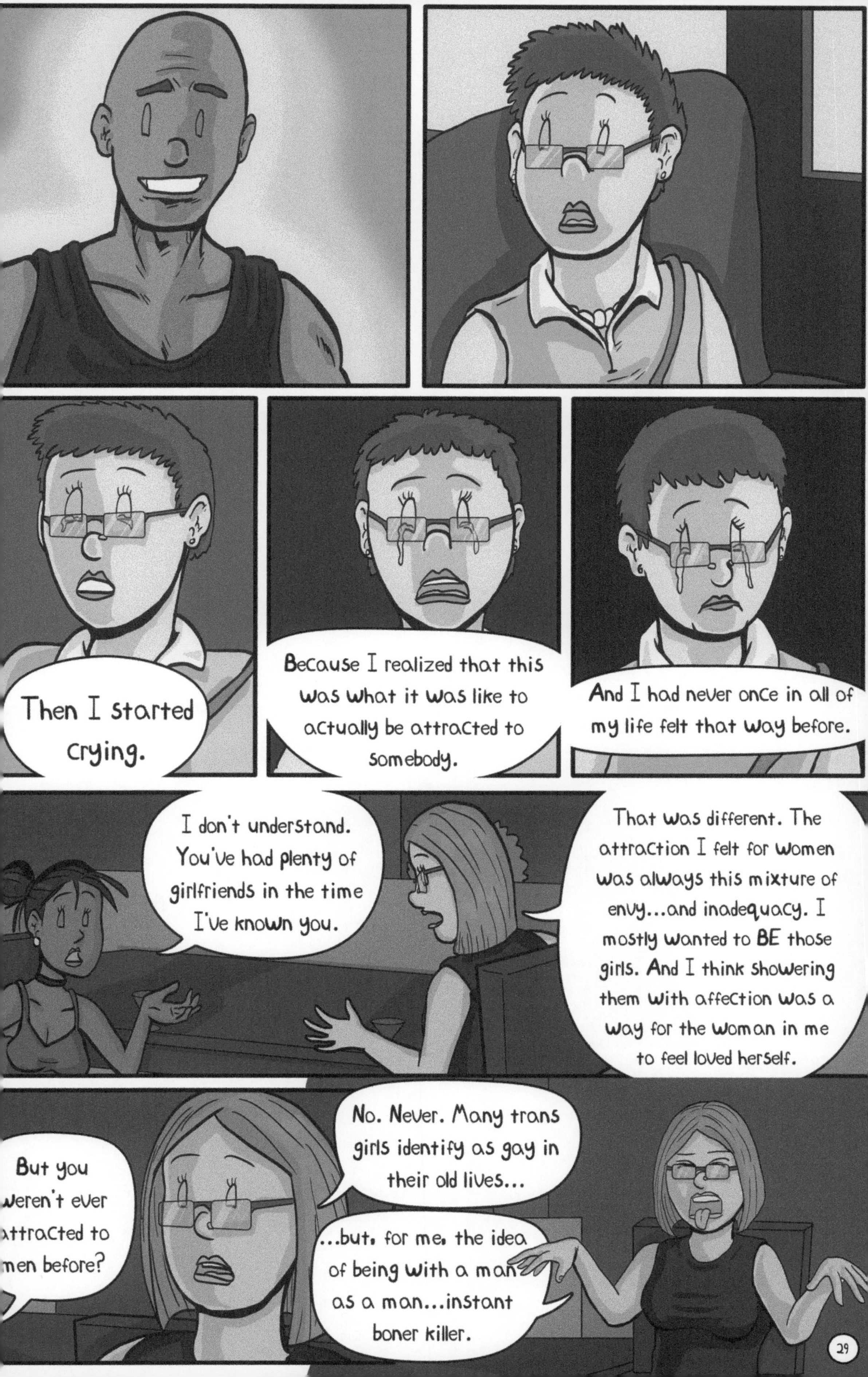

Then I started crying.
Because I realized that this was what it was like to actually be attracted to somebody.
And I had never once in all of my life felt that way before.
I don't understand. You've had plenty of girlfriends in the time I've known you.
That was different. The attraction I felt for women was always this mixture of envy...and inadequacy. I mostly wanted to BE those girls. And I think showering them with affection was a way for the woman in me to feel loved herself.
But you weren't ever attracted to men before?
No. Never. Many trans girls identify as gay in their old lives...
...but, for me, the idea of being with a man as a man...instant boner killer.

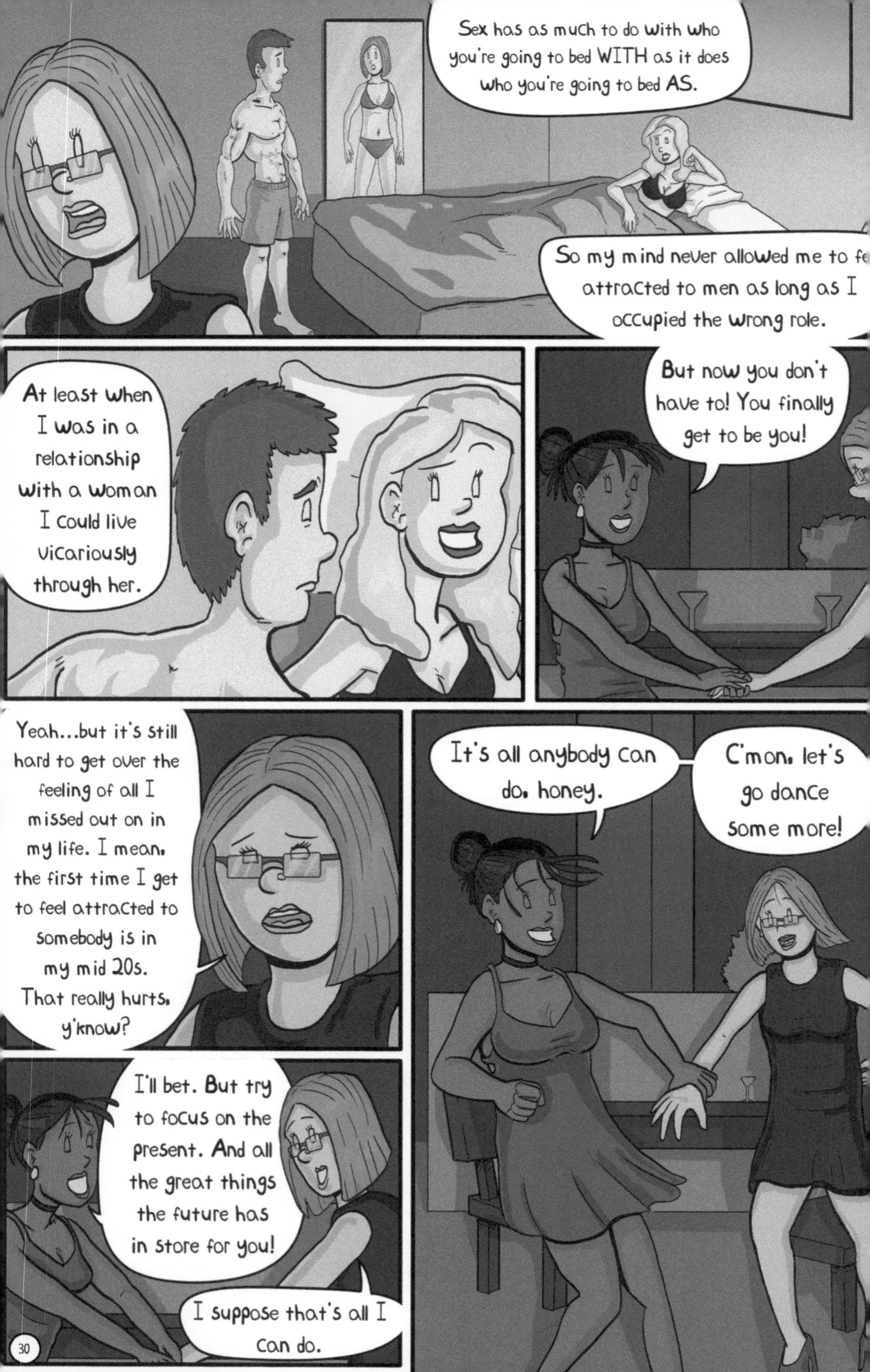

Sex has as much to do with who you're going to bed WITH as it does who you're going to bed AS.
So my mind never allowed me to fe attracted to men as long as I occupied the wrong role.
At least when I was in a relationship with a woman I could live vicariously through her.
But now you don't have to! You finally get to be you!
Yeah...but it's still hard to get over the feeling of all I missed out on in my life. I mean, the first time I get to feel attracted to somebody is in my mid 20s. That really hurts, y'know?
I'll bet. But try to focus on the present. And all the great things the future has in store for you!
I suppose that's all I can do.
It's all anybody can do, honey.
C'mon, let's go dance some more!

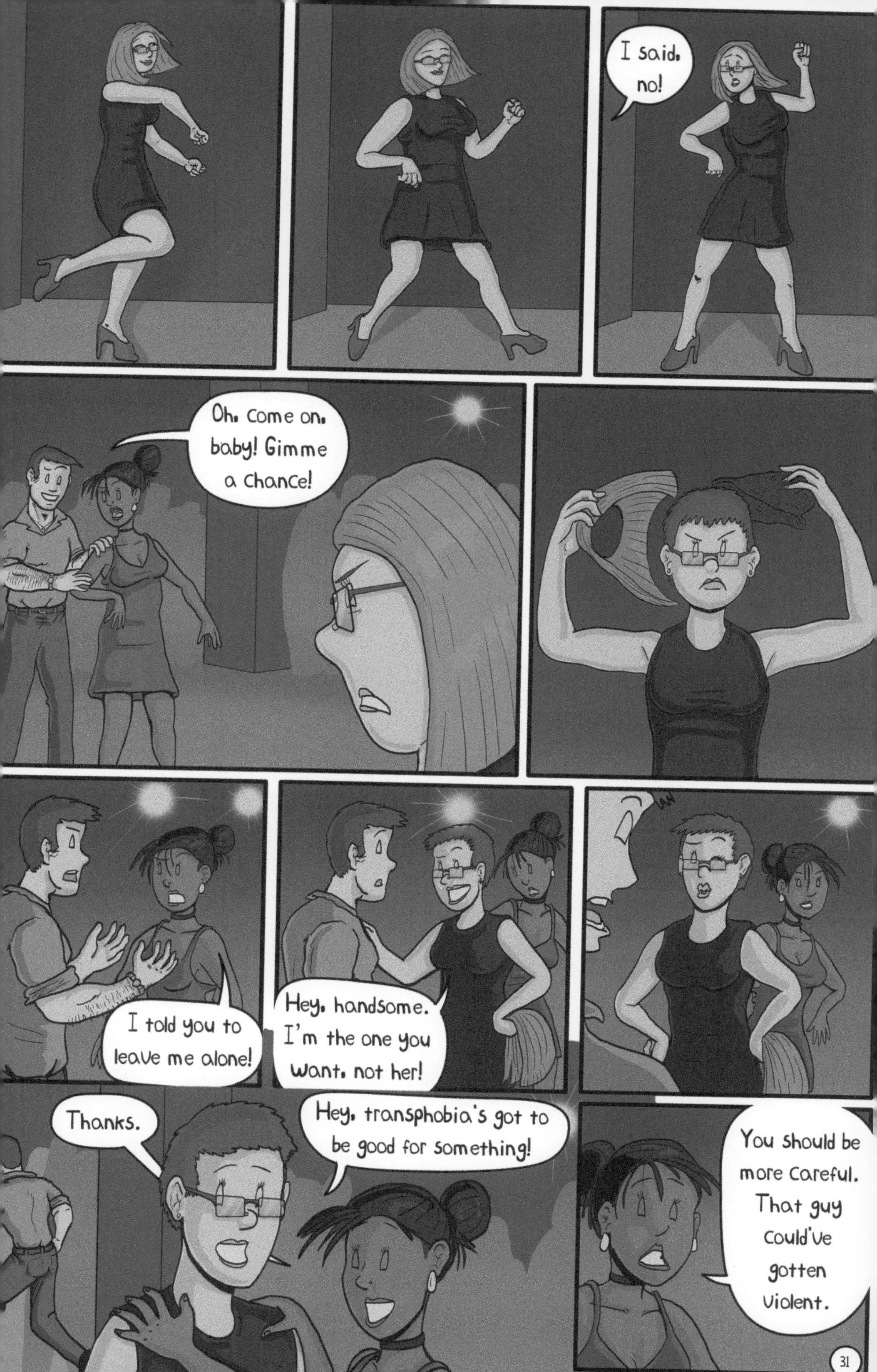
I said, no!
Oh, come on, baby! Gimme a chance!
I told you to leave me alone!
Hey, handsome. I'm the one you want, not her!
Thanks.
Hey, transphobia's got to be good for something!
You should be more careful. That guy could've gotten violent.

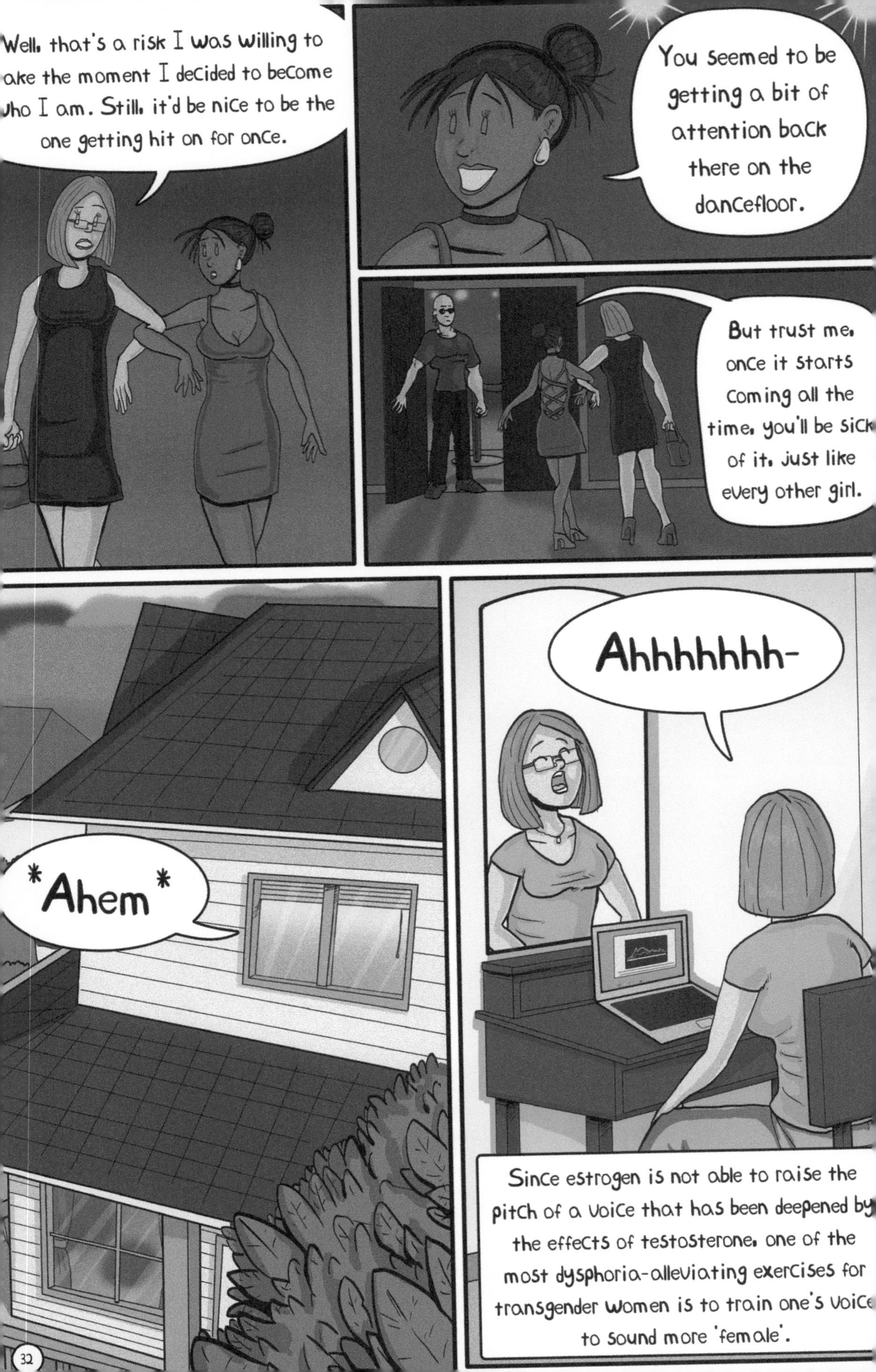

Well, that's a risk I was willing to ake the moment I decided to become who I am. Still, it'd be nice to be the one getting hit on for once.
You seemed to be getting a bit of attention back there on the dancefloor.
But trust me, once it starts coming all the time, you'll be sick of it, just like every other girl.
Ahem
Ahhhhhhh-
Since estrogen is not able to raise the pitch of a voice that has been deepened by the effects of testosterone, one of the most dysphoria-alleviating exercises for transgender women is to train one's voice to sound more 'female'.

Since cis females tend to have a voice box roughly half the size of cis males...

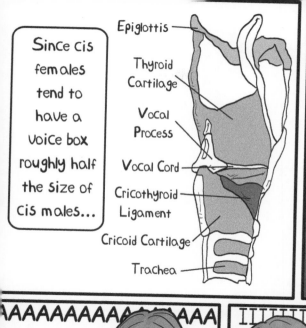

Epiglottis

Thyroid Cartilage

Vocal Process

Vocal Cord

Cricothyroid Ligament

Cricoid Cartilage

Trachea

...much of the training involved in voice feminization is to gain control over the muscles of the throat to be able to constrict and release the voice box at will.

AAAAAAAAAAAAAAAAAA AAAAAAAA AA AAAAAAA A AAAAAAA A AAAAAAA A AAAAAAAA AA AAAAAA AAAA

IIIIIIIIIIIIII IIIIIII IIIIII IIIII IIIIIII IIIIIII II II

OOOOOOOOOOOOOOOOOO OOOOOOO OOOOOO OOOOO OOOOO OOOOO OOOOOO OOOOOO

This effectively reduces its working size by half while also allowing the throat to be opened up to give the voice a 'breathy' quality frequently found in female voices.

While not all transgender people opt to change their voices...

EEEE E E E E E E E

...it is fully possible for a transgender woman to re-learn how to speak like a typical cisgender woman, allowing her to [be] more comfortable in her identity as well [a]s fit in with society's expectations of what a woman 'should' sound like.

Can you please stop making those annoying sounds?

Um, sure! Once I have a voice that isn't emotionally upsetting to speak with!

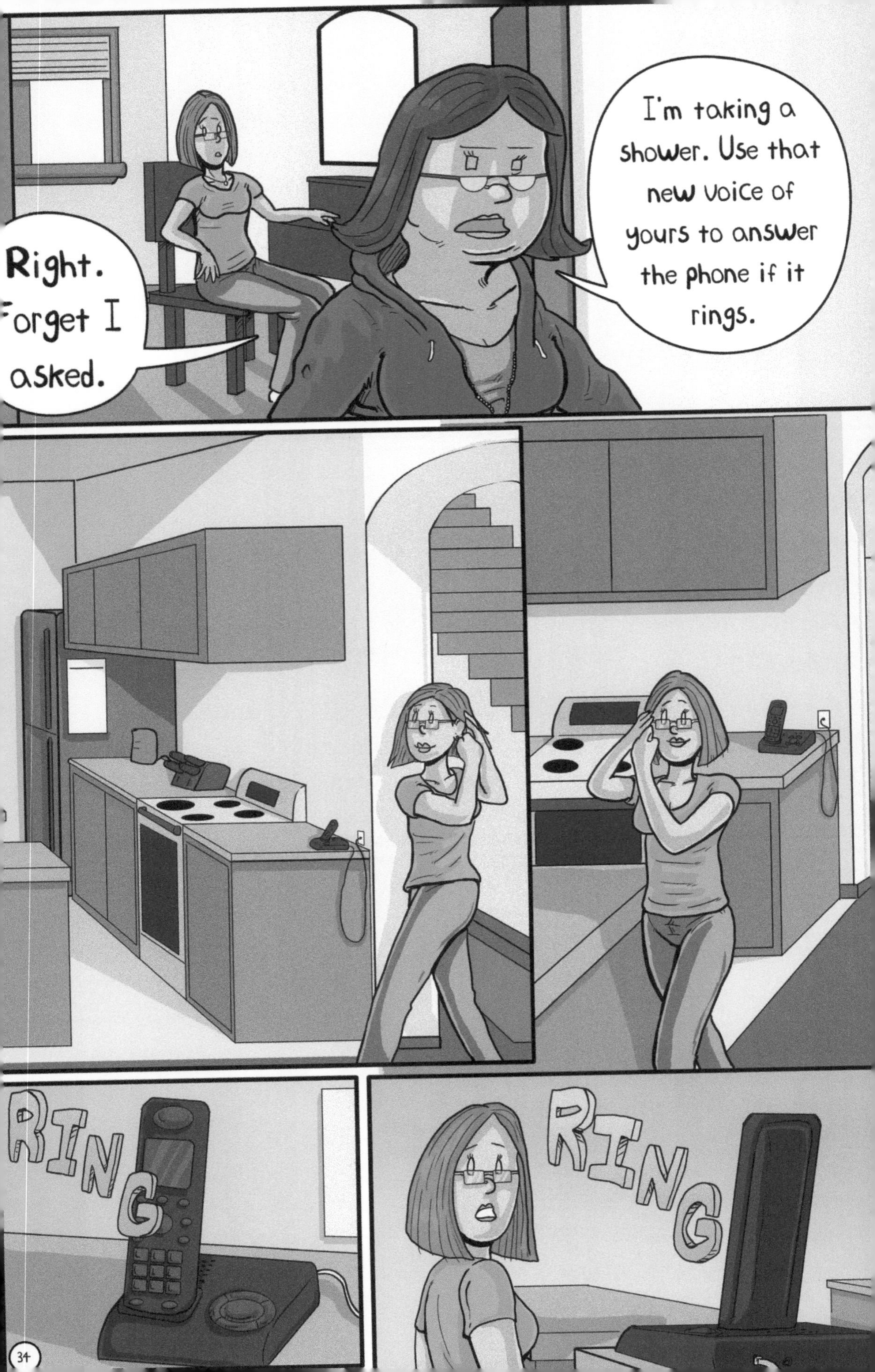

I'm taking a shower. Use that new voice of yours to answer the phone if it rings.
Right. Forget I asked.
RING
RING

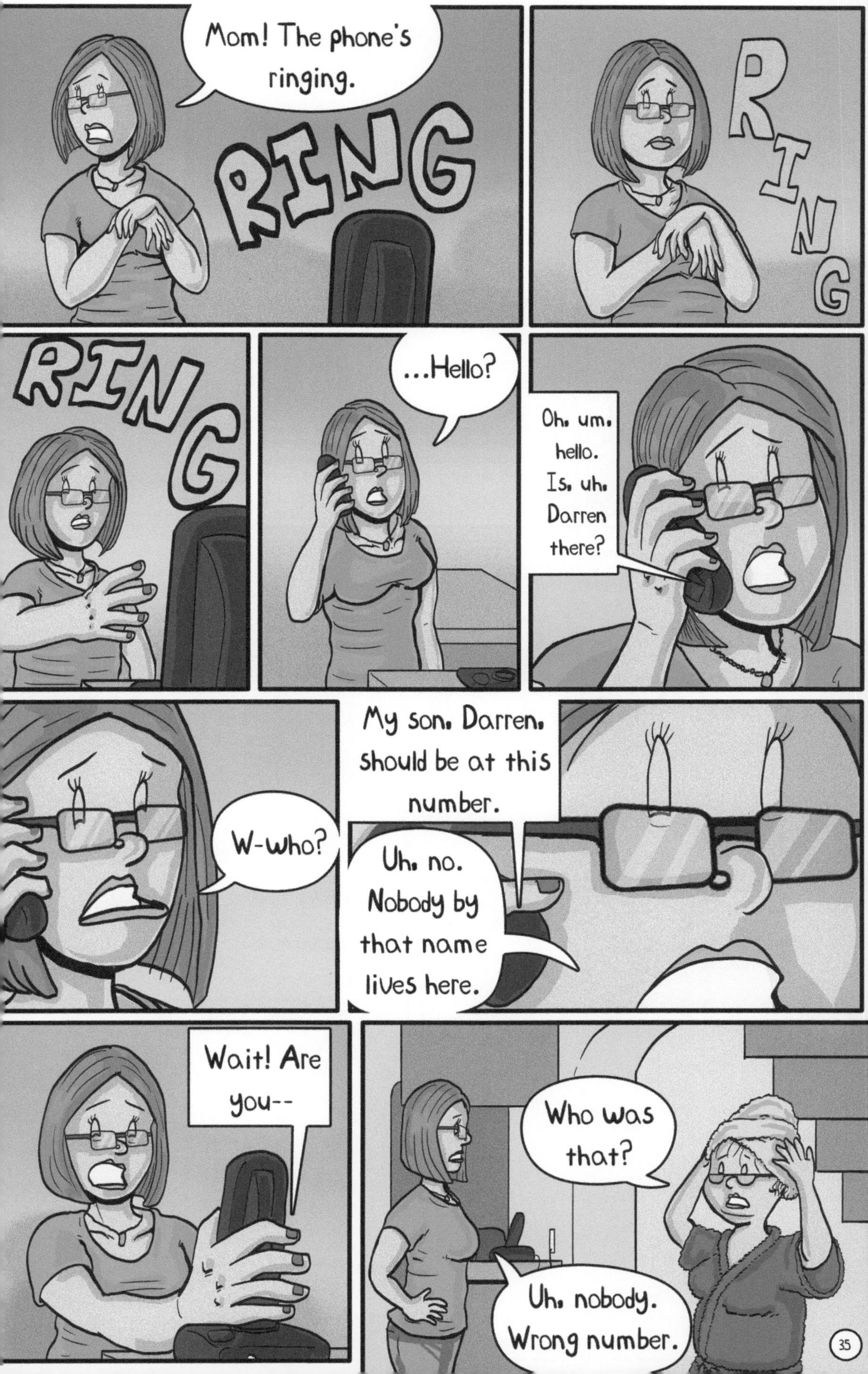
Mom! The phone's ringing.
RING
RING
RING
...Hello?
Oh, um, hello. Is, uh, Darren there?
W-who?
My son, Darren, should be at this number.
Uh, no. Nobody by that name lives here.
Wait! Are you--
Who was that?
Uh, nobody. Wrong number.

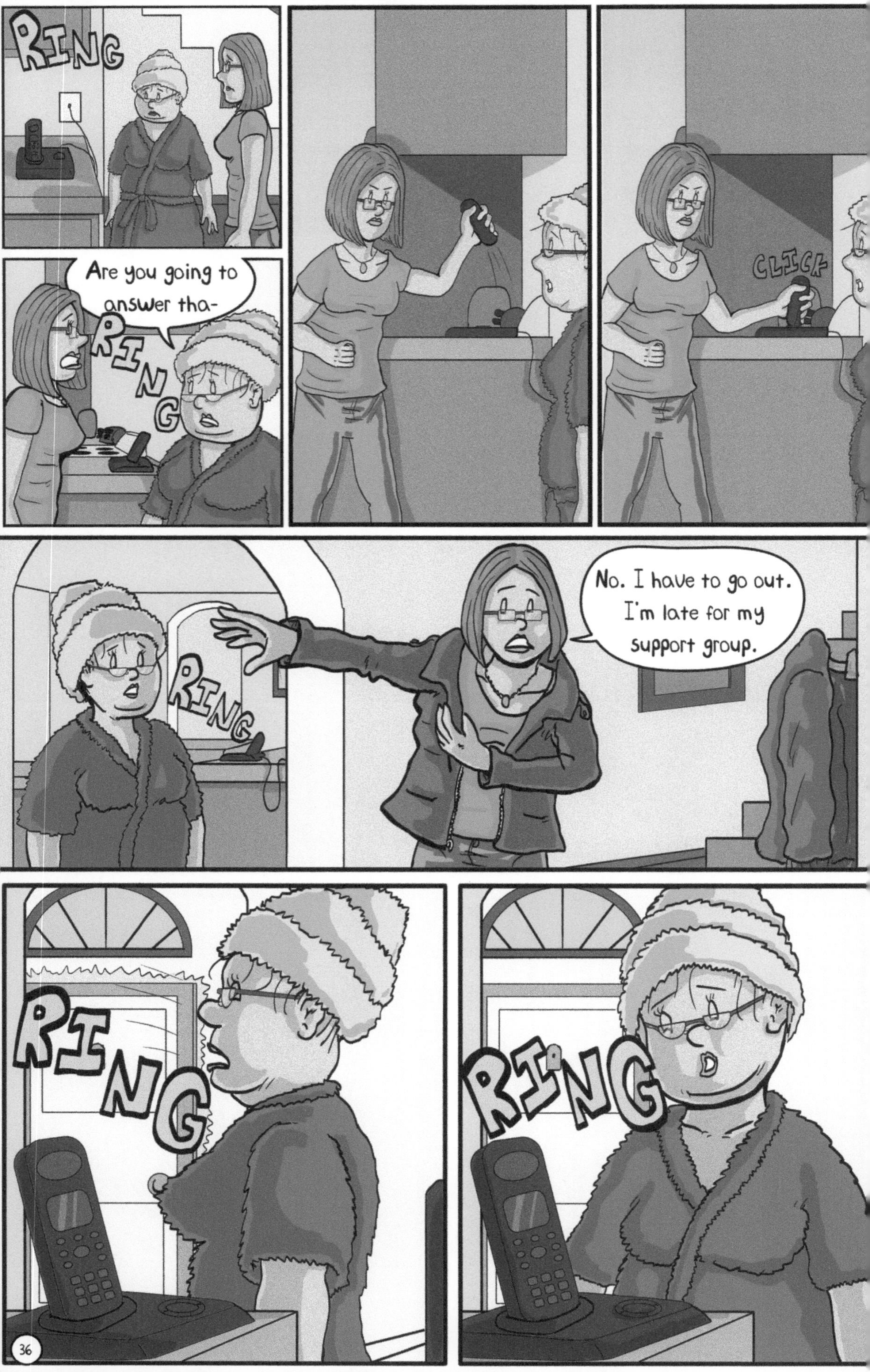
RING
Are you going to answer tha-
RING
CLICK
No. I have to go out. I'm late for my support group.
RING
RING
RING

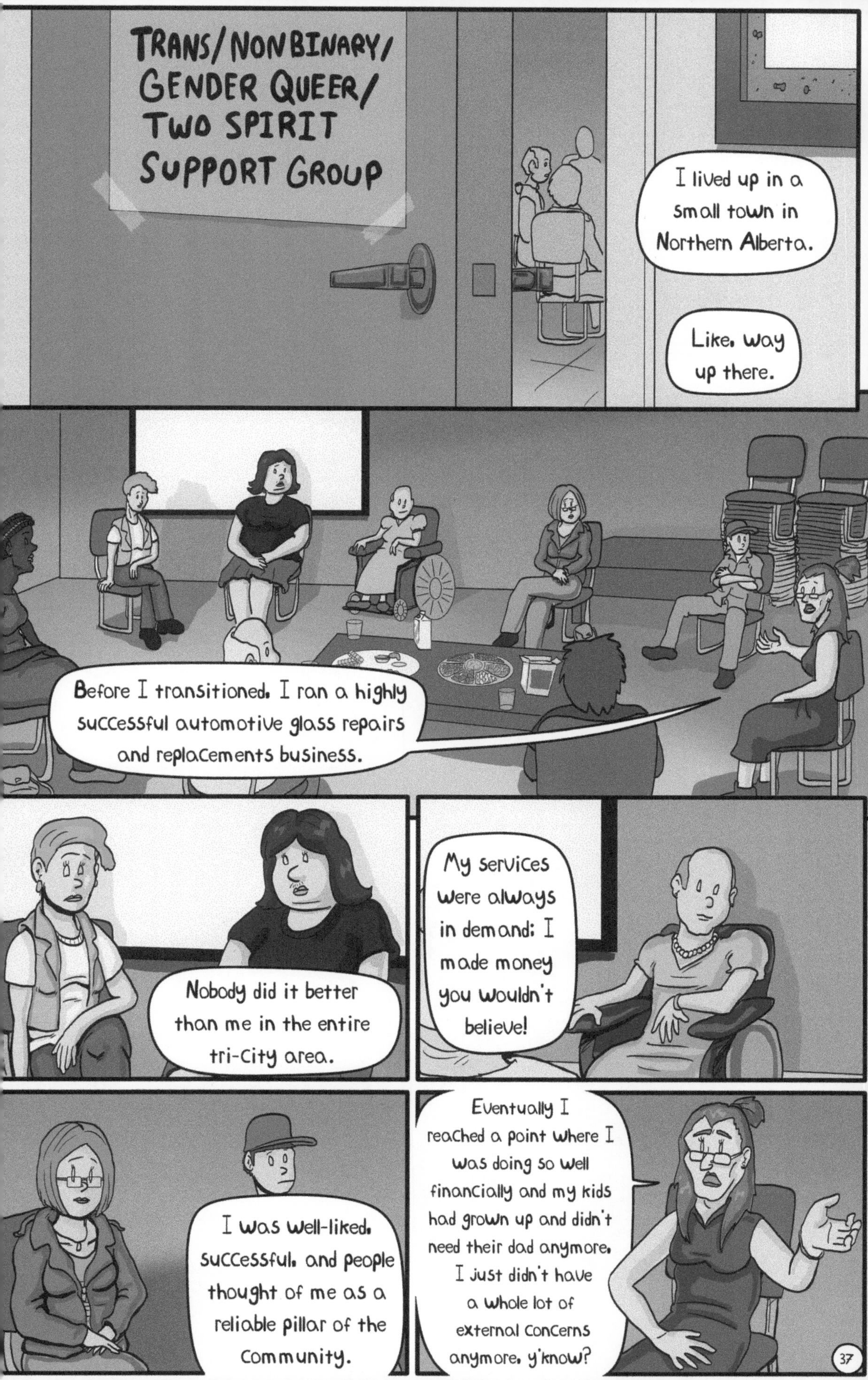
TRANS/NONBINARY/ GENDER QUEER/ TWO SPIRIT SUPPORT GROUP
I lived up in a small town in Northern Alberta.
Like, way up there.
Before I transitioned, I ran a highly successful automotive glass repairs and replacements business.
Nobody did it better than me in the entire tri-city area.
My services were always in demand; I made money you wouldn't believe!
I was well-liked, successful, and people thought of me as a reliable pillar of the community.
Eventually I reached a point where I was doing so well financially and my kids had grown up and didn't need their dad anymore. I just didn't have a whole lot of external concerns anymore, y'know?

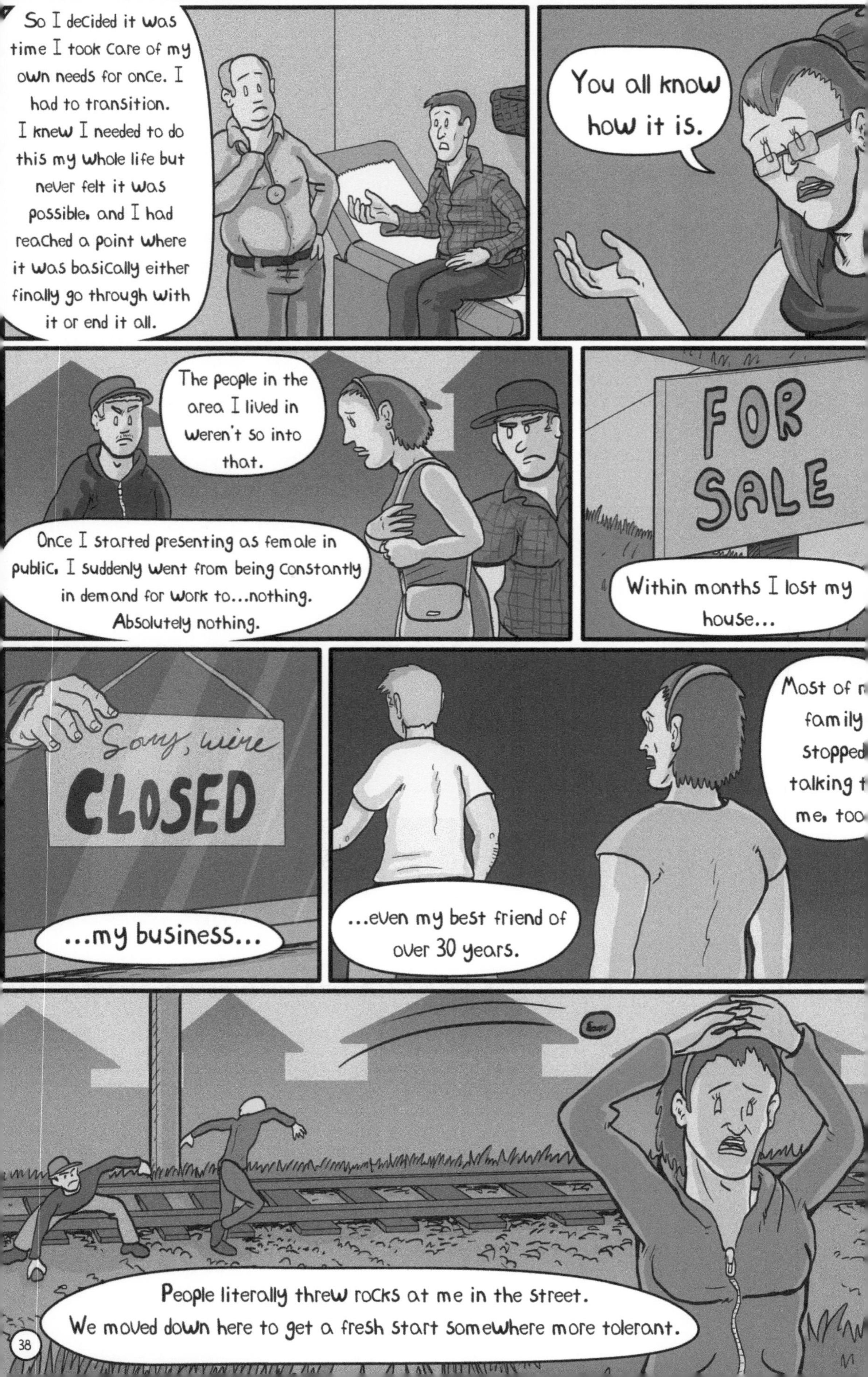

So I decided it was time I took care of my own needs for once. I had to transition. I knew I needed to do this my whole life but never felt it was possible, and I had reached a point where it was basically either finally go through with it or end it all.
You all know how it is.
The people in the area I lived in weren't so into that.
Once I started presenting as female in public, I suddenly went from being constantly in demand for work to...nothing. Absolutely nothing.
FOR SALE
Within months I lost my house...
Sorry, we're
CLOSED
...my business...
...even my best friend of over 30 years.
Most of m
family
stopped
talking t
me, too
People literally threw rocks at me in the street.
We moved down here to get a fresh start somewhere more tolerant.

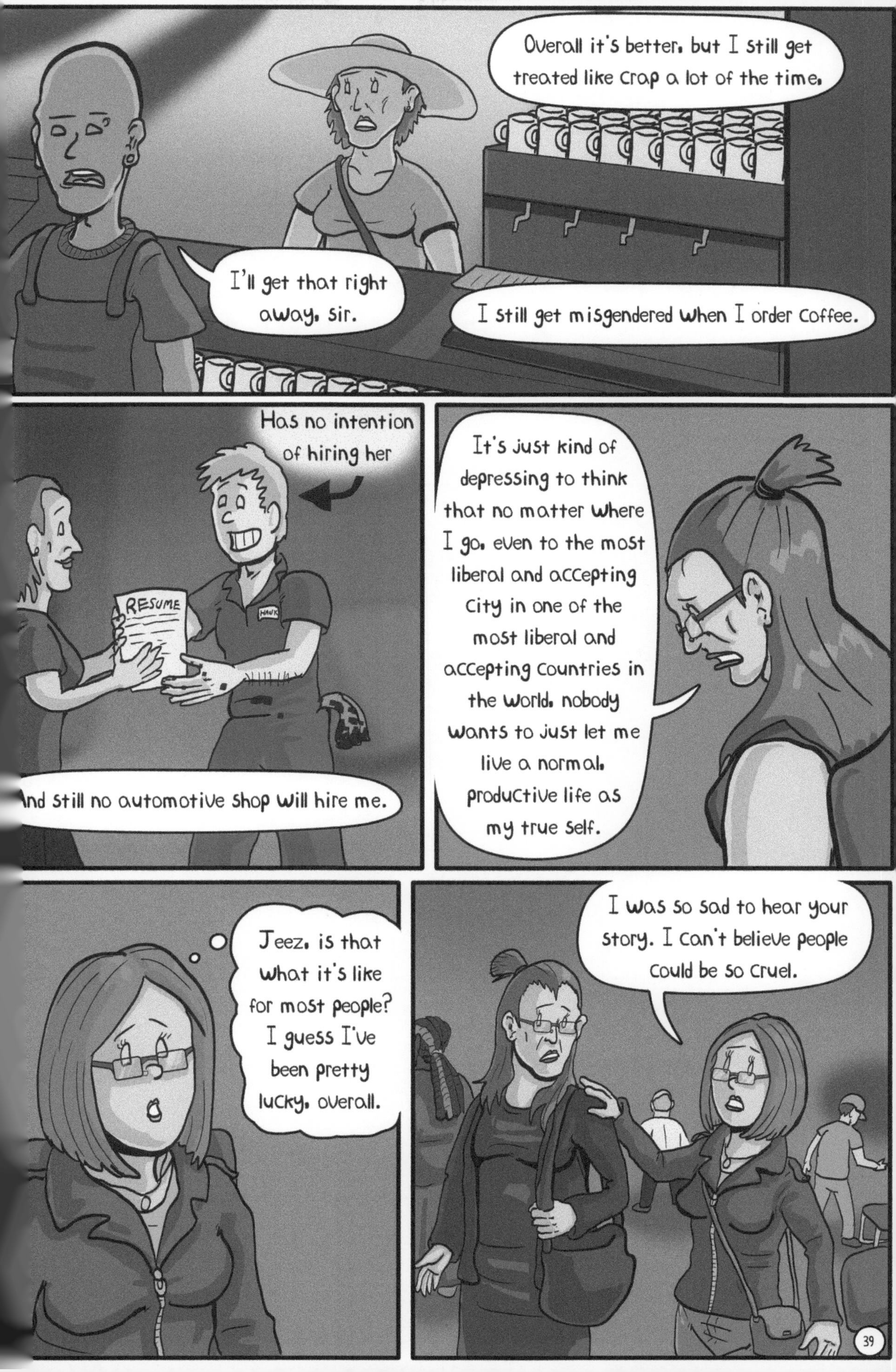
Overall it's better, but I still get treated like crap a lot of the time.
I'll get that right away, sir.
I still get misgendered when I order coffee.
Has no intention of hiring her
RESUME
HANK
And still no automotive shop will hire me.
It's just kind of depressing to think that no matter where I go, even to the most liberal and accepting city in one of the most liberal and accepting countries in the world, nobody wants to just let me live a normal, productive life as my true self.
Jeez, is that what it's like for most people? I guess I've been pretty lucky, overall.
I was so sad to hear your story. I can't believe people could be so cruel.

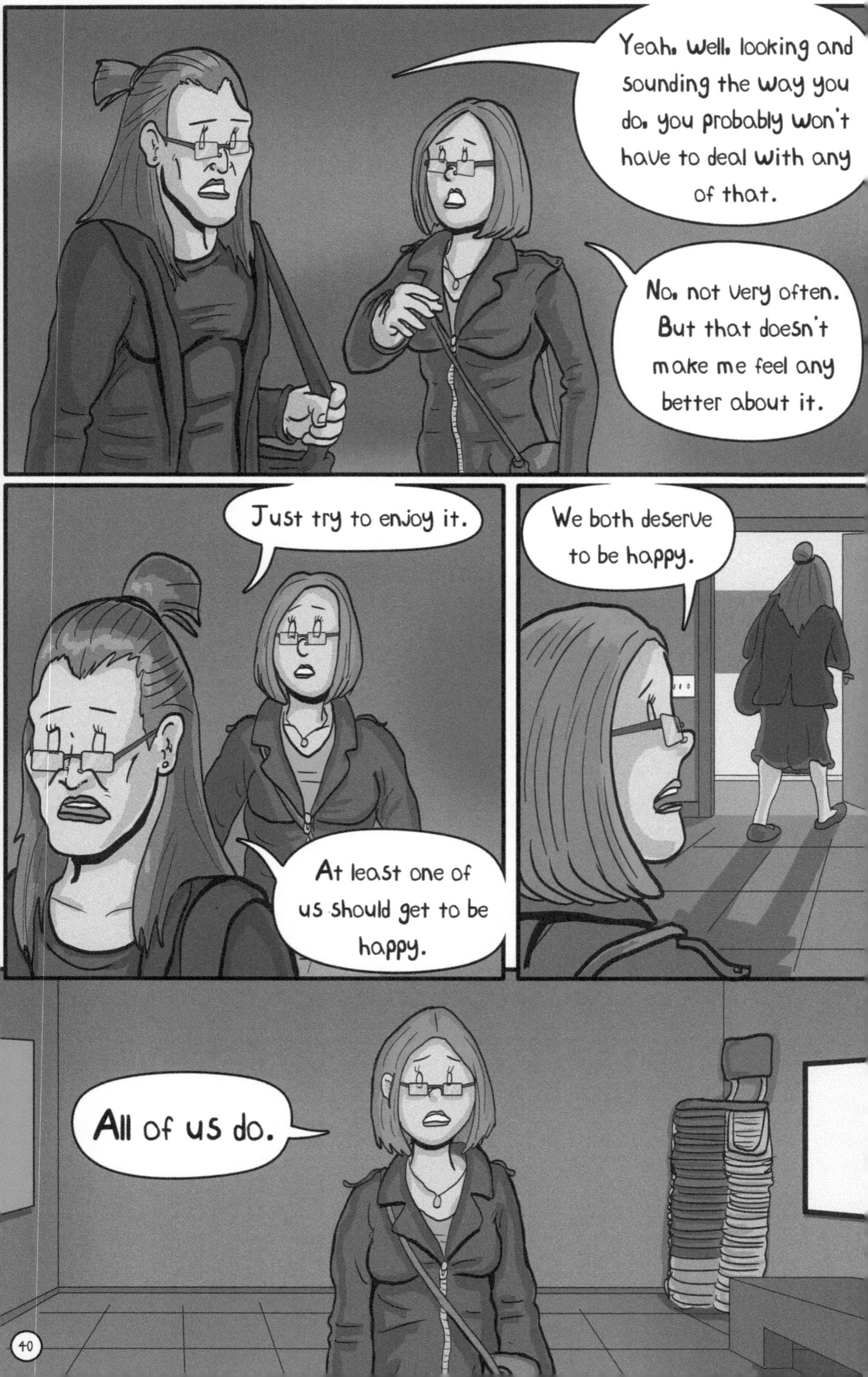
Yeah, well, looking and sounding the way you do, you probably won't have to deal with any of that.
No, not very often. But that doesn't make me feel any better about it.
Just try to enjoy it.
At least one of us should get to be happy.
We both deserve to be happy.
All of us do.

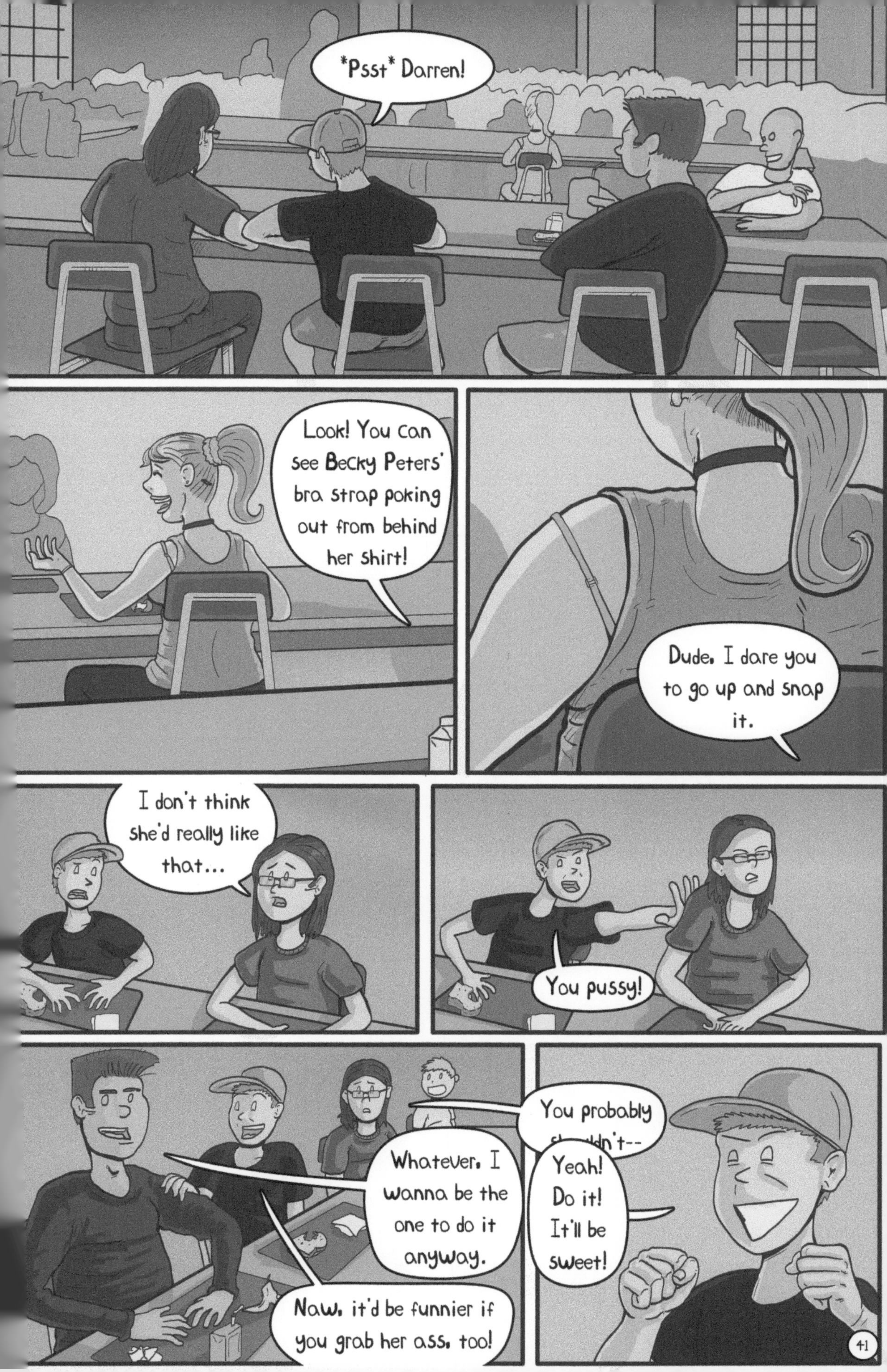
Psst Darren!
Look! You can see Becky Peters' bra strap poking out from behind her shirt!
Dude. I dare you to go up and snap it.
I don't think she'd really like that...
You pussy!
Whatever. I wanna be the one to do it anyway.
Naw. it'd be funnier if you grab her ass, too!
You probably
Yeah! Do it! It'll be sweet!

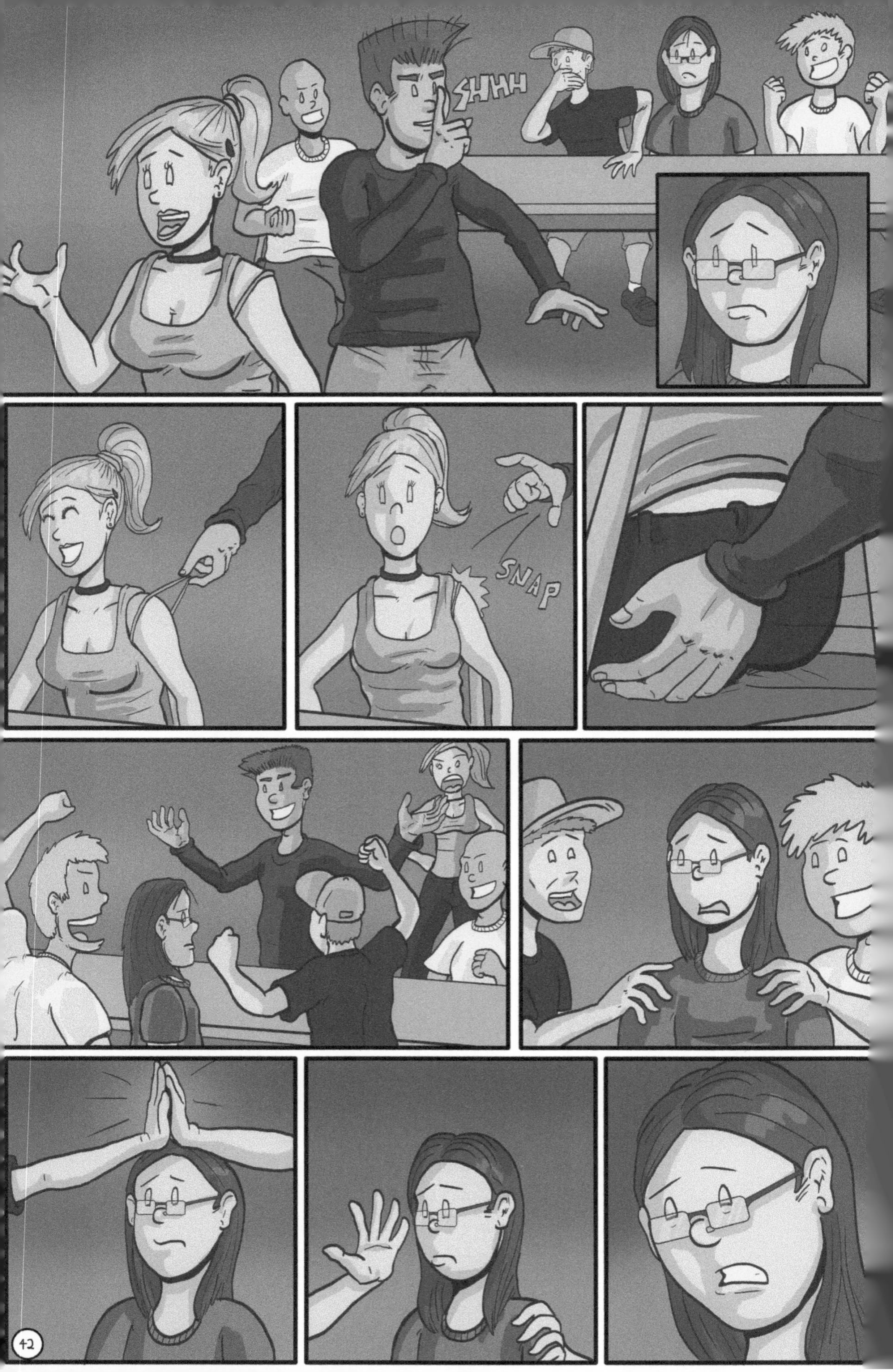
SHHH
SNAP

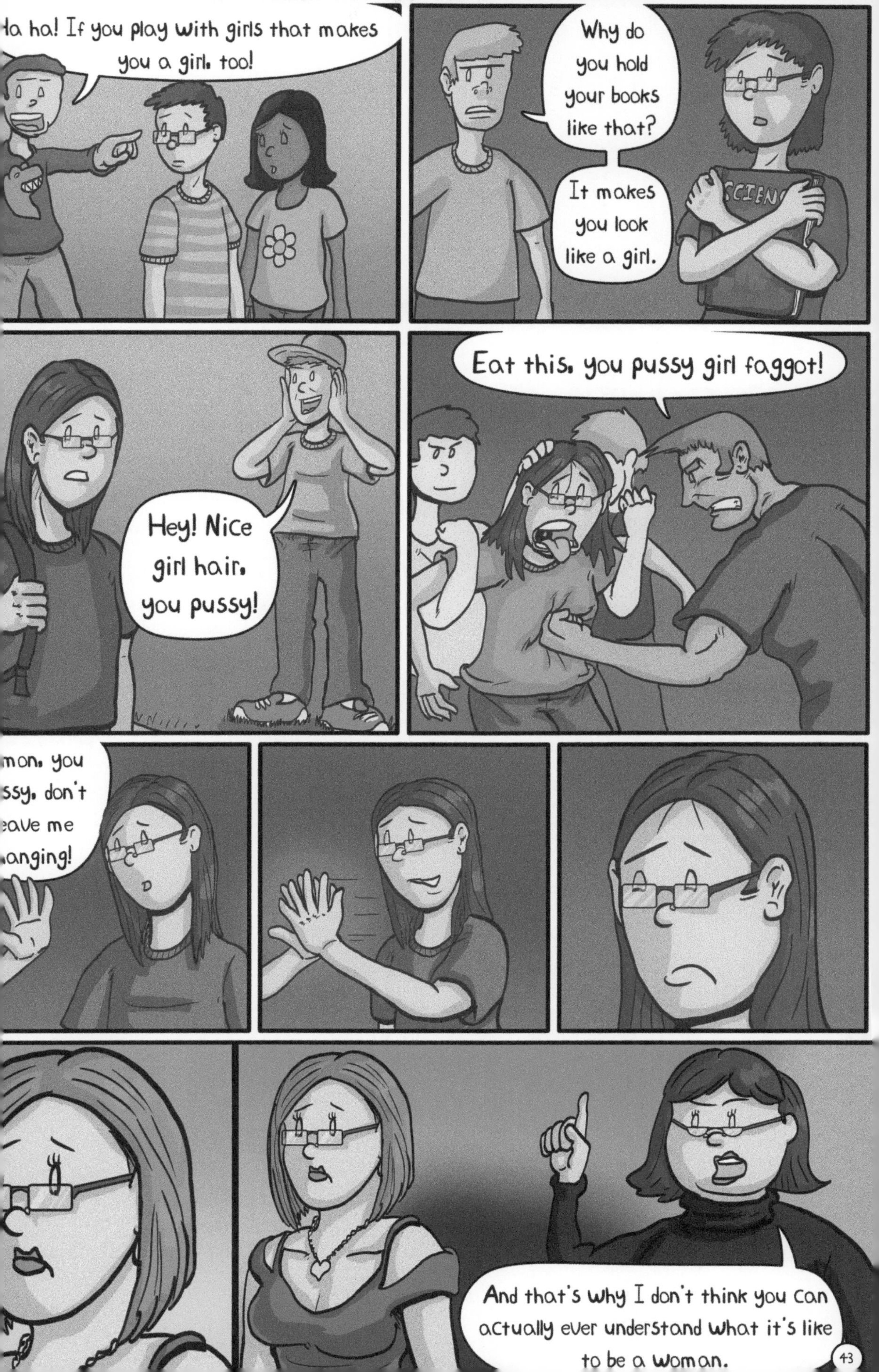

Ha ha! If you play with girls that makes you a girl, too!
Why do you hold your books like that?
It makes you look like a girl.
SCIENC
Hey! Nice girl hair, you pussy!
Eat this, you pussy girl faggot!
mon, you ssy, don't eave me anging!
And that's why I don't think you can actually ever understand what it's like to be a woman.

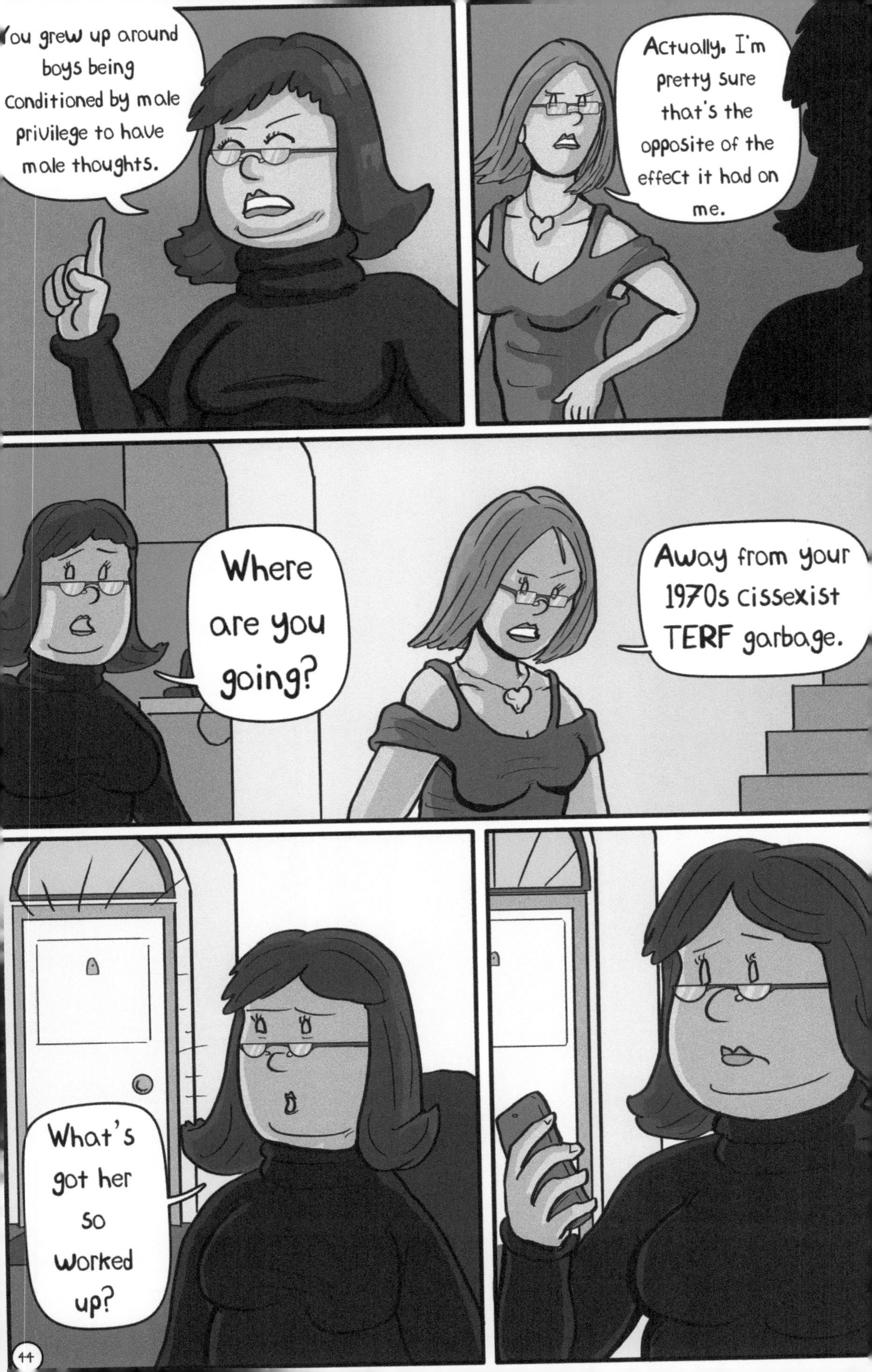
You grew up around boys being conditioned by male privilege to have male thoughts.
Actually, I'm pretty sure that's the opposite of the effect it had on me.
Where are you going?
Away from your 1970s cissexist TERF garbage.
What's got her so worked up?

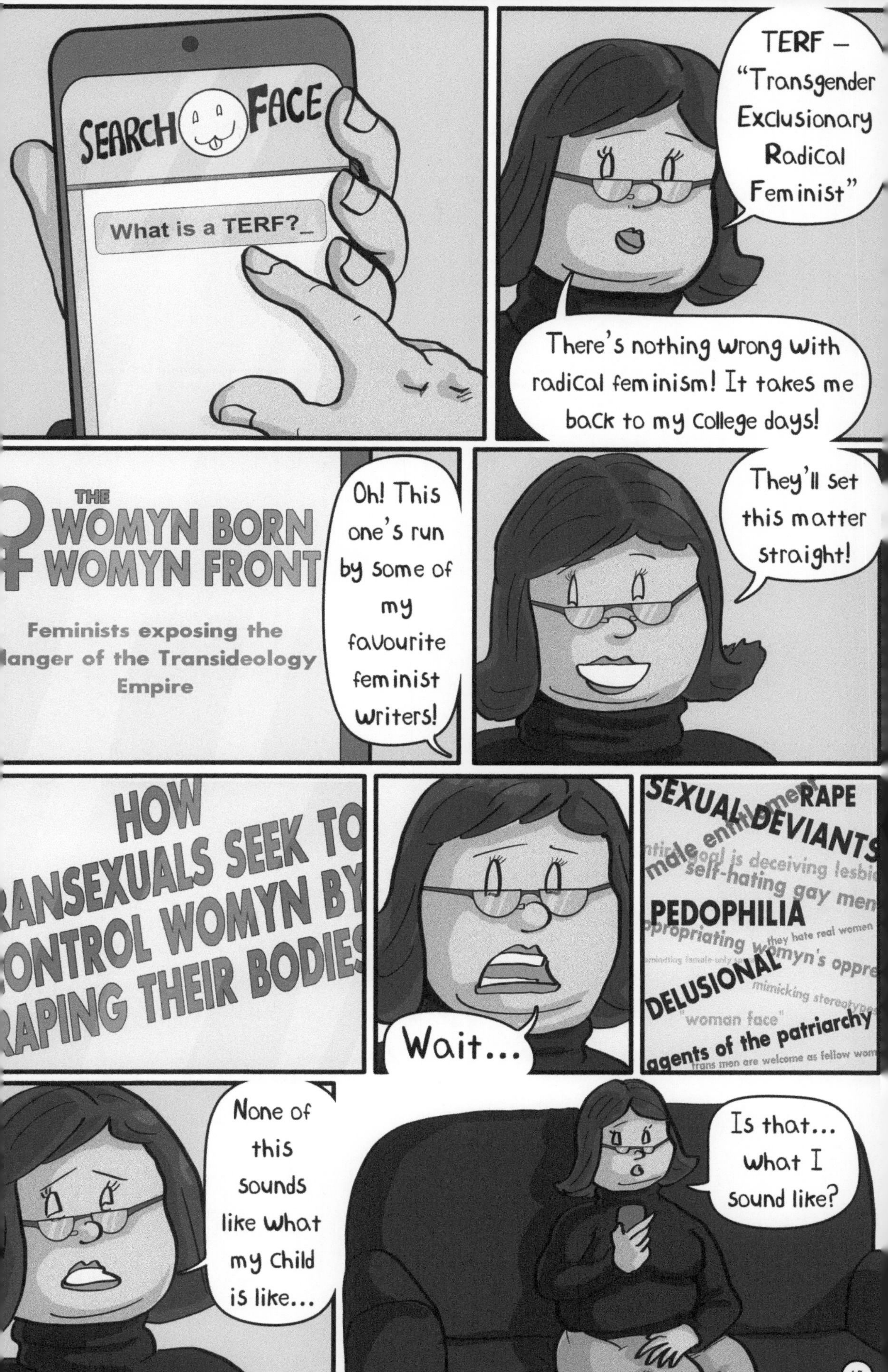
SEARCH FACE
What is a TERF?_
TERF – "Transgender Exclusionary Radical Feminist"
There's nothing wrong with radical feminism! It takes me back to my college days!
THE WOMYN BORN WOMYN FRONT
Feminists exposing the
anger of the Transideology
Empire
Oh! This one's run by some of my favourite feminist writers!
They'll set this matter straight!
HOW
RANSEXUALS SEEK TO
CONTROL WOMYN BY
RAPING THEIR BODIES
Wait...
SEXUAL
RAPE
DEVIANTS
male entitlement
goal is deceiving lesbi
self-hating gay men
PEDOPHILIA
ppropriating womyn's oppre
they hate real women
DELUSIONAL
mimicking stereotypes
"woman face"
agents of the patriarchy
trans men are welcome as fellow wom
None of this sounds like what my child is like...
Is that... what I sound like?

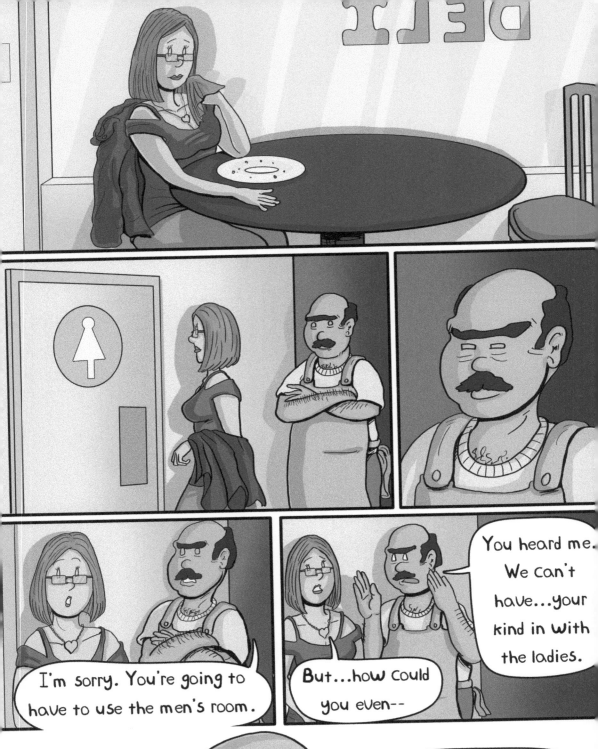

I'm sorry. You're going to have to use the men's room.

But...how could you even--

You heard me. We can't have...your kind in with the ladies.

Excuse me, but which washroom should I use?

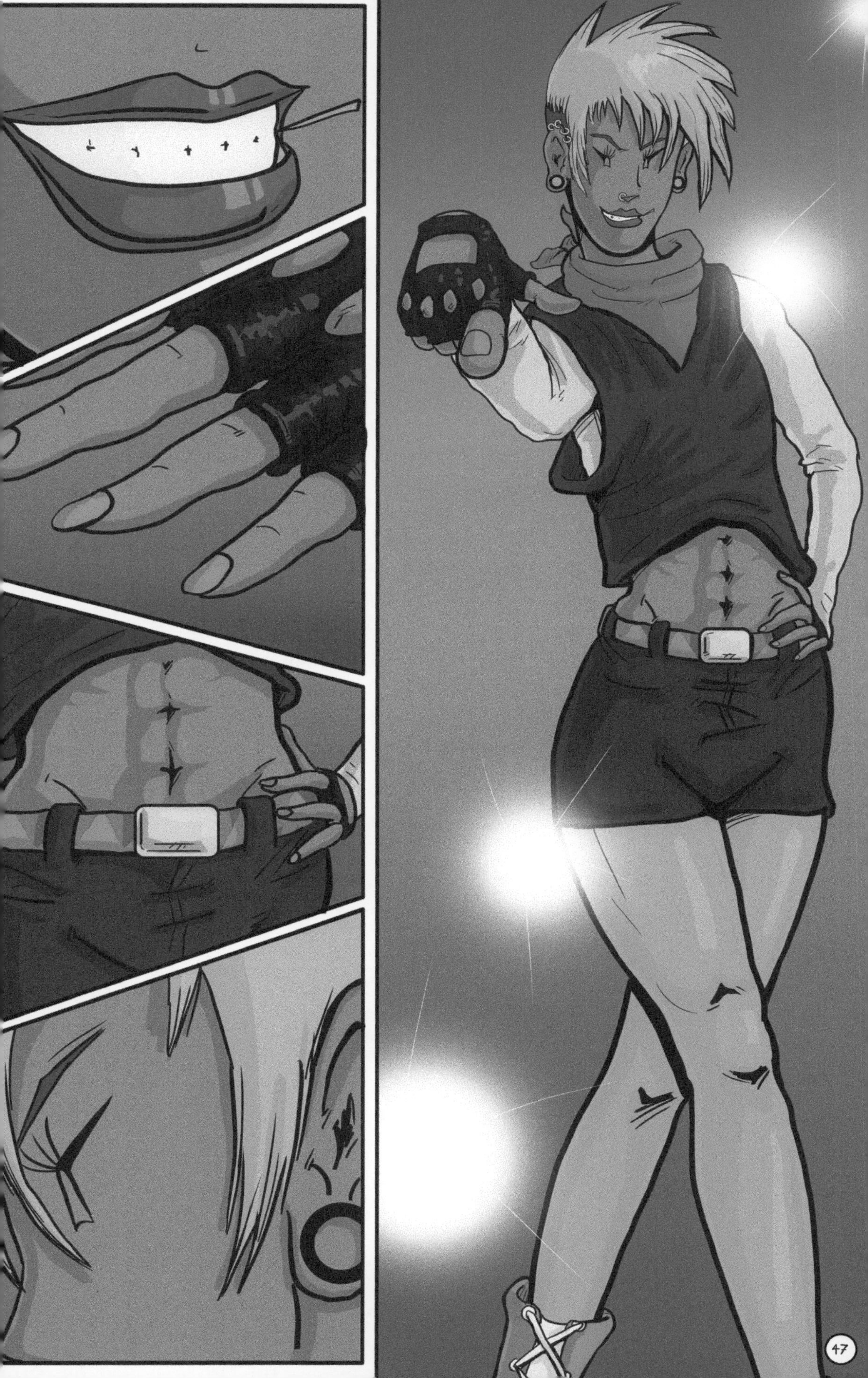

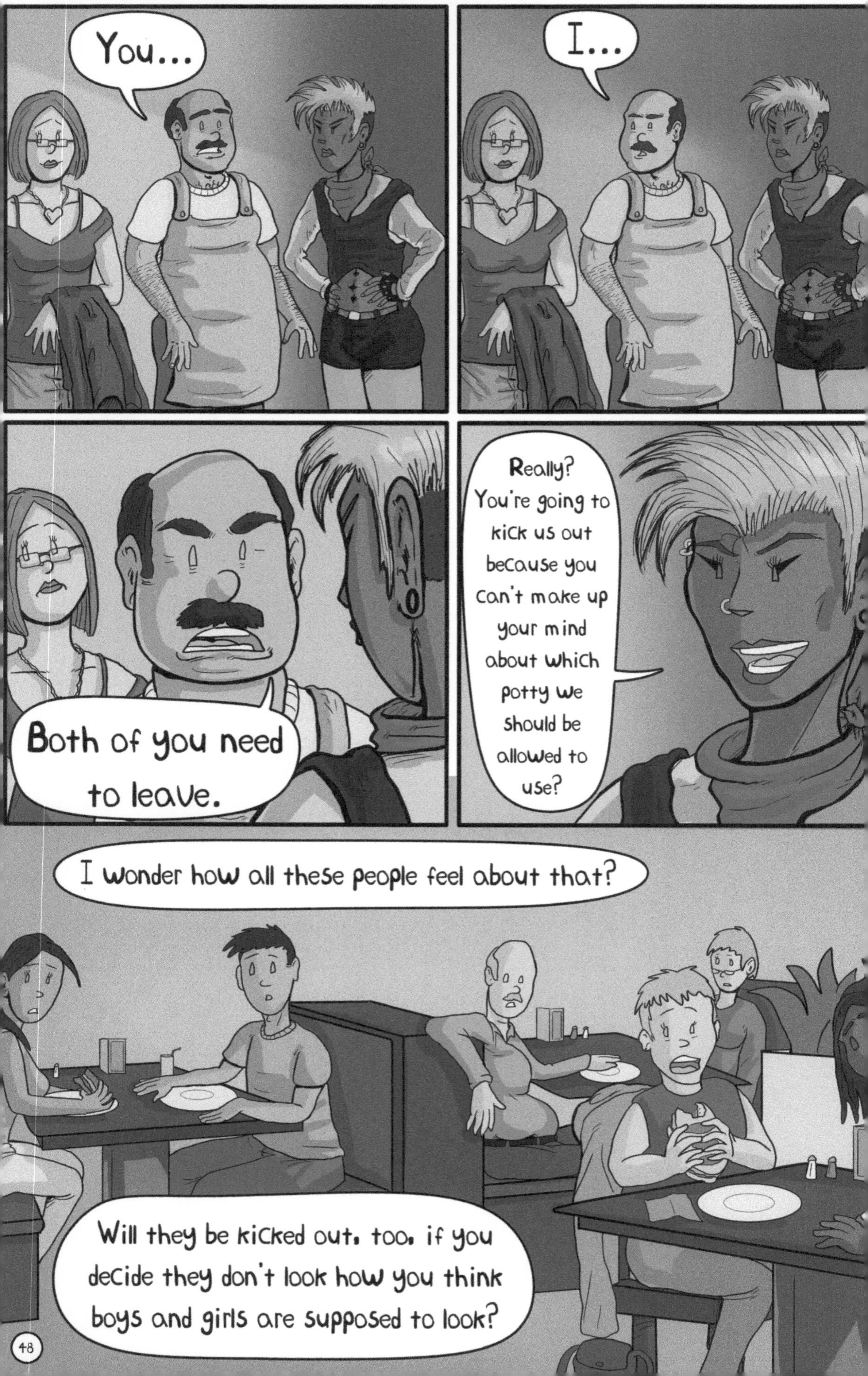
You...
I...
Both of you need to leave.
Really? You're going to kick us out because you can't make up your mind about which potty we should be allowed to use?
I wonder how all these people feel about that?
Will they be kicked out, too, if you decide they don't look how you think boys and girls are supposed to look?

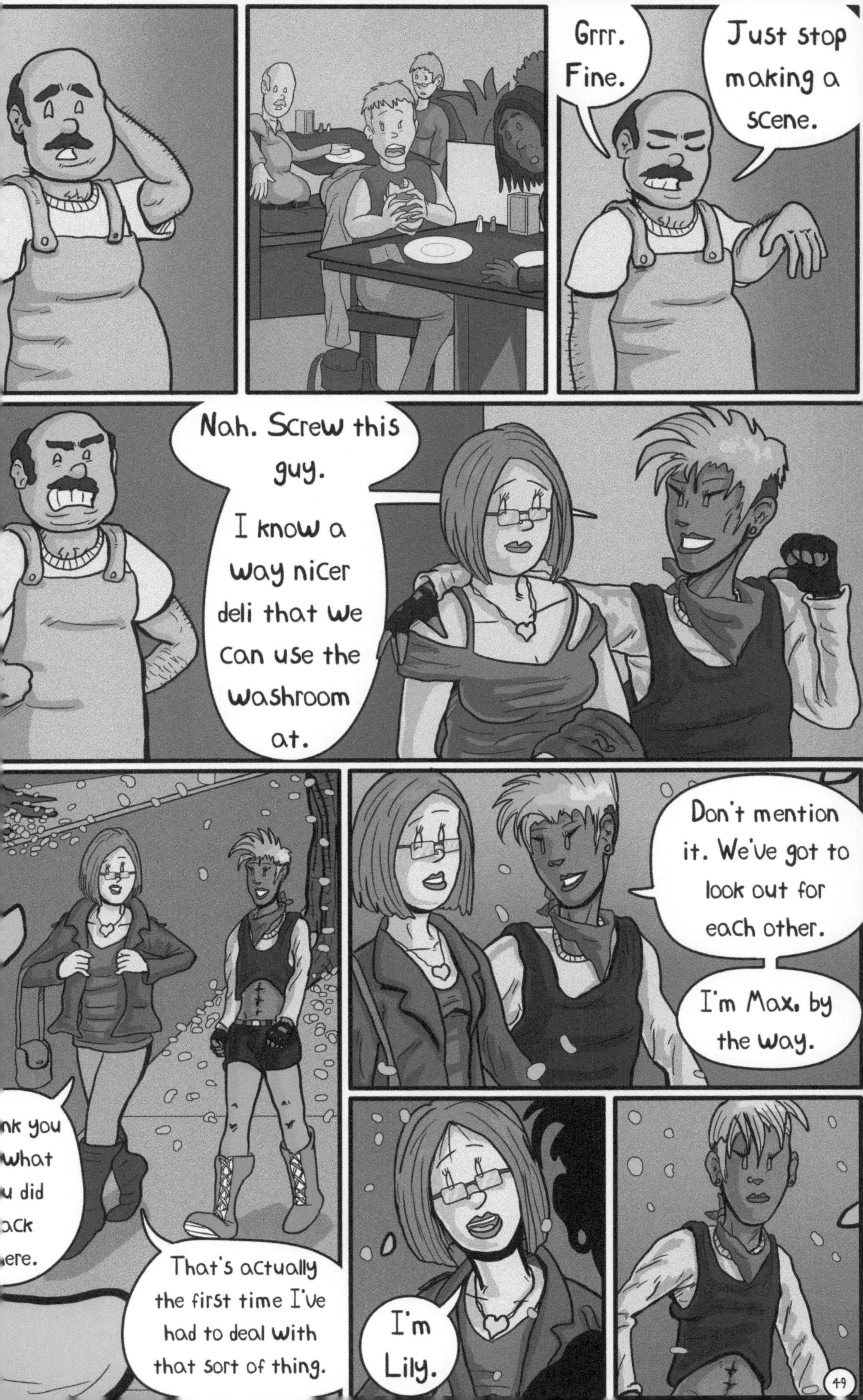
Grrr. Fine.
Just stop making a scene.
Nah. Screw this guy.
I know a way nicer deli that we can use the washroom at.
Don't mention it. We've got to look out for each other.
I'm Max, by the way.
That's actually the first time I've had to deal with that sort of thing.
I'm Lily.

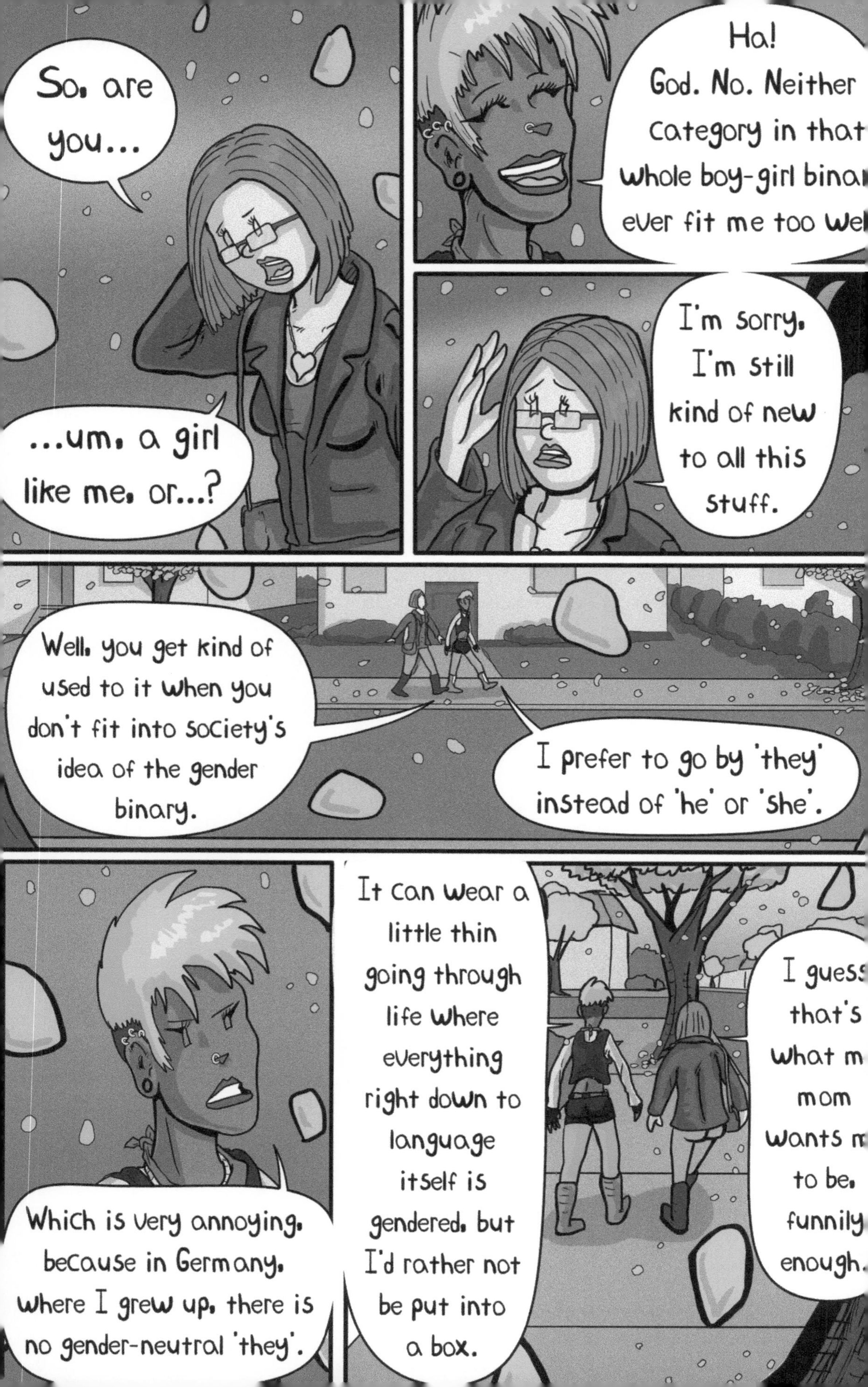
So, are you...
...um, a girl like me, or...?
Ha! God. No. Neither category in that whole boy-girl bina ever fit me too we
I'm sorry. I'm still kind of new to all this stuff.
Well, you get kind of used to it when you don't fit into society's idea of the gender binary.
I prefer to go by 'they' instead of 'he' or 'she'.
Which is very annoying, because in Germany, where I grew up, there is no gender-neutral 'they'.
It can wear a little thin going through life where everything right down to language itself is gendered, but I'd rather not be put into a box.
I gues that's what m mom wants m to be, funnily enough.

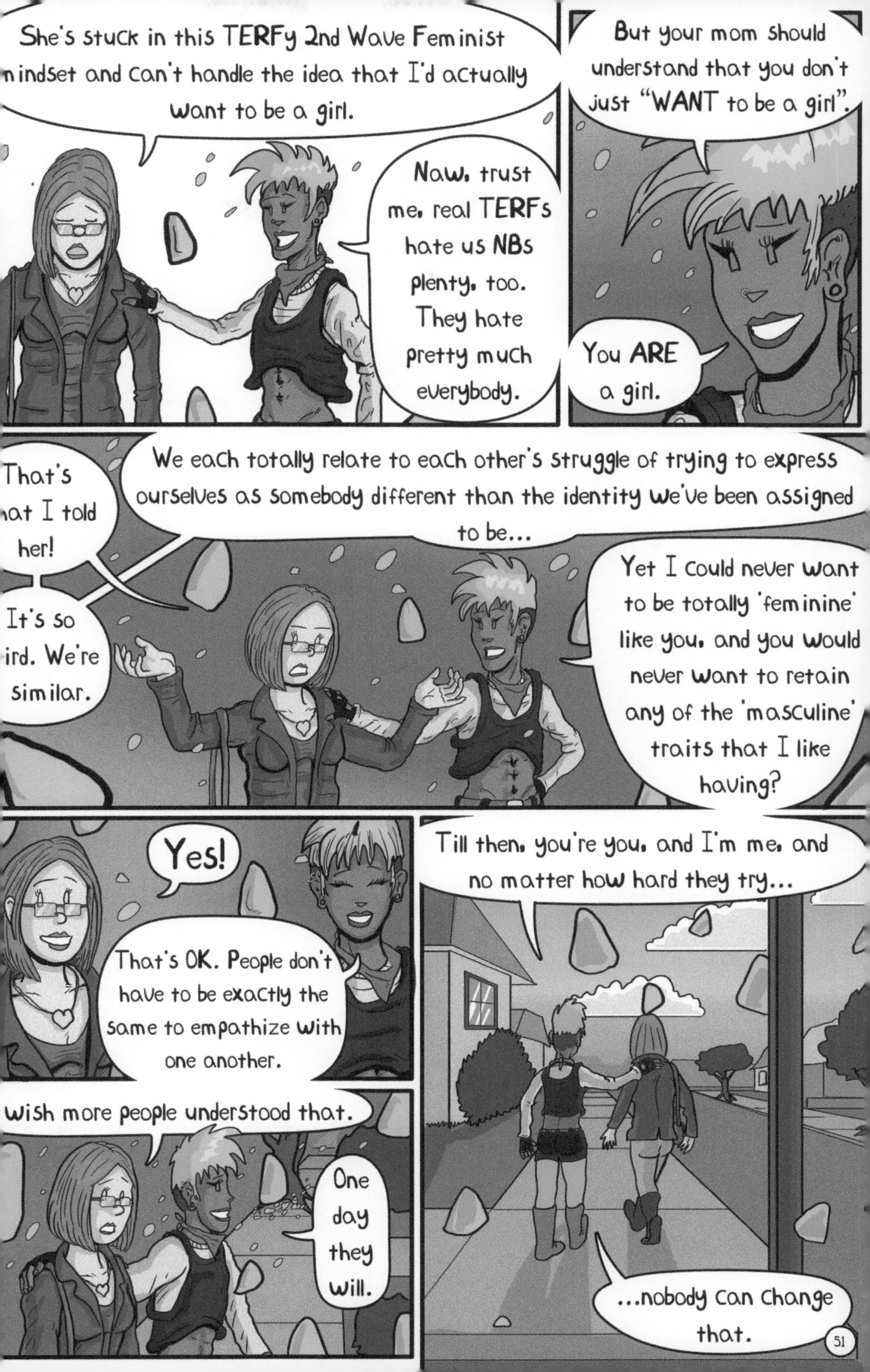

She's stuck in this TERFy 2nd Wave Feminist nindset and can't handle the idea that I'd actually want to be a girl.
Naw, trust me, real TERFs hate us NBs plenty, too. They hate pretty much everybody.
But your mom should understand that you don't just "WANT to be a girl".
You ARE a girl.
That's at I told her!
It's so ird. We're similar.
We each totally relate to each other's struggle of trying to express ourselves as somebody different than the identity we've been assigned to be...
Yet I could never want to be totally 'feminine' like you, and you would never want to retain any of the 'masculine' traits that I like having?
Yes!
That's OK. People don't have to be exactly the same to empathize with one another.
wish more people understood that.
One day they will.
Till then, you're you, and I'm me, and no matter how hard they try...
...nobody can change that.

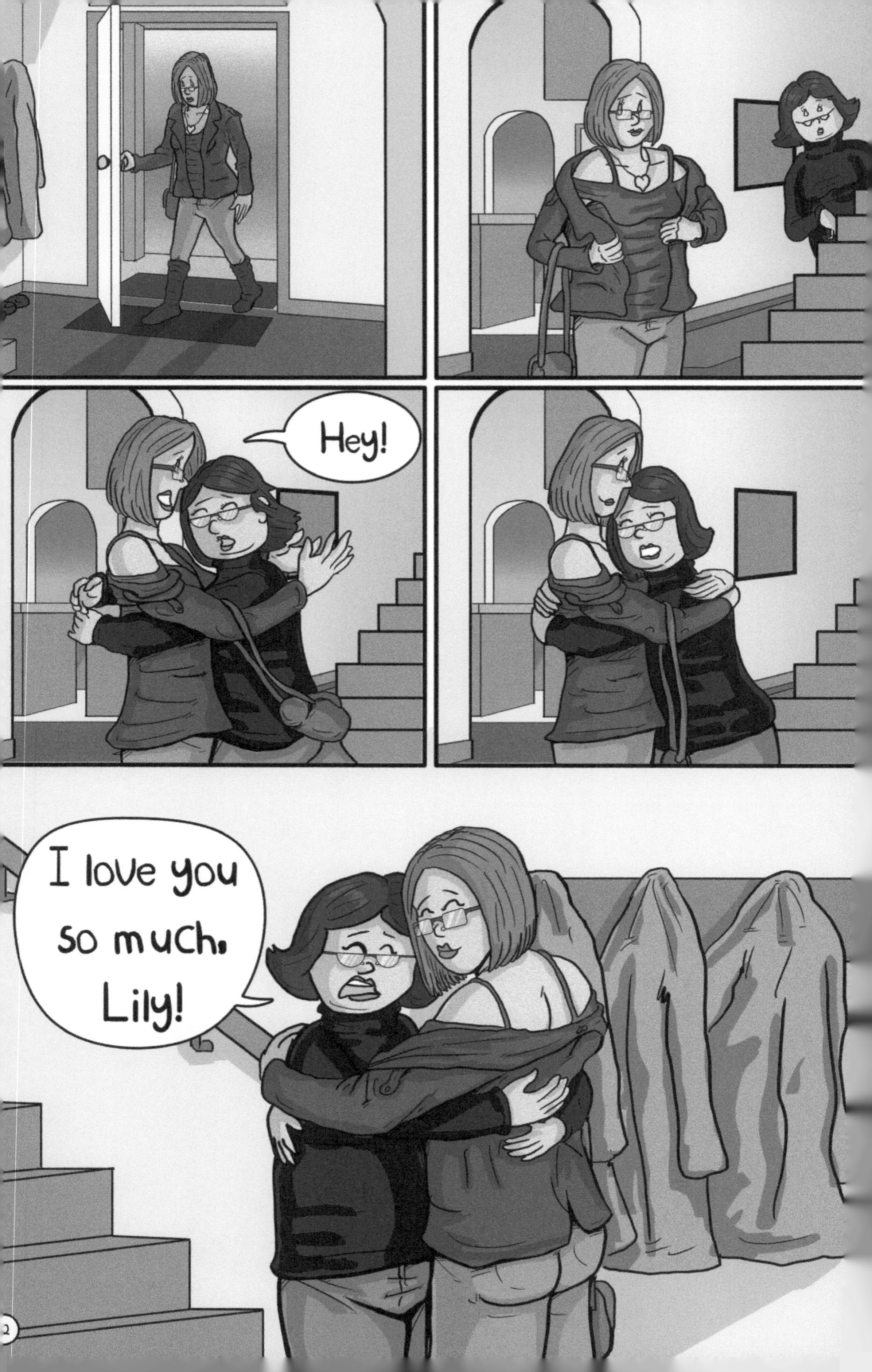
Hey!
I love you so much, Lily!

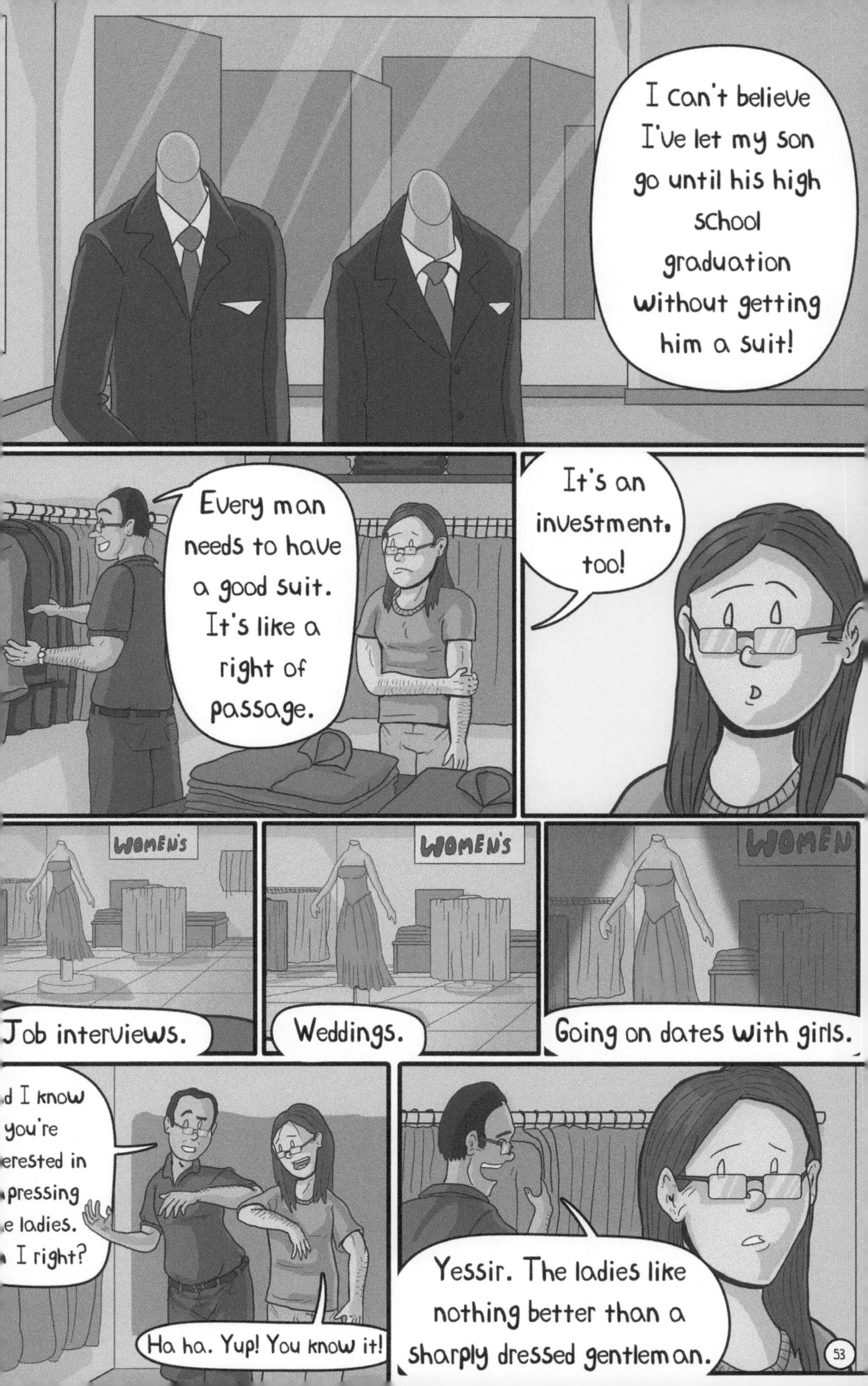

I can't believe I've let my son go until his high school graduation without getting him a suit!
Every man needs to have a good suit. It's like a right of passage.
It's an investment, too!
WOMEN'S
Job interviews.
WOMEN'S
Weddings.
WOMEN
Going on dates with girls.
d I know you're erested in pressing e ladies. I right?
Ha ha. Yup! You know it!
Yessir. The ladies like nothing better than a sharply dressed gentleman.

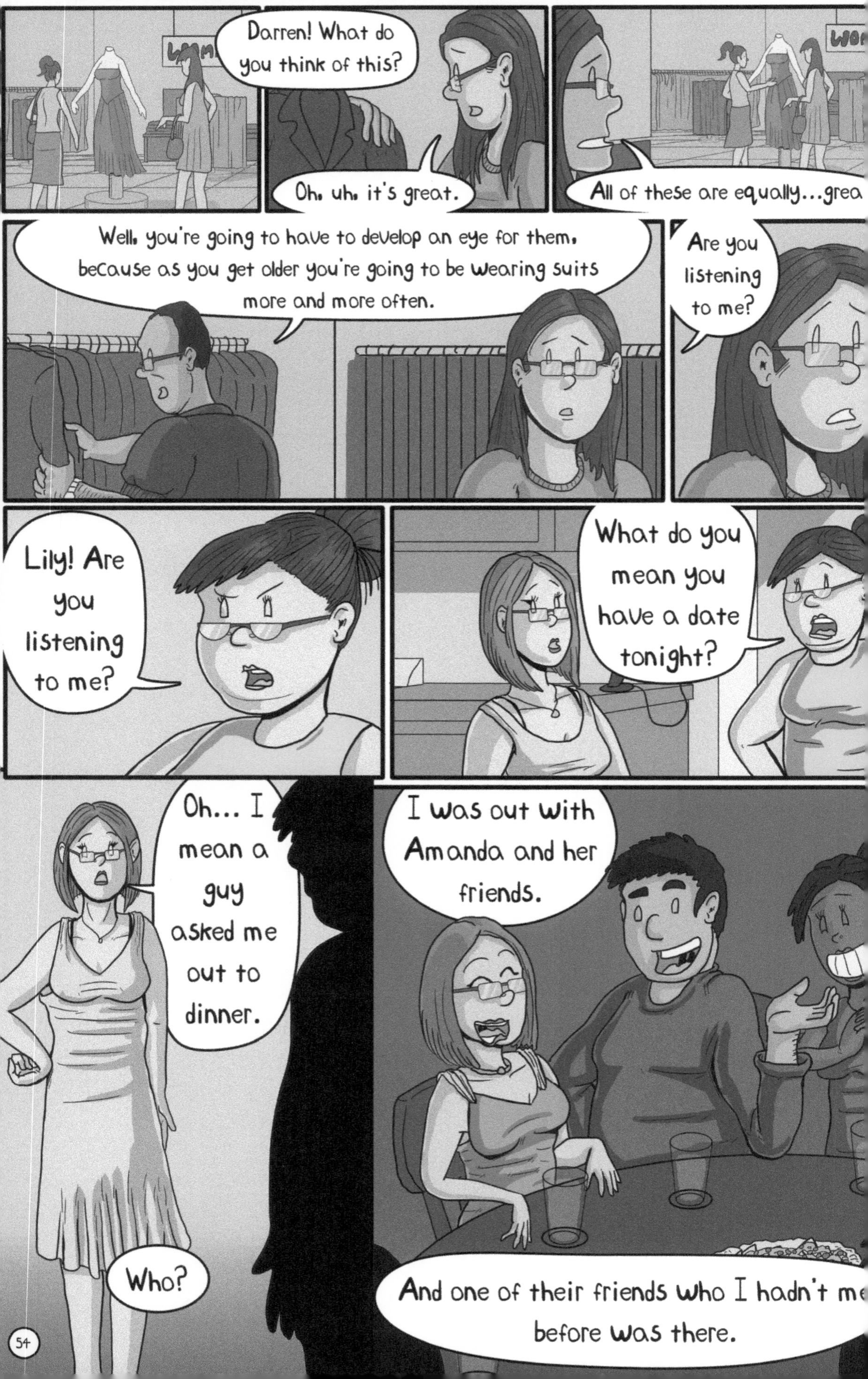
Darren! What do you think of this?
Oh, uh, it's great.
All of these are equally...grea
Well, you're going to have to develop an eye for them, because as you get older you're going to be wearing suits more and more often.
Are you listening to me?
Lily! Are you listening to me?
What do you mean you have a date tonight?
Oh... I mean a guy asked me out to dinner.
Who?
I was out with Amanda and her friends.
And one of their friends who I hadn't me
before was there.

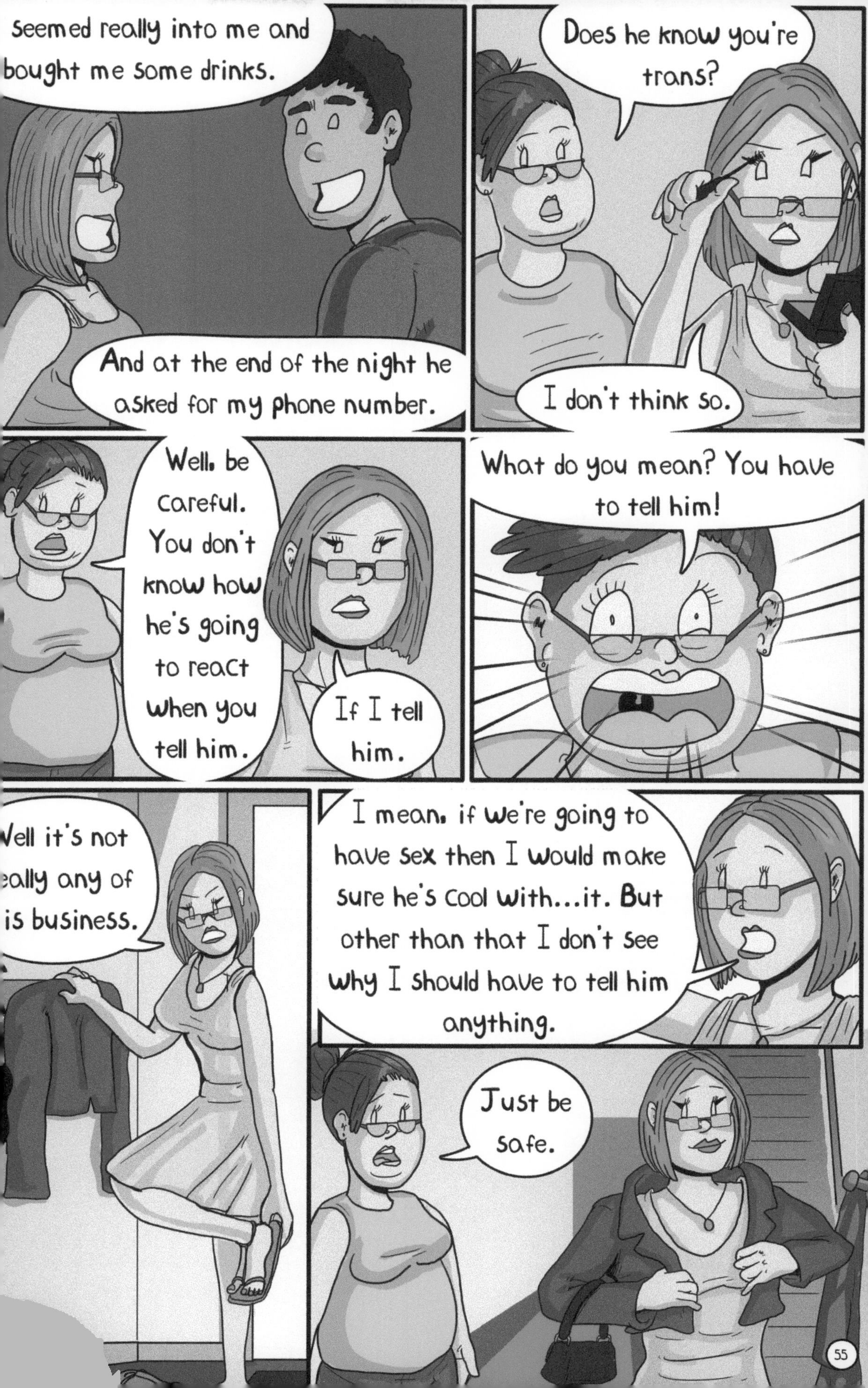

Seemed really into me and bought me some drinks.
And at the end of the night he asked for my phone number.
Does he know you're trans?
I don't think so.
Well, be careful. You don't know how he's going to react when you tell him.
If I tell him.
What do you mean? You have to tell him!
ell it's not eally any of is business.
I mean, if we're going to have sex then I would make sure he's cool with...it. But other than that I don't see why I should have to tell him anything.
Just be safe.

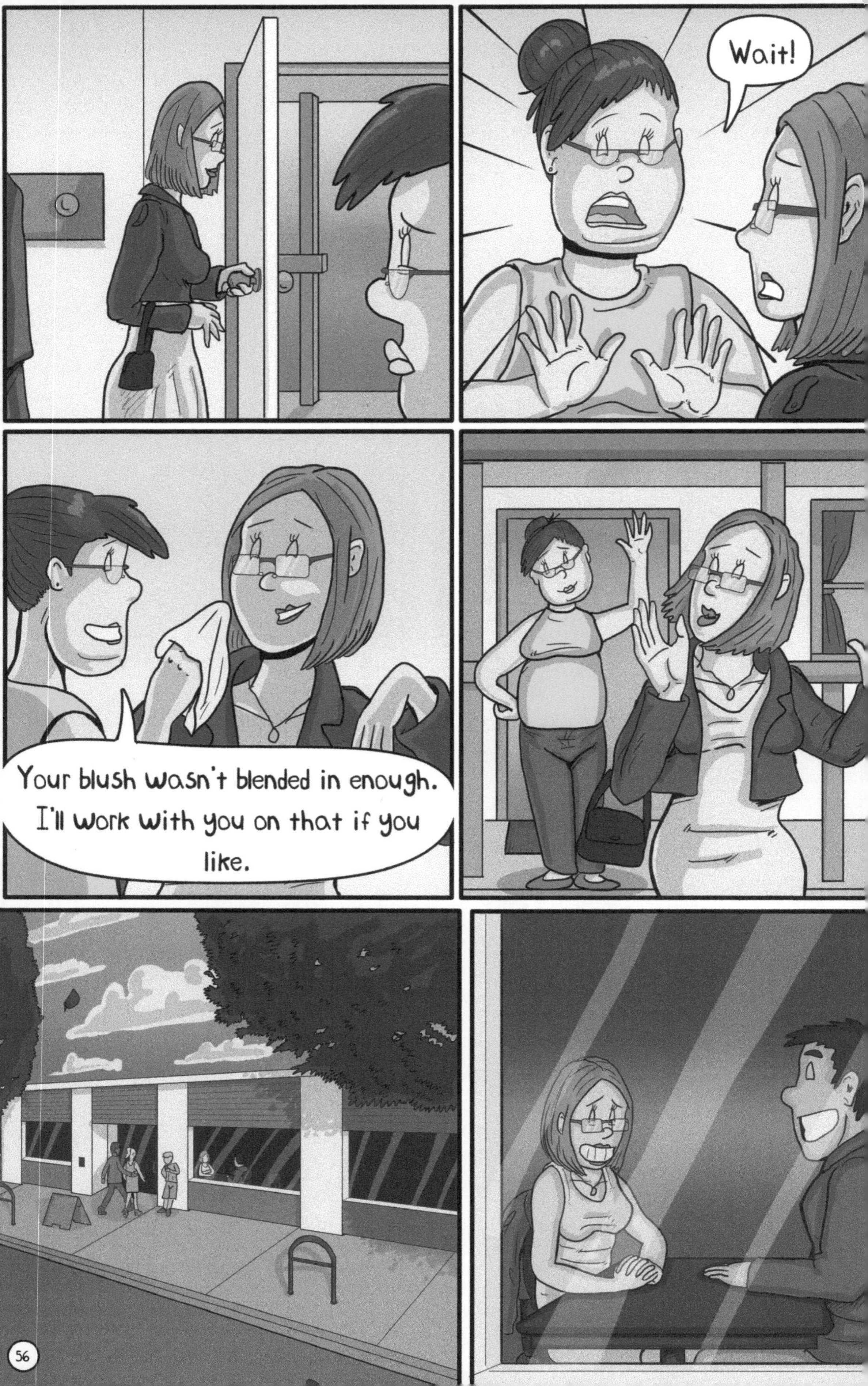
Wait!
Your blush wasn't blended in enough. I'll work with you on that if you like.

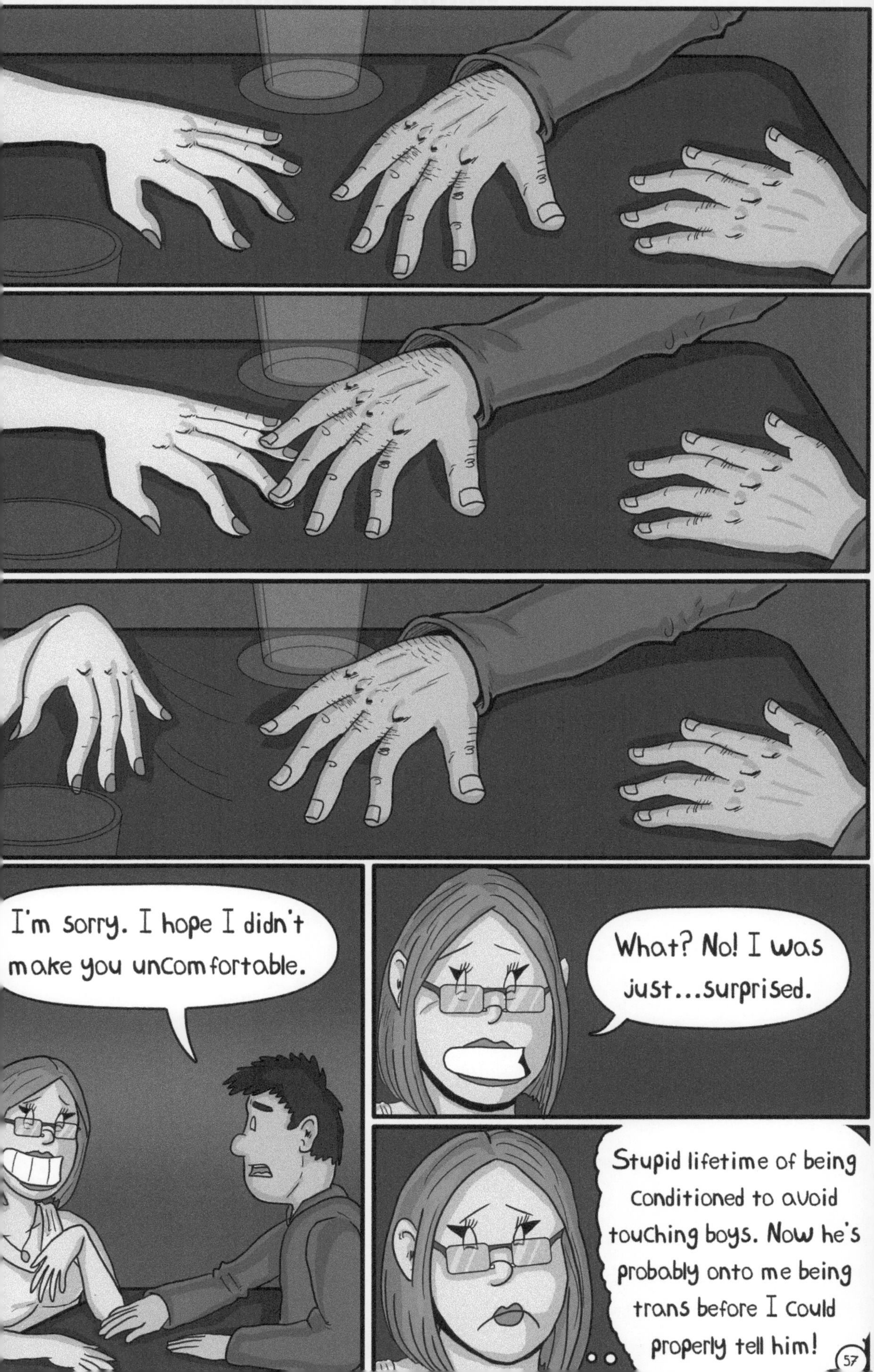
I'm sorry. I hope I didn't make you uncomfortable.
What? No! I was just...surprised.
Stupid lifetime of being conditioned to avoid touching boys. Now he's probably onto me being trans before I could properly tell him!

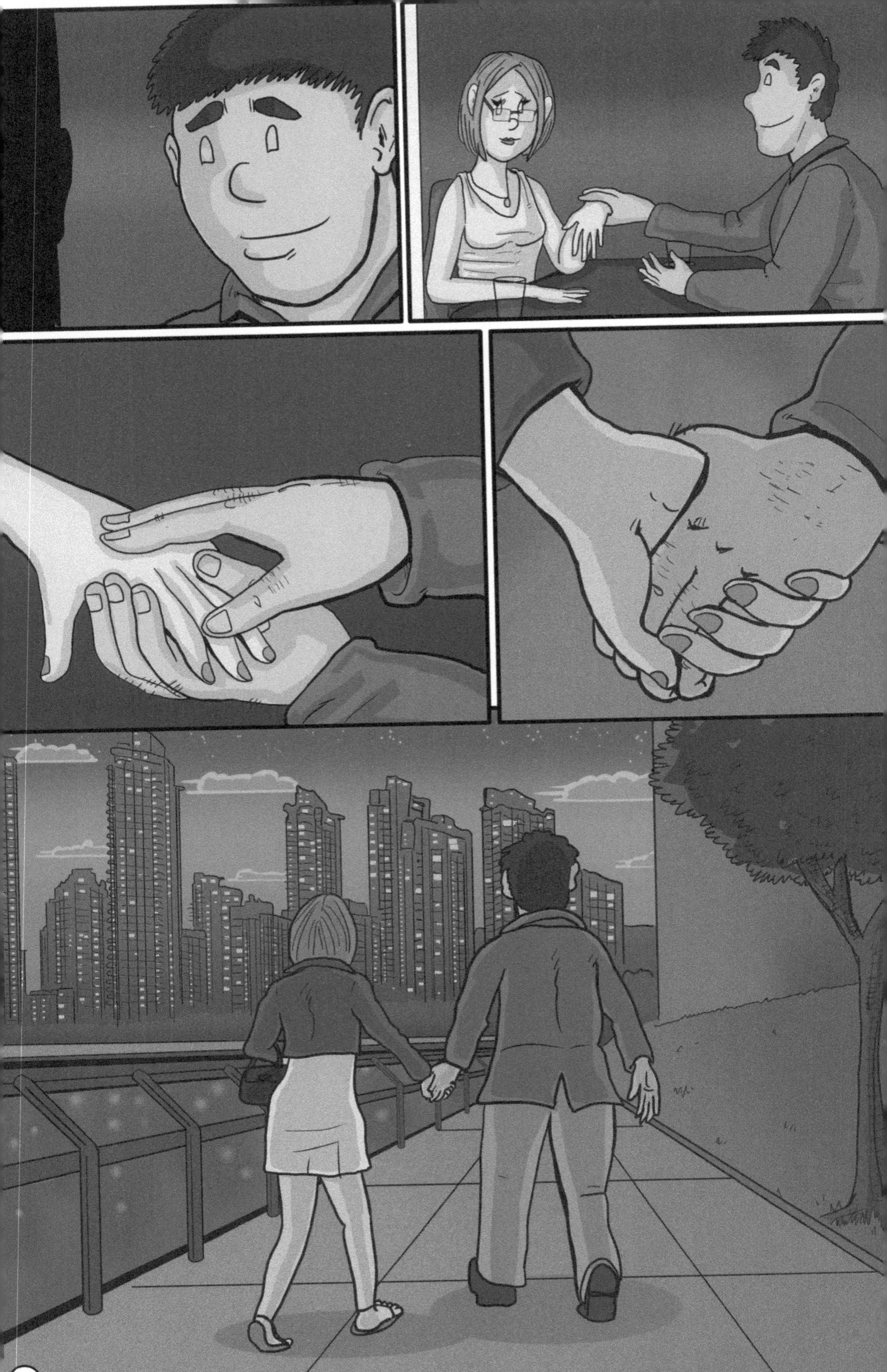

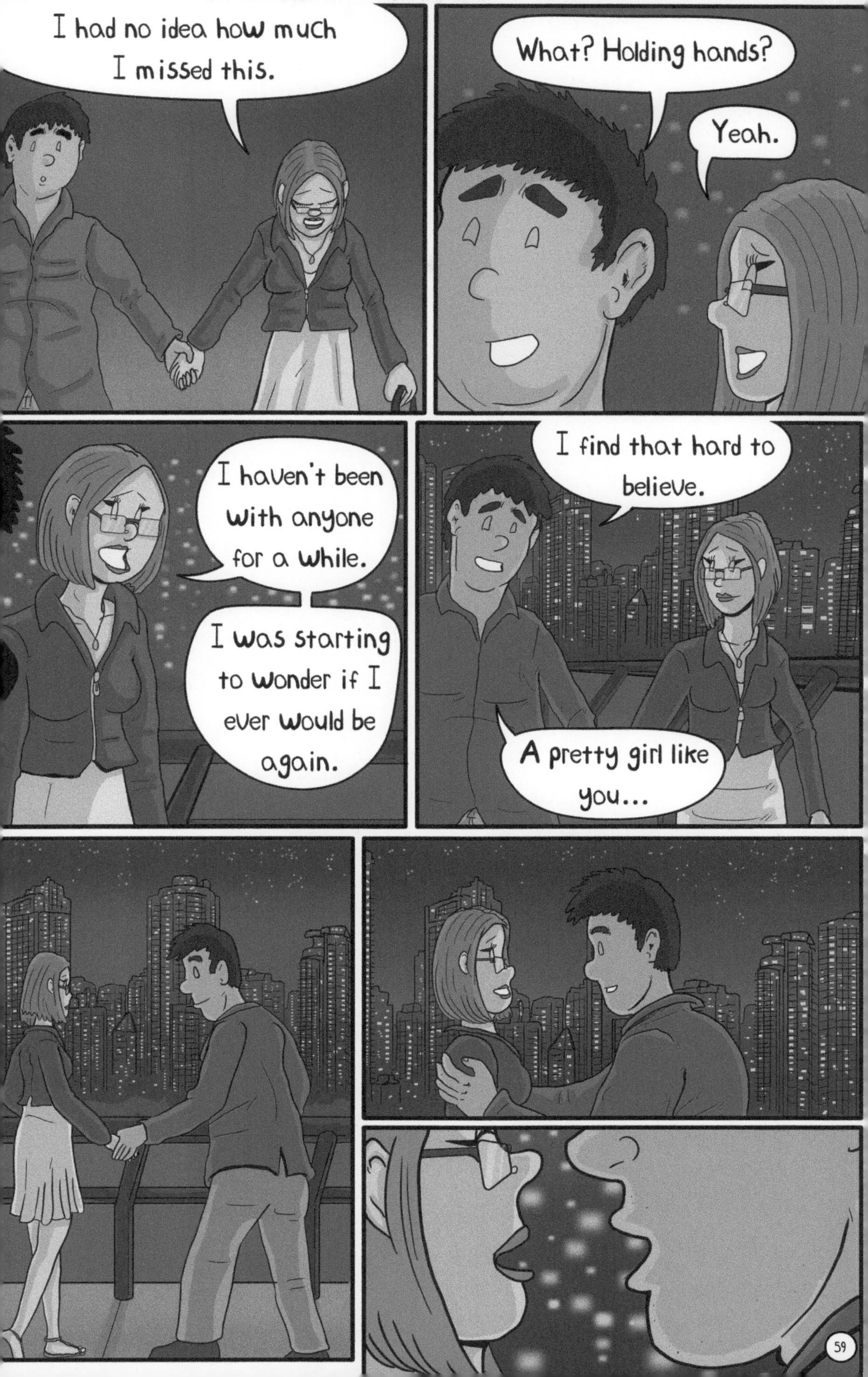
I had no idea how much I missed this.
What? Holding hands?
Yeah.
I haven't been with anyone for a while.
I was starting to wonder if I ever would be again.
I find that hard to believe.
A pretty girl like you...

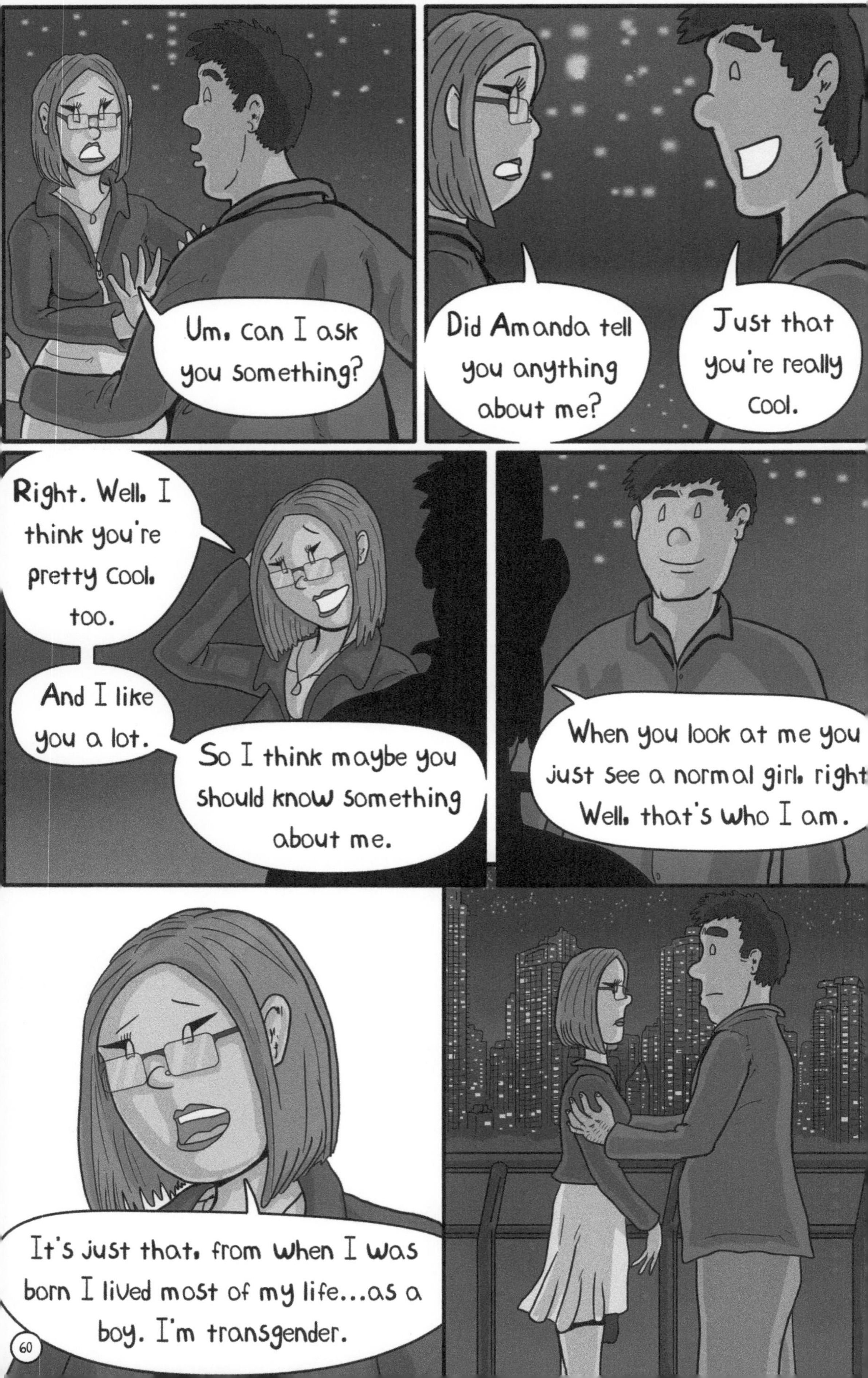

Um, can I ask you something?
Did Amanda tell you anything about me?
Just that you're really cool.
Right. Well, I think you're pretty cool, too.
And I like you a lot.
So I think maybe you should know something about me.
When you look at me you just see a normal girl, right
Well, that's who I am.
It's just that, from when I was born I lived most of my life...as a boy. I'm transgender.

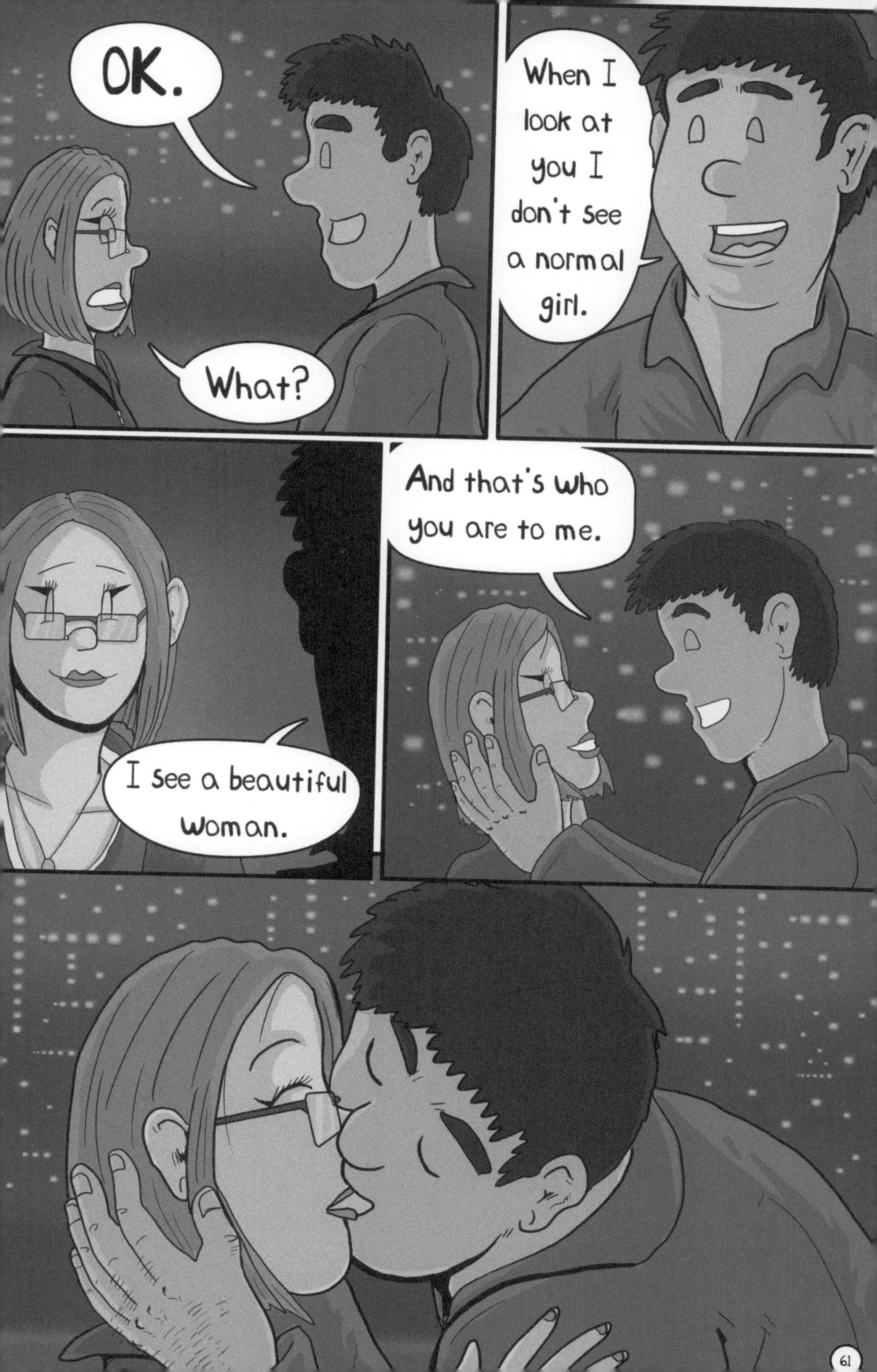
OK.
What?
When I look at you I don't see a normal girl.
I see a beautiful woman.
And that's who you are to me.

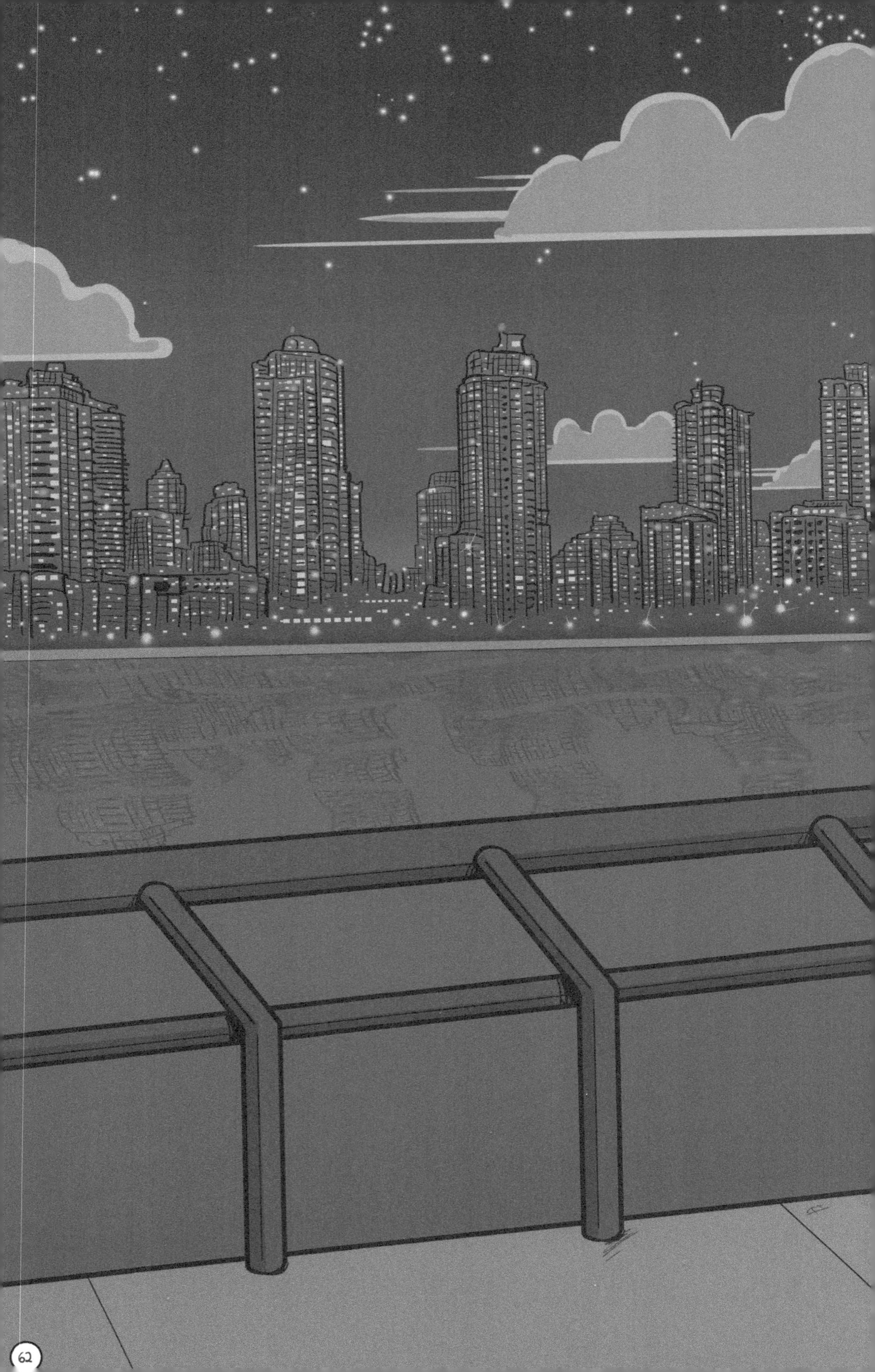

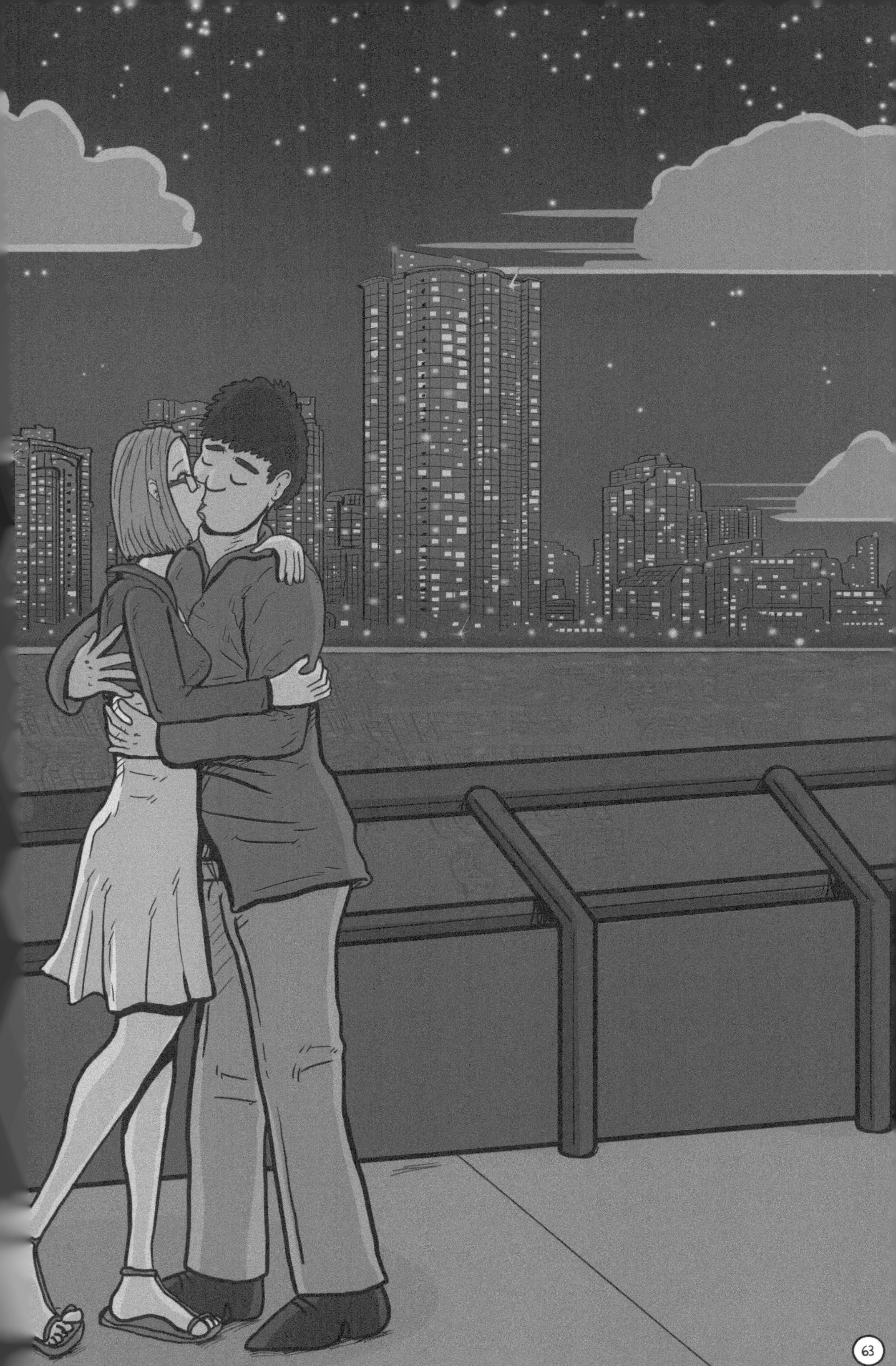

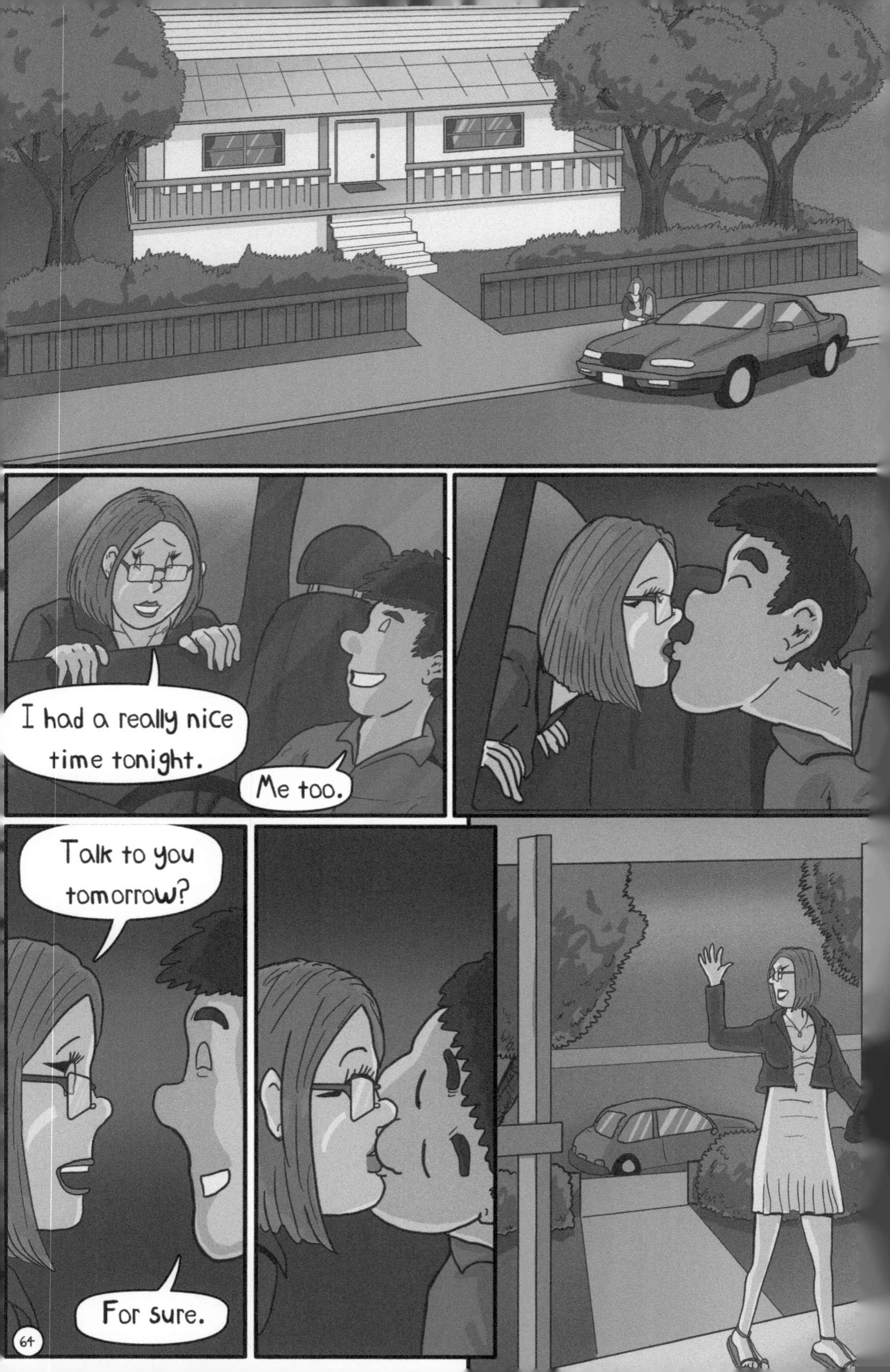

I had a really nice time tonight.
Me too.
Talk to you tomorrow?
For sure.

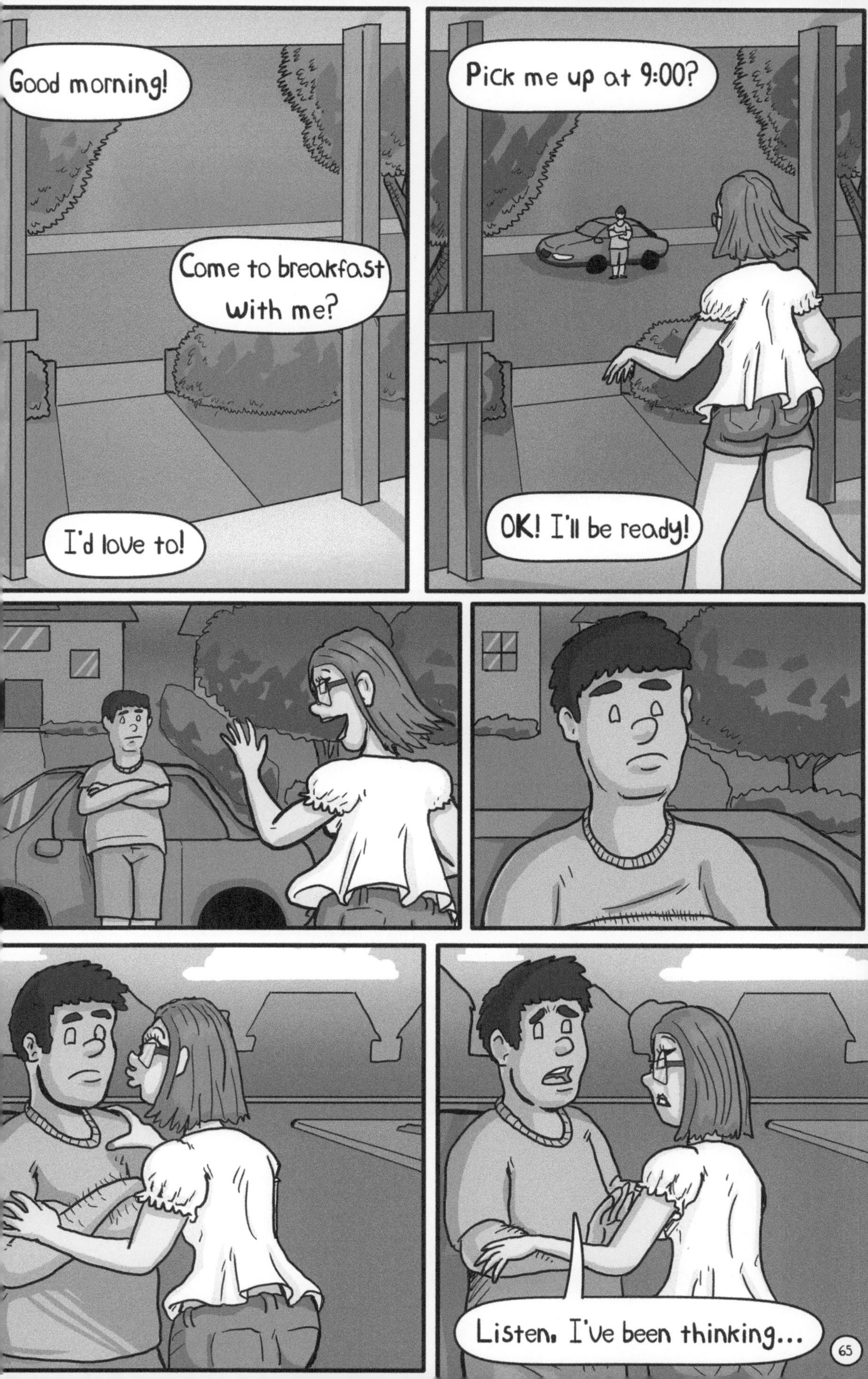
Good morning!
Come to breakfast with me?
I'd love to!
Pick me up at 9:00?
OK! I'll be ready!
Listen. I've been thinking...

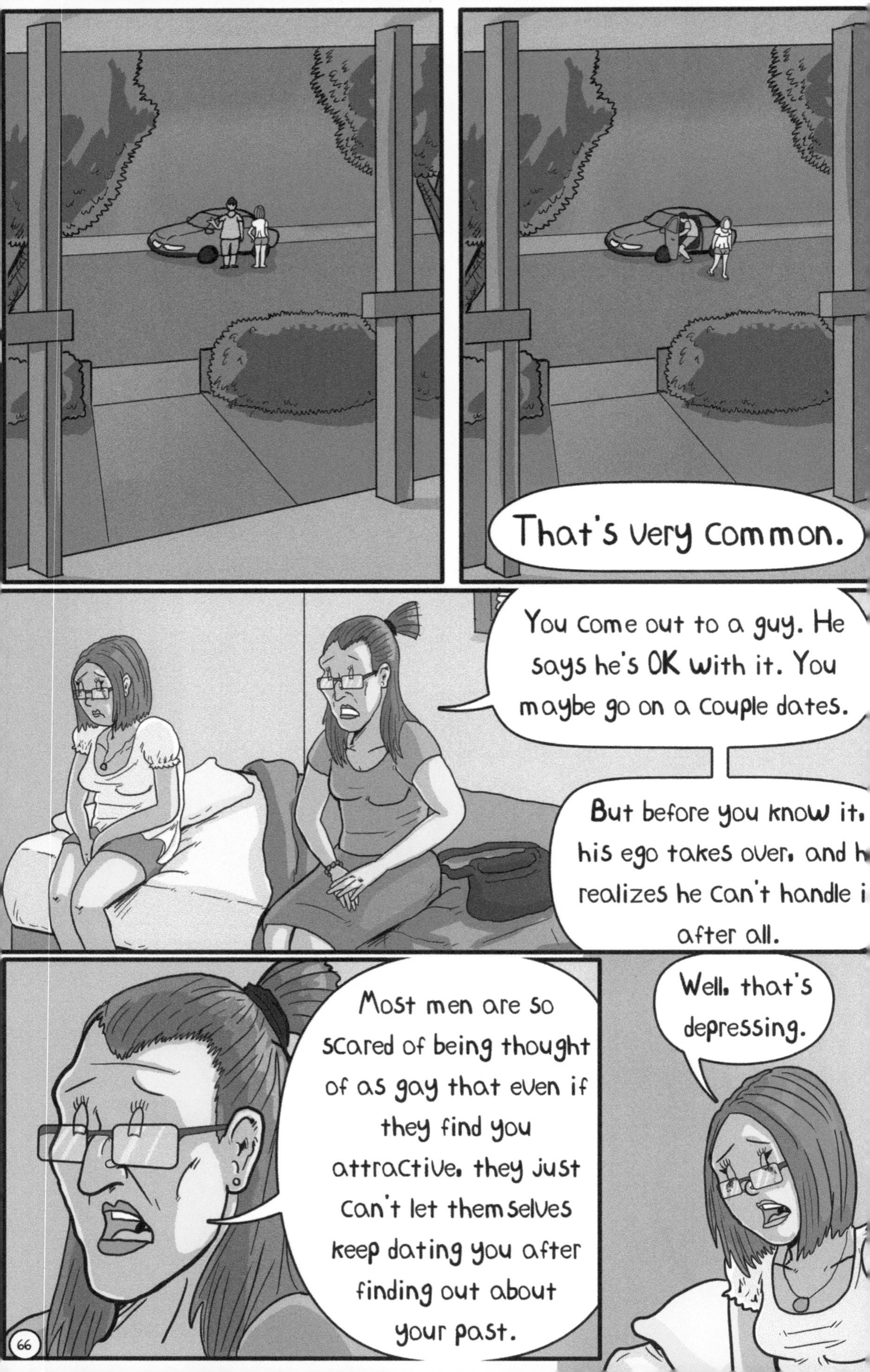
That's very common.
You come out to a guy. He says he's OK with it. You maybe go on a couple dates.
But before you know it, his ego takes over, and h realizes he can't handle i after all.
Most men are so scared of being thought of as gay that even if they find you attractive, they just can't let themselves keep dating you after finding out about your past.
Well, that's depressing.

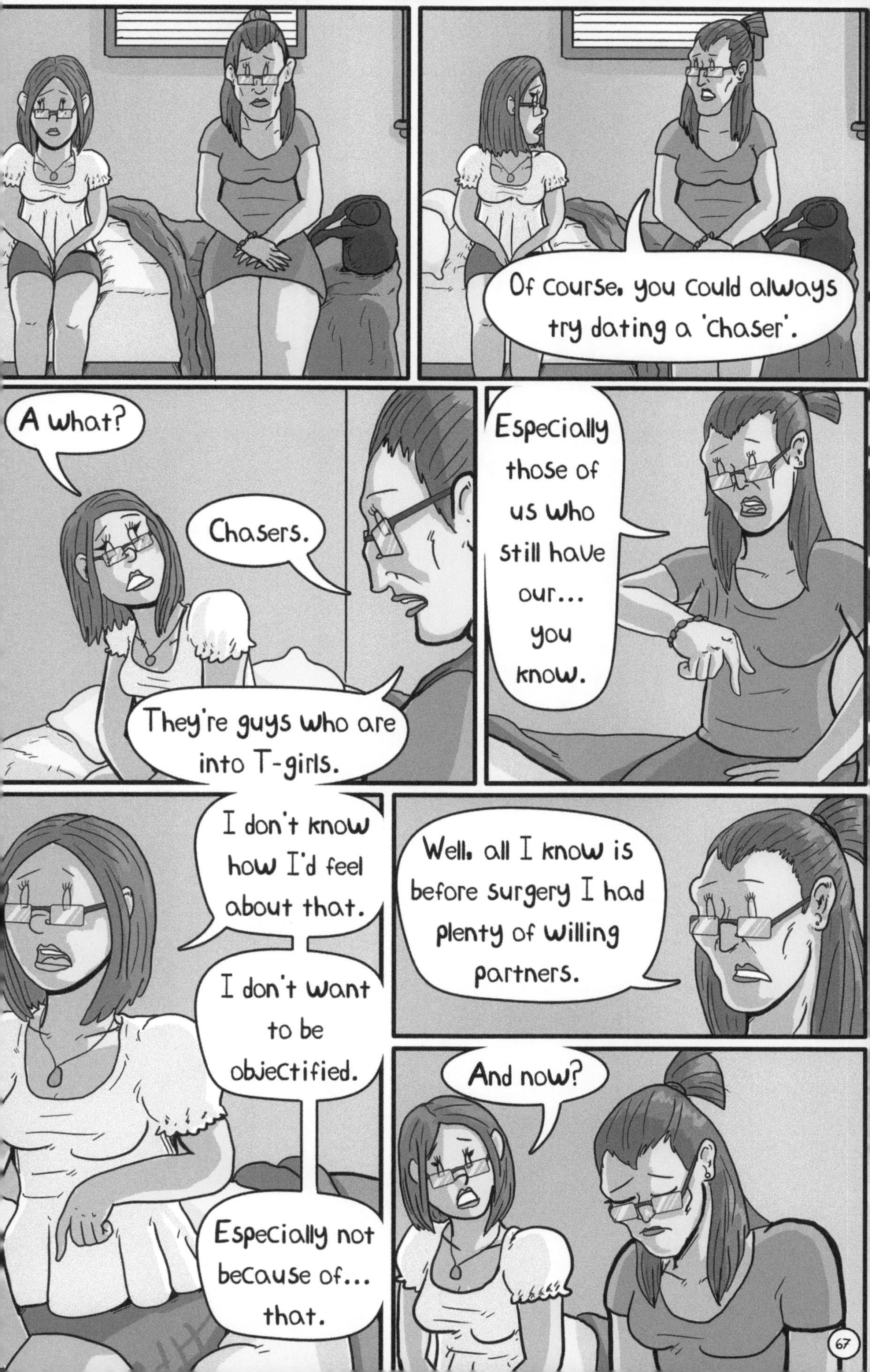

Of course, you could always try dating a 'chaser'.
A what?
Chasers.
They're guys who are into T-girls.
Especially those of us who still have our... you know.
I don't know how I'd feel about that.
I don't want to be objectified.
Especially not because of... that.
Well, all I know is before surgery I had plenty of willing partners.
And now?

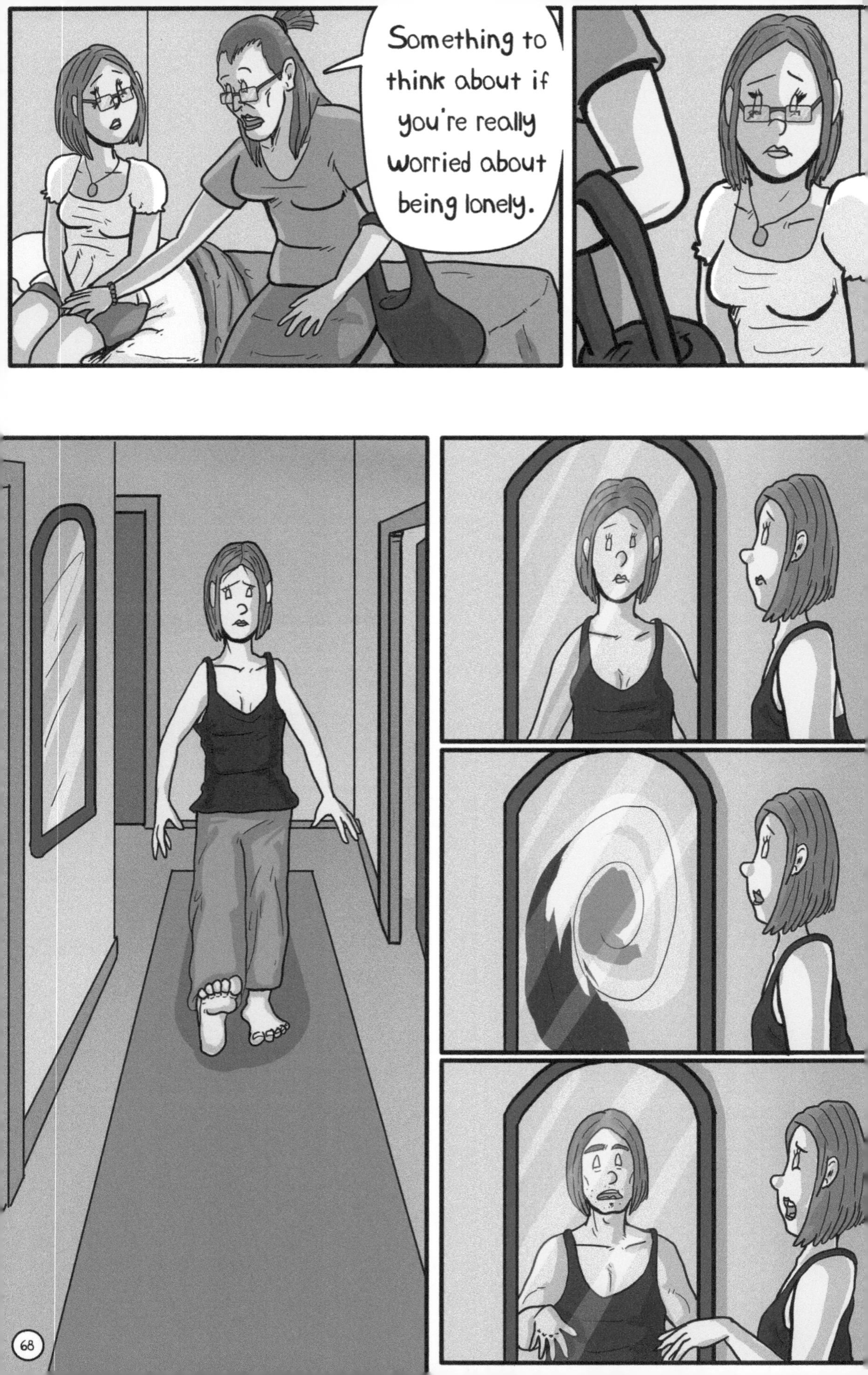
Something to think about if you're really worried about being lonely.

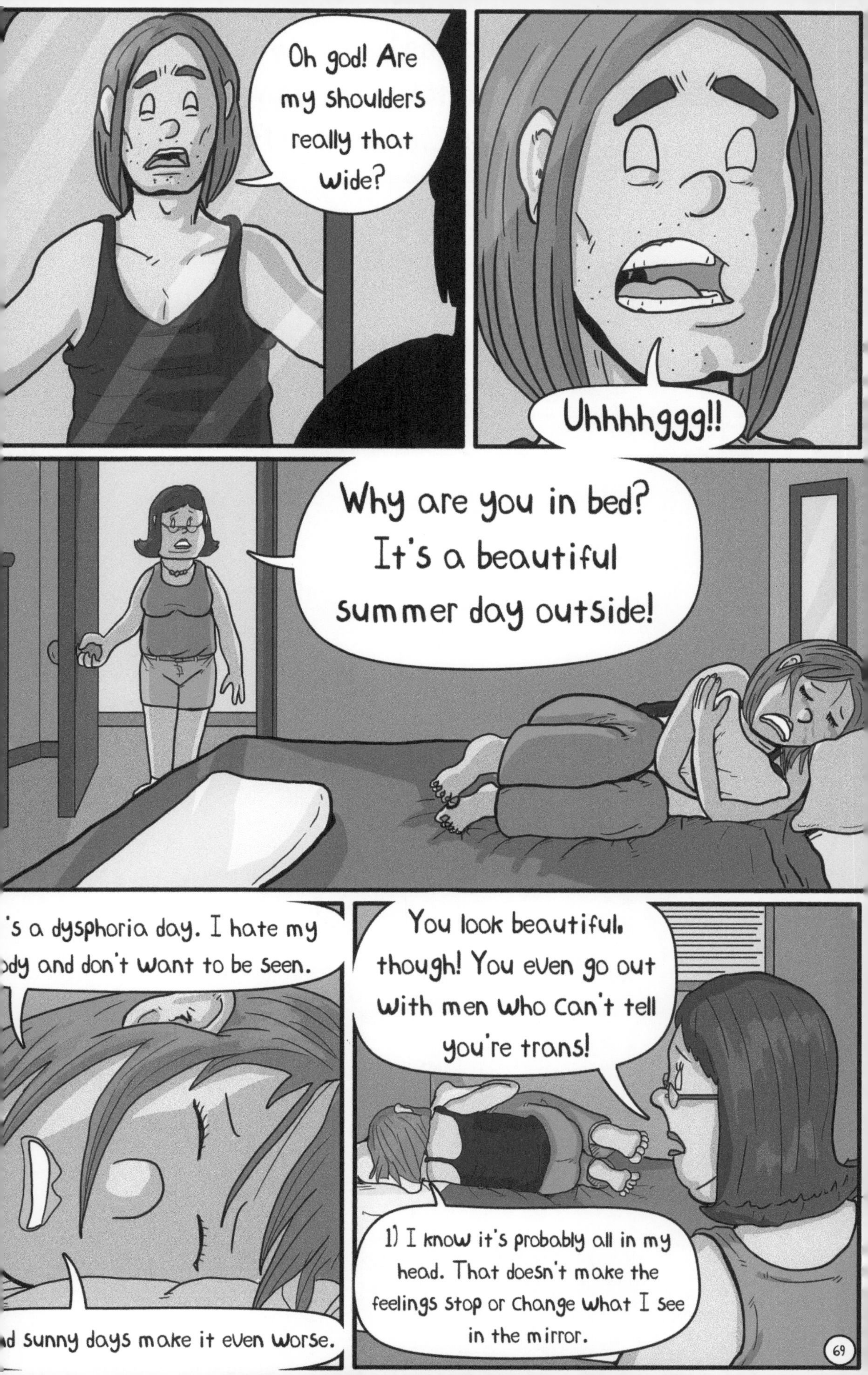
Oh god! Are my shoulders really that wide?
Uhhhhggg!!
Why are you in bed? It's a beautiful summer day outside!
'S a dysphoria day. I hate my ody and don't want to be seen.
d sunny days make it even worse.
You look beautiful, though! You even go out with men who can't tell you're trans!
1) I know it's probably all in my head. That doesn't make the feelings stop or change what I see in the mirror.

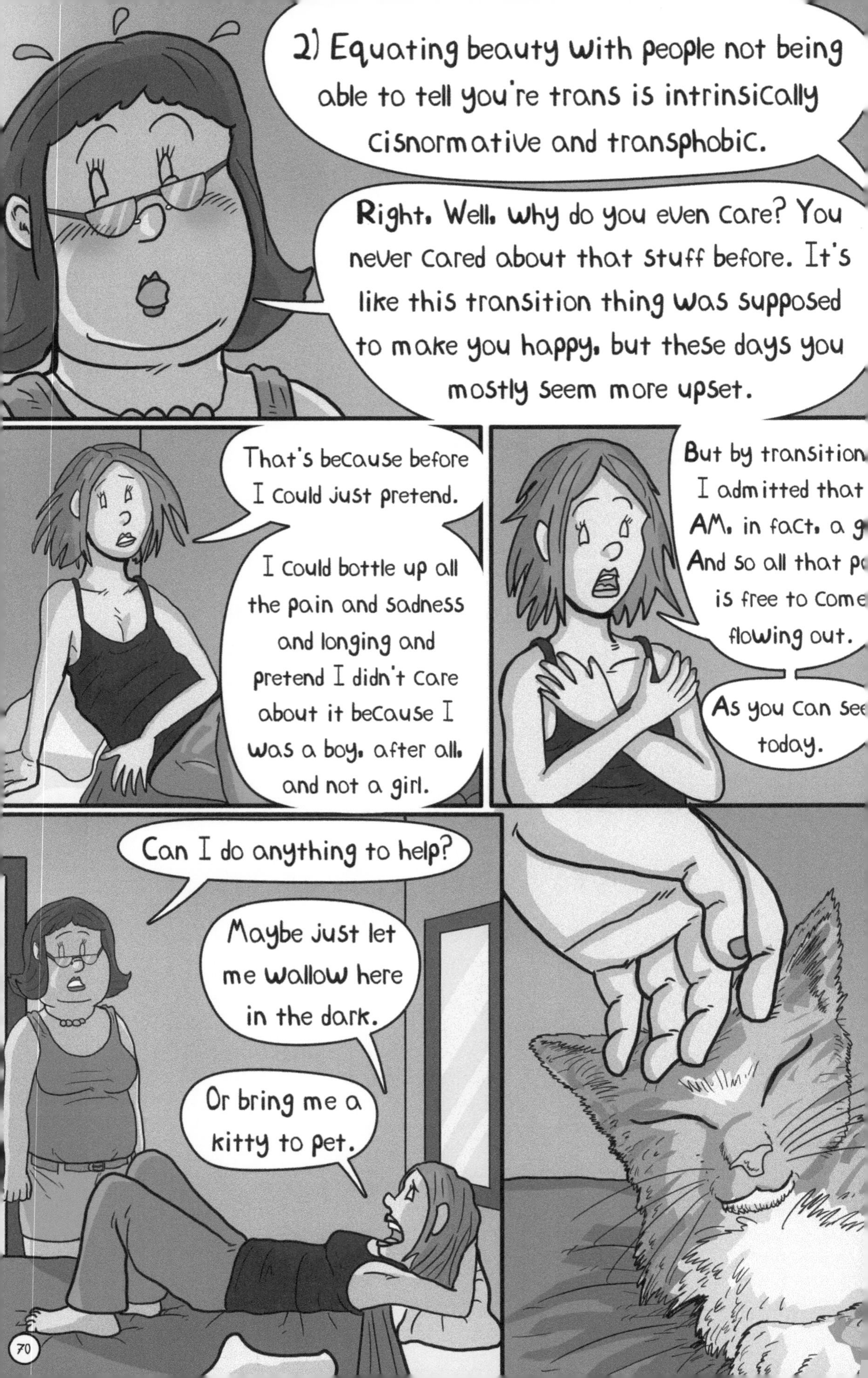
2) Equating beauty with people not being able to tell you're trans is intrinsically cisnormative and transphobic.
Right. Well. why do you even care? You never cared about that stuff before. It's like this transition thing was supposed to make you happy. but these days you mostly seem more upset.
That's because before I could just pretend.
I could bottle up all the pain and sadness and longing and pretend I didn't care about it because I was a boy. after all. and not a girl.
But by transition
I admitted that
AM. in fact. a
And so all that
is free to come
flowing out.
As you can se
today.
Can I do anything to help?
Maybe just let me wallow here in the dark.
Or bring me a kitty to pet.

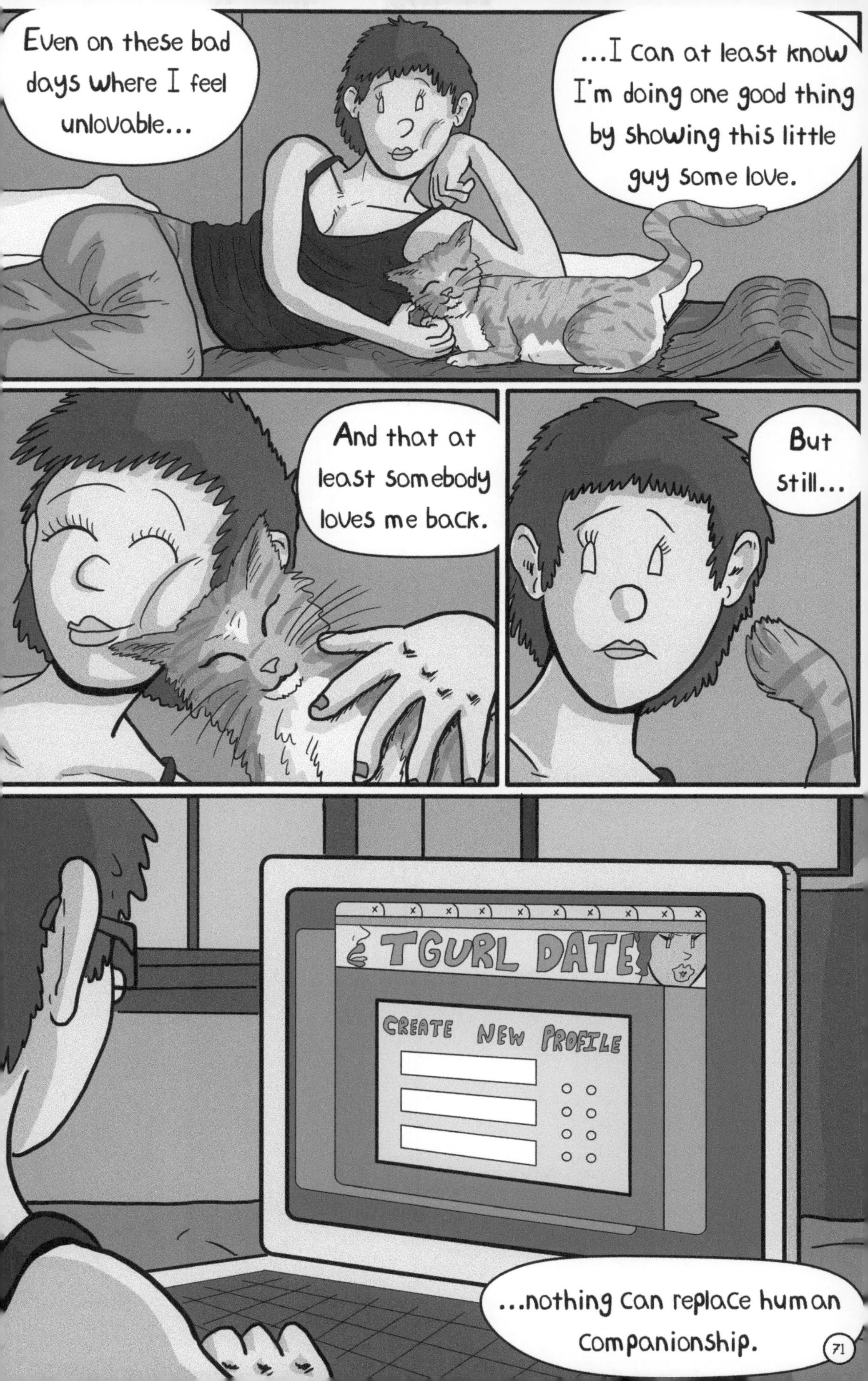

Even on these bad days where I feel unlovable...
...I can at least know I'm doing one good thing by showing this little guy some love.
And that at least somebody loves me back.
But still...
TGURL DATE
CREATE NEW PROFILE
...nothing can replace human companionship.

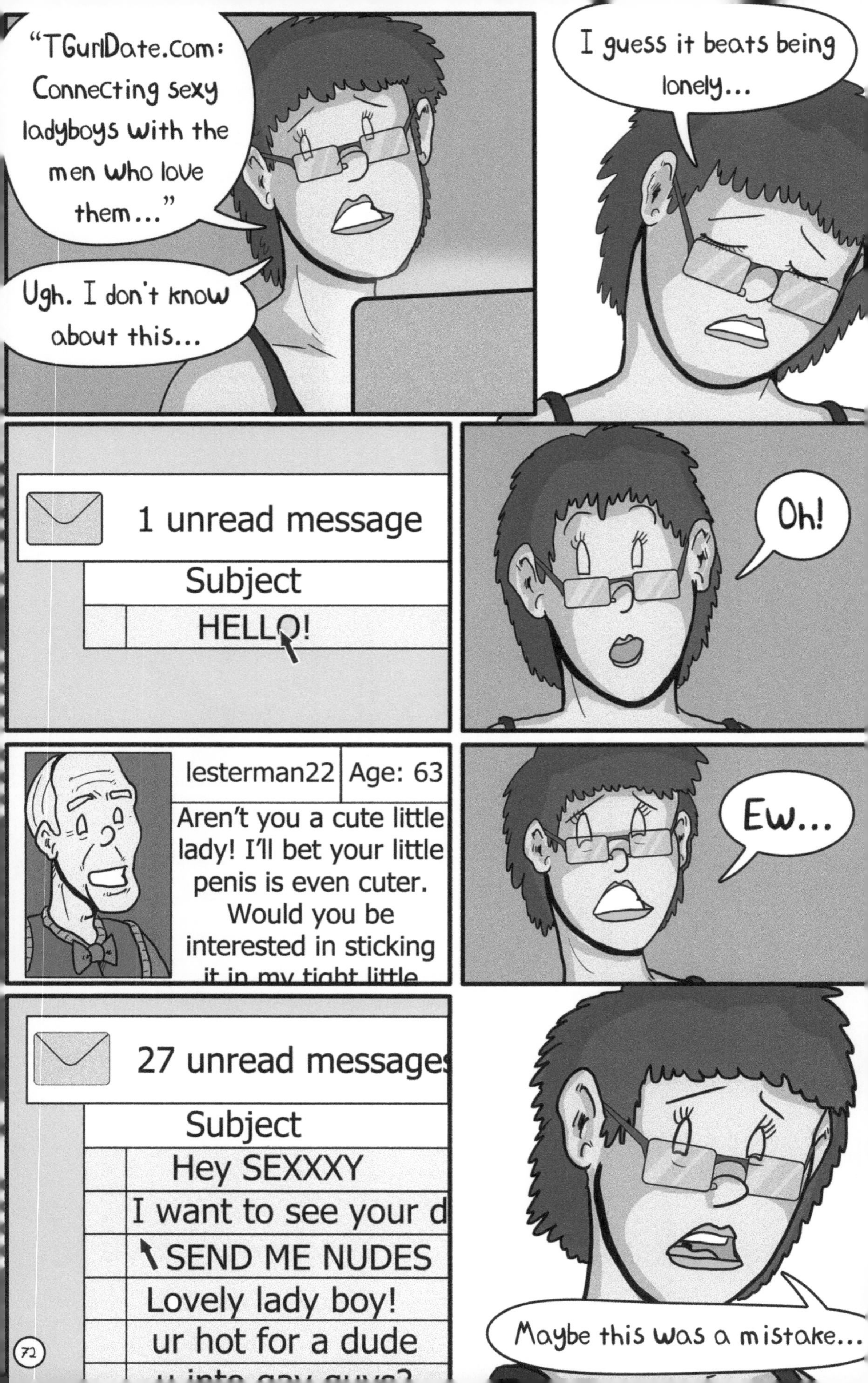

"TGurlDate.com: Connecting sexy ladyboys with the men who love them..."
Ugh. I don't know about this...
I guess it beats being lonely...
1 unread message
Subject
HELLO!
Oh!
lesterman22
Age: 63
Aren't you a cute little lady! I'll bet your little penis is even cuter. Would you be interested in sticking
Ew...
27 unread message
Subject
Hey SEXXXY
I want to see your d
SEND ME NUDES
Lovely lady boy!
ur hot for a dude
Maybe this was a mistake...

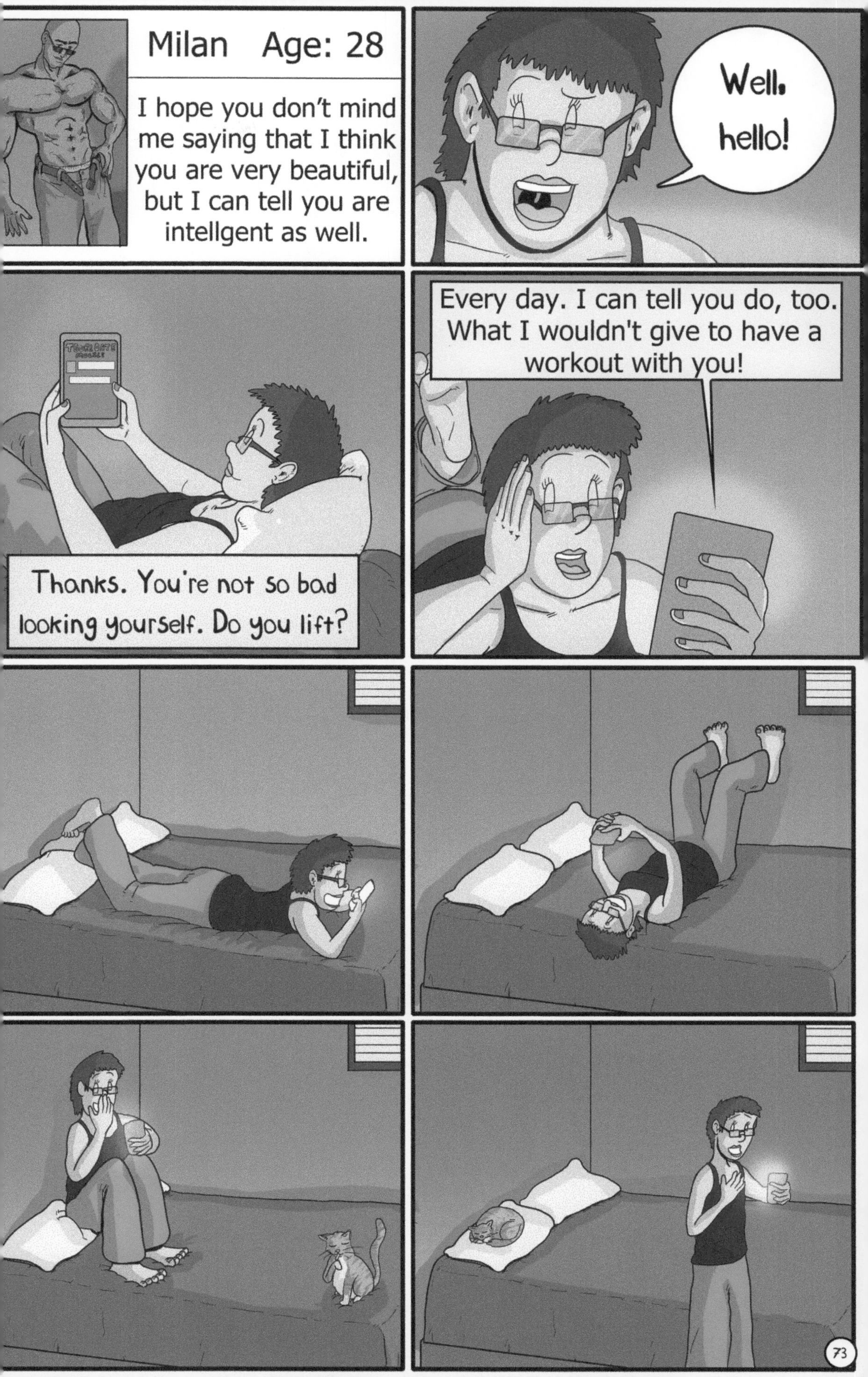
Milan Age: 28
I hope you don't mind me saying that I think you are very beautiful, but I can tell you are intellgent as well.
Well, hello!
Thanks. You're not so bad looking yourself. Do you lift?
Every day. I can tell you do, too. What I wouldn't give to have a workout with you!

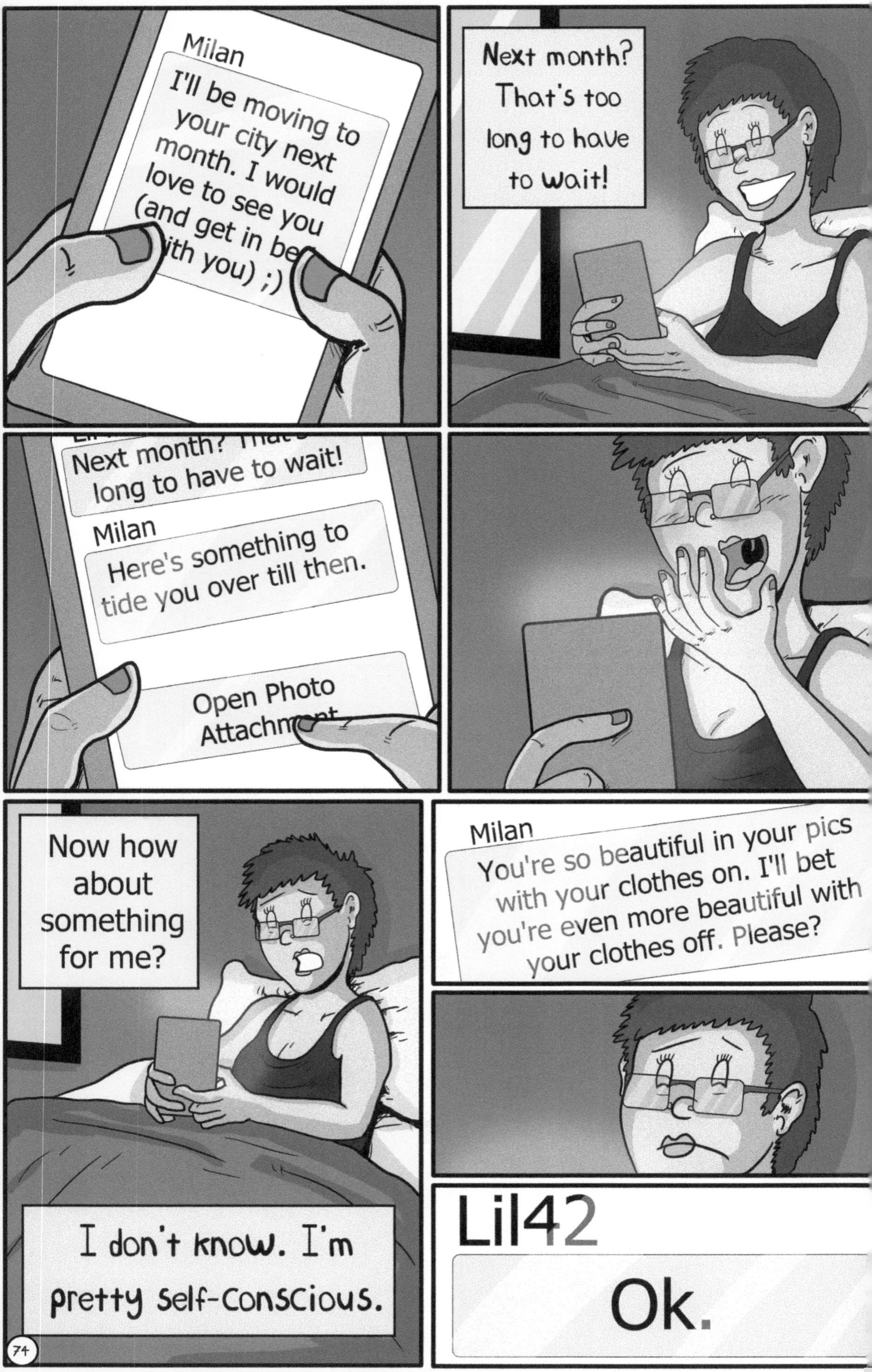

Milan
I'll be moving to your city next month. I would love to see you (and get in be
ith you) ;)
Next month? That's too long to have to wait!
Next month?
long to have to wait!
Milan
Here's something to tide you over till then.
Open Photo Attachm
Now how about something for me?
I don't know. I'm pretty self-conscious.
Milan
You're so beautiful in your pics with your clothes on. I'll bet you're even more beautiful with your clothes off. Please?
Lil42
Ok.

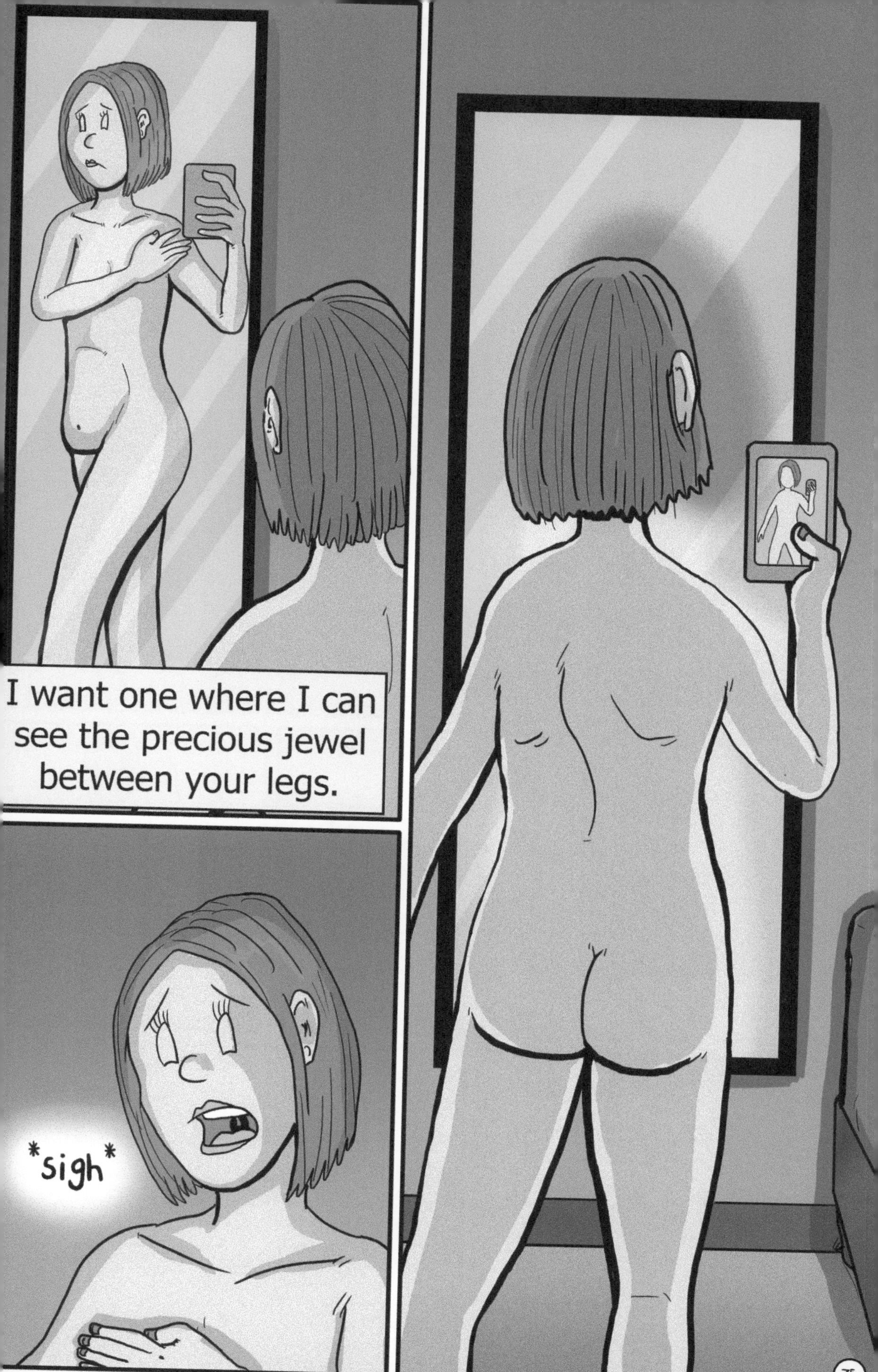

I want one where I can see the precious jewel between your legs.
sigh

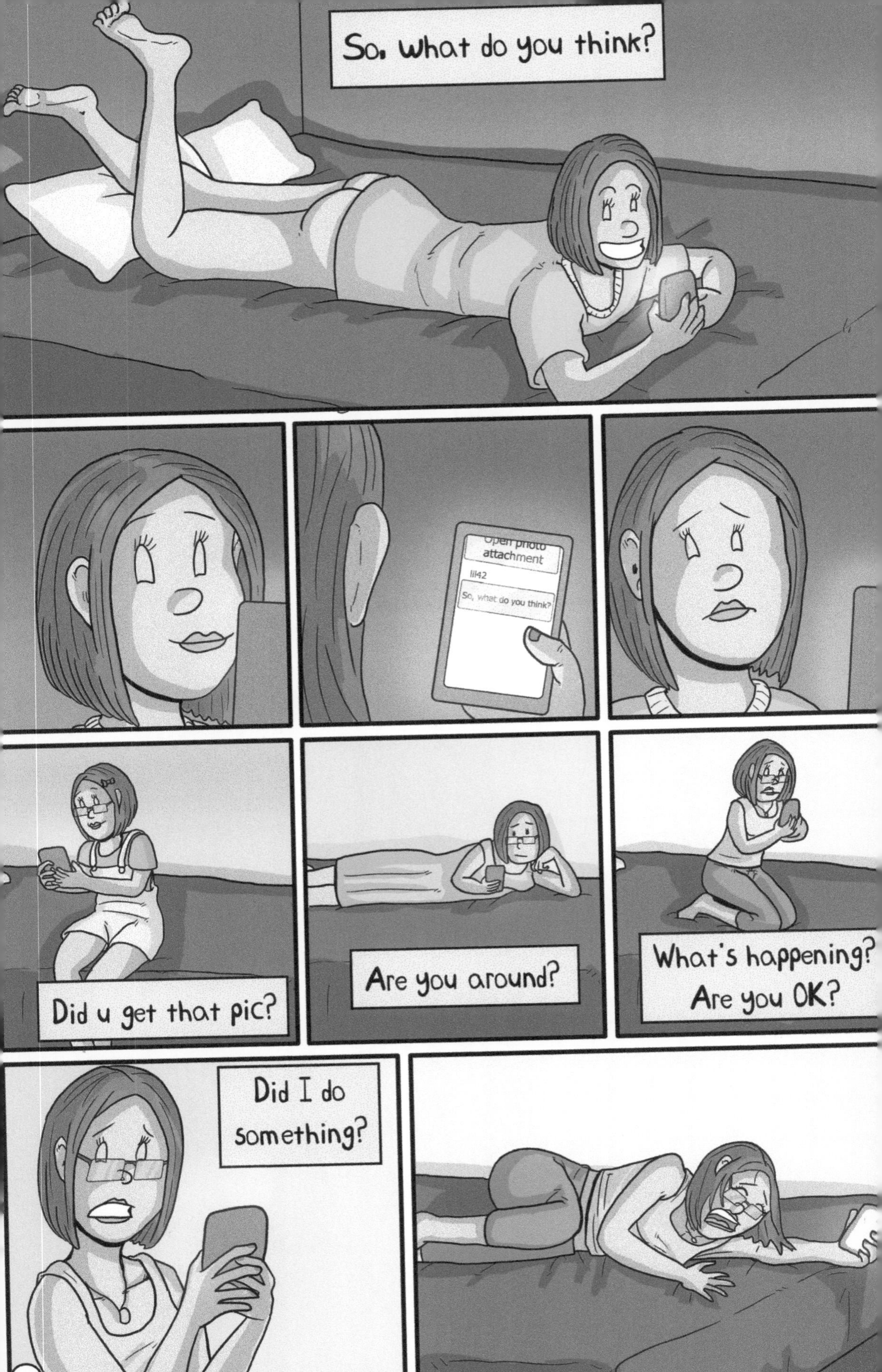
So, what do you think?
attachment
lil42
So, what do you think?
Did u get that pic?
Are you around?
What's happening? Are you OK?
Did I do something?

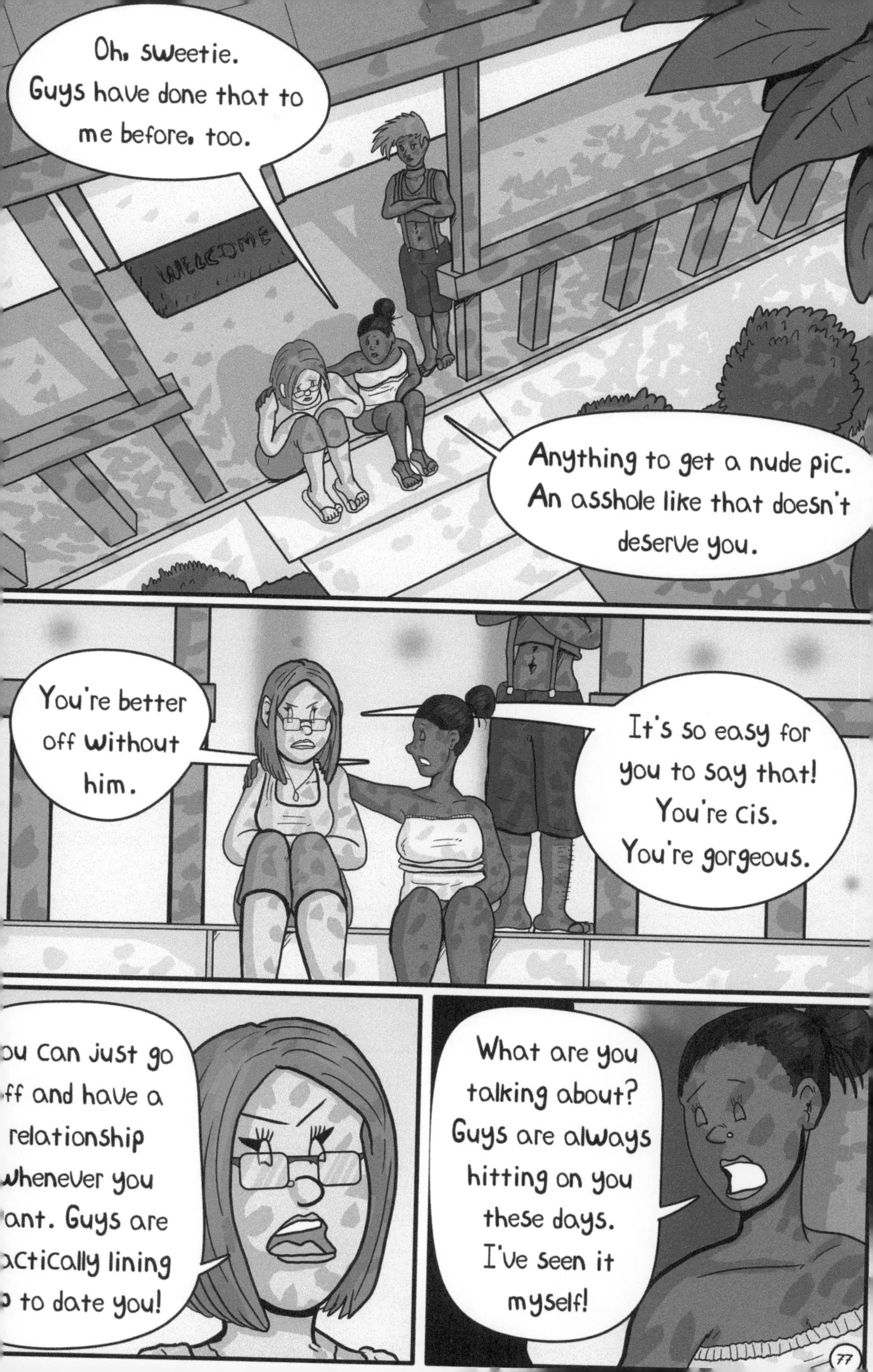
Oh, sweetie. Guys have done that to me before, too.
WELCOME
Anything to get a nude pic. An asshole like that doesn't deserve you.
You're better off without him.
It's so easy for you to say that! You're cis. You're gorgeous.
ou can just go ff and have a relationship whenever you ant. Guys are acticlly lining to date you!
What are you talking about? Guys are always hitting on you these days. I've seen it myself!

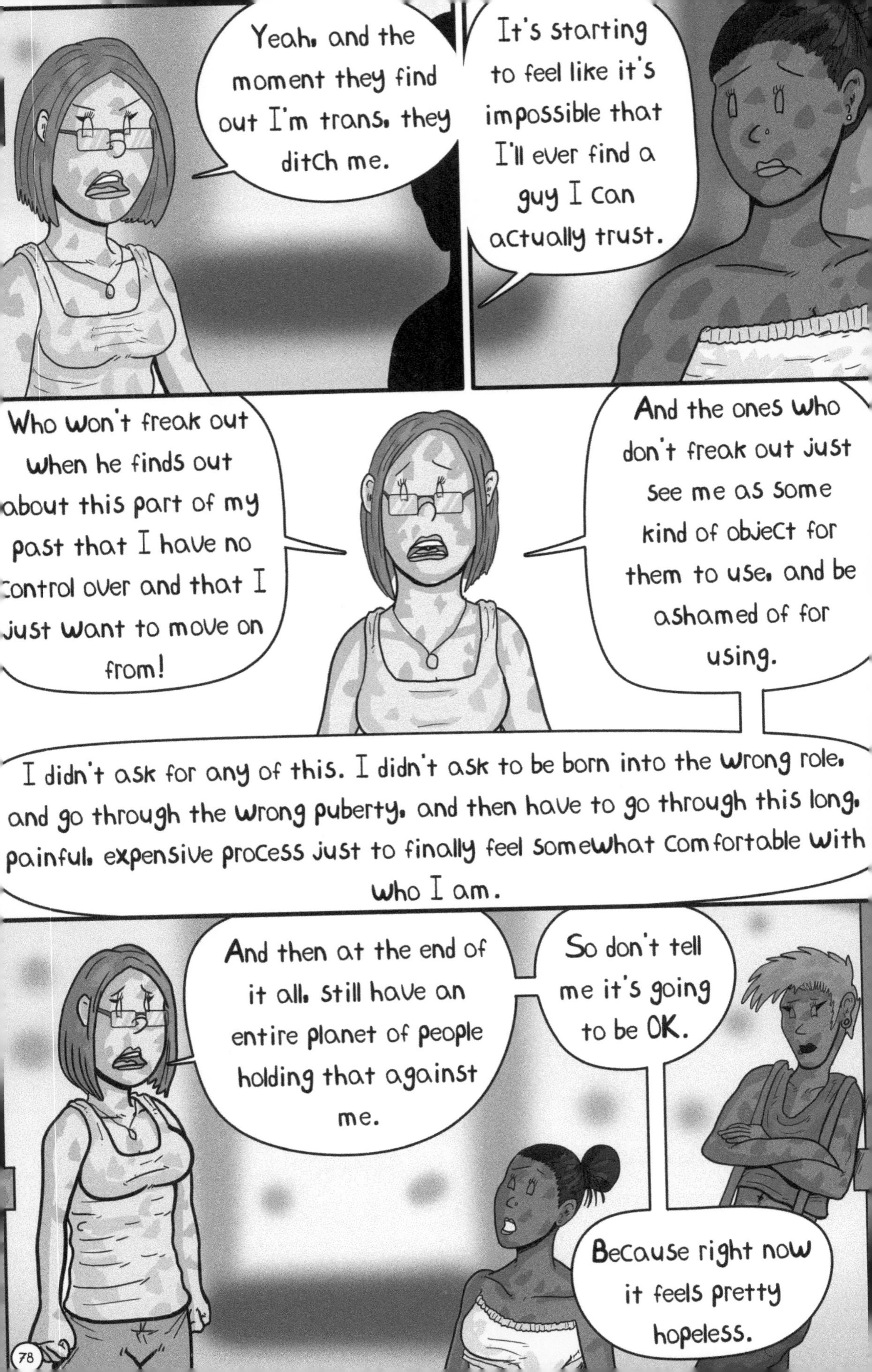
Yeah, and the moment they find out I'm trans, they ditch me.
It's starting to feel like it's impossible that I'll ever find a guy I can actually trust.
Who won't freak out when he finds out about this part of my past that I have no control over and that I just want to move on from!
And the ones who don't freak out just see me as some kind of object for them to use, and be ashamed of for using.
I didn't ask for any of this. I didn't ask to be born into the wrong role, and go through the wrong puberty, and then have to go through this long, painful, expensive process just to finally feel somewhat comfortable with who I am.
And then at the end of it all, still have an entire planet of people holding that against me.
So don't tell me it's going to be OK.
Because right now it feels pretty hopeless.

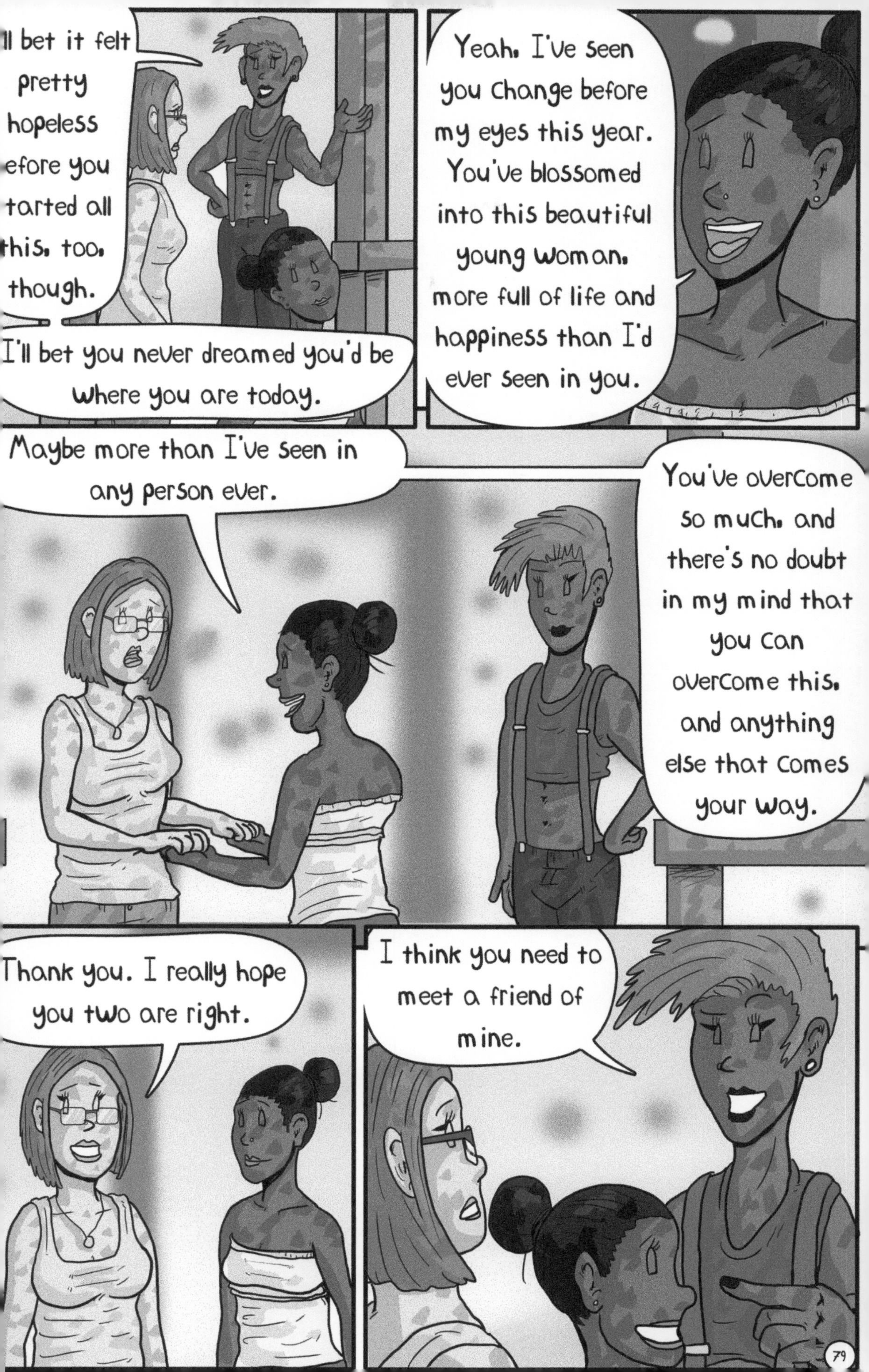
ll bet it felt pretty hopeless efore you tarted all this, too, though.
I'll bet you never dreamed you'd be where you are today.
Yeah, I've seen you change before my eyes this year. You've blossomed into this beautiful young woman, more full of life and happiness than I'd ever seen in you.
Maybe more than I've seen in any person ever.
You've overcome so much, and there's no doubt in my mind that you can overcome this, and anything else that comes your way.
Thank you. I really hope you two are right.
I think you need to meet a friend of mine.
79

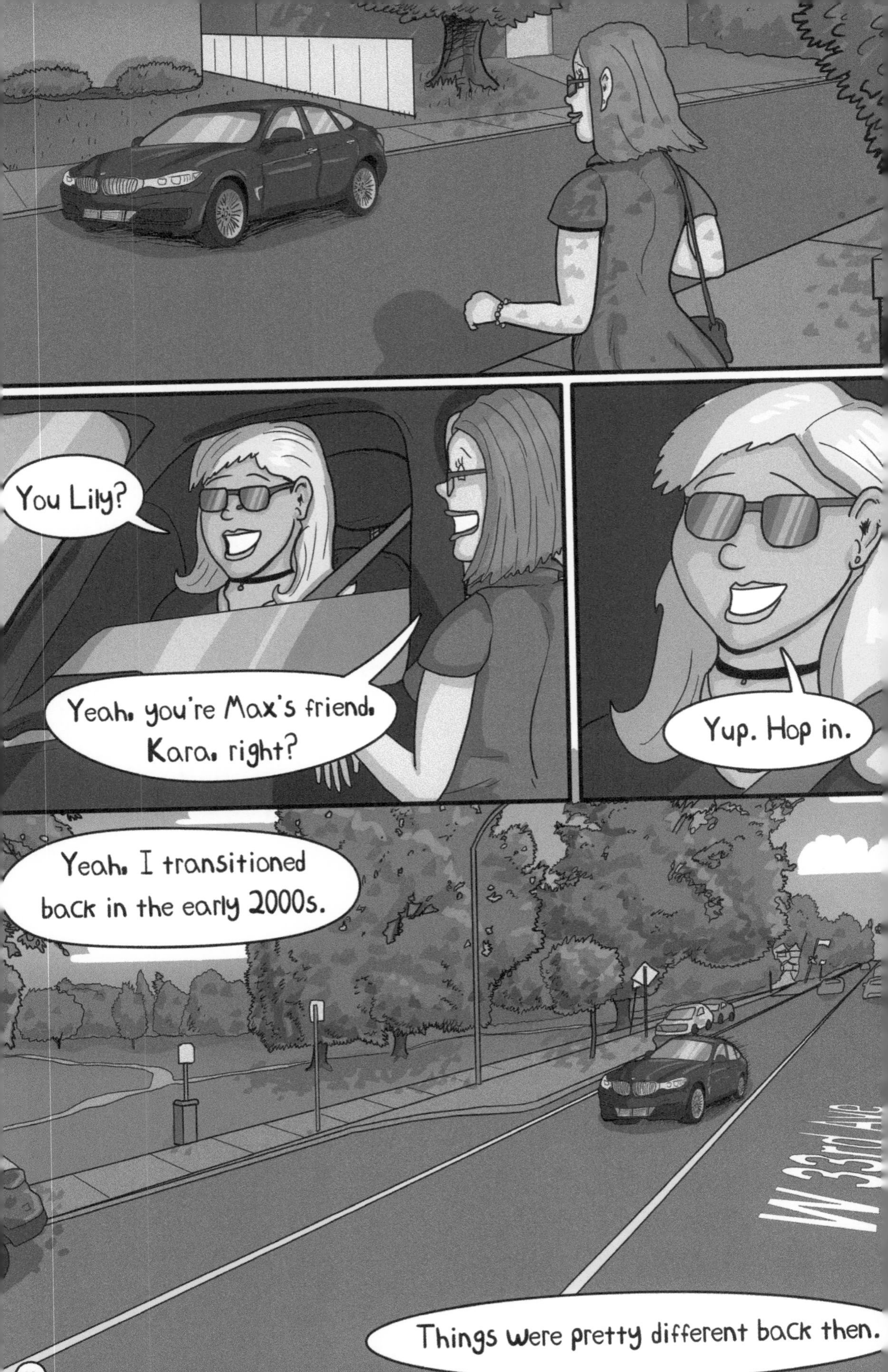
You Lily?
Yeah, you're Max's friend, Kara, right?
Yup. Hop in.
Yeah, I transitioned back in the early 2000s.
W 33rd Ave
Things were pretty different back then.

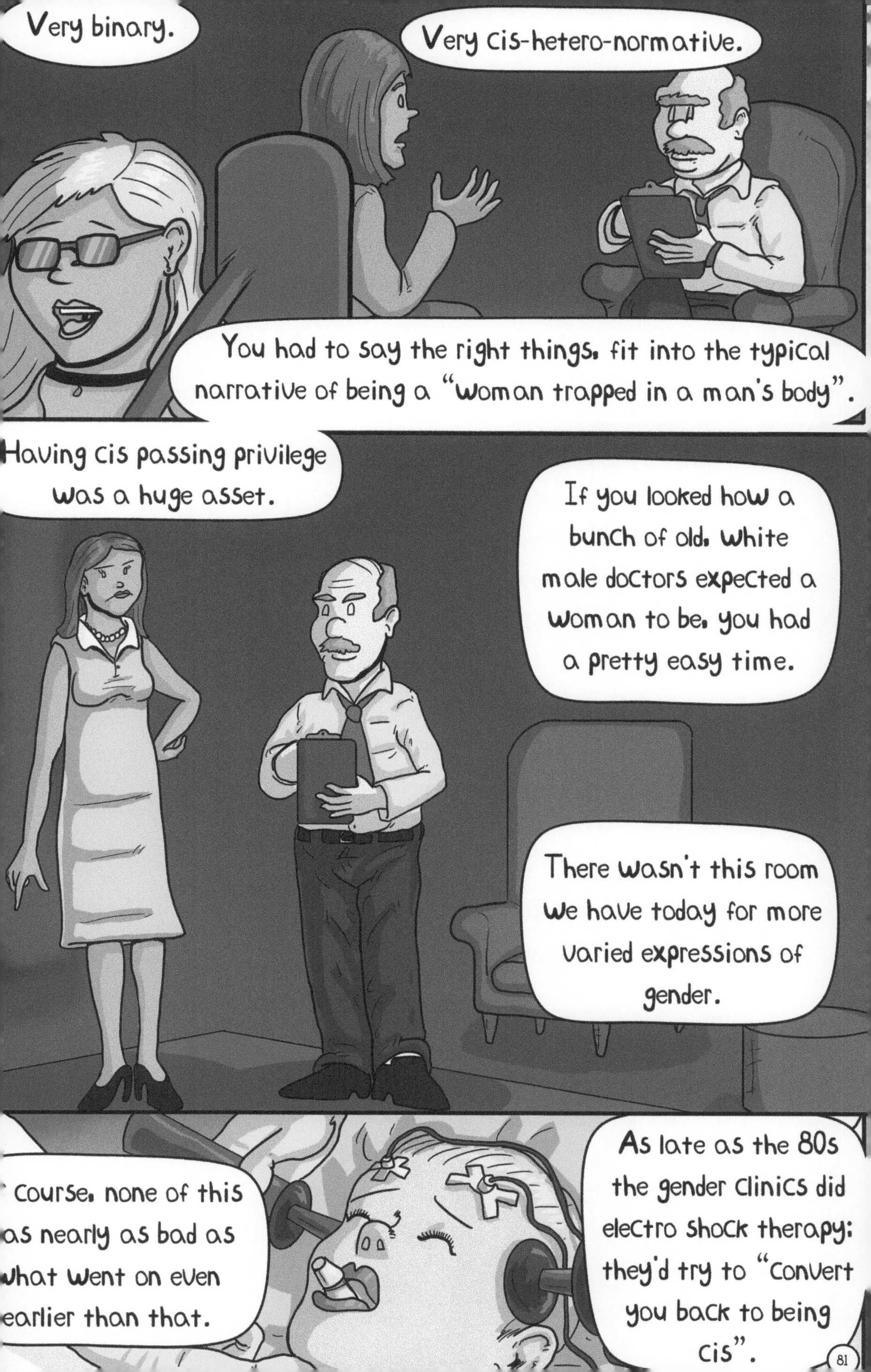
Very binary.
Very cis-hetero-normative.
You had to say the right things, fit into the typical narrative of being a "woman trapped in a man's body".
Having cis passing privilege was a huge asset.
If you looked how a bunch of old, white male doctors expected a woman to be, you had a pretty easy time.
There wasn't this room we have today for more varied expressions of gender.
course, none of this as nearly as bad as what went on even earlier than that.
As late as the 80s the gender clinics did electro shock therapy; they'd try to "convert you back to being cis".
81

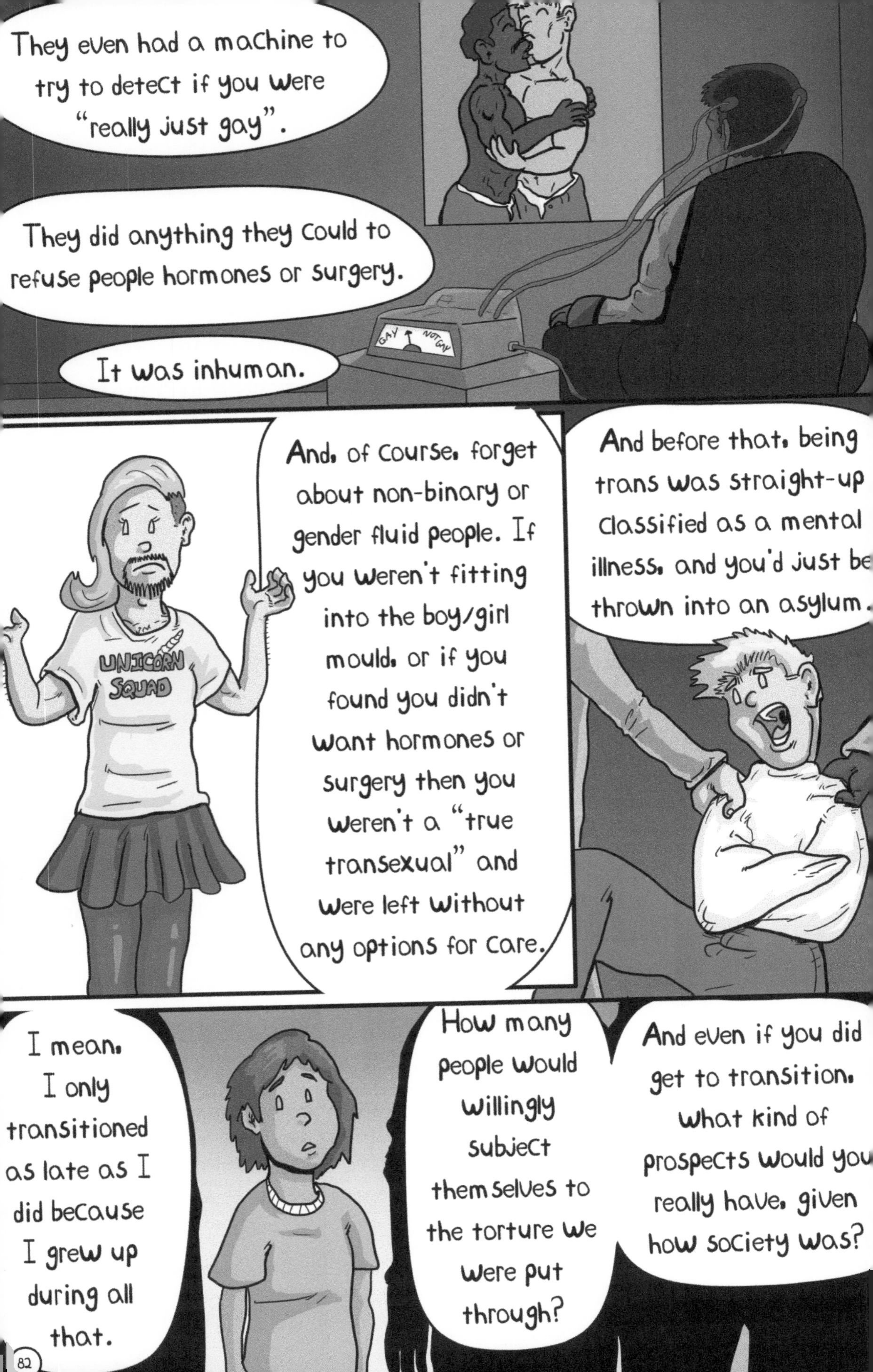
They even had a machine to try to detect if you were "really just gay".
They did anything they could to refuse people hormones or surgery.
It was inhuman.
GAY
NOT GAY
And, of course, forget about non-binary or gender fluid people. If you weren't fitting into the boy/girl mould, or if you found you didn't want hormones or surgery then you weren't a "true transexual" and were left without any options for care.
UNICORN SQUAD
And before that, being trans was straight-up classified as a mental illness, and you'd just be thrown into an asylum.
I mean, I only transitioned as late as I did because I grew up during all that.
How many people would willingly subject themselves to the torture we were put through?
And even if you did get to transition, what kind of prospects would you really have, given how society was?

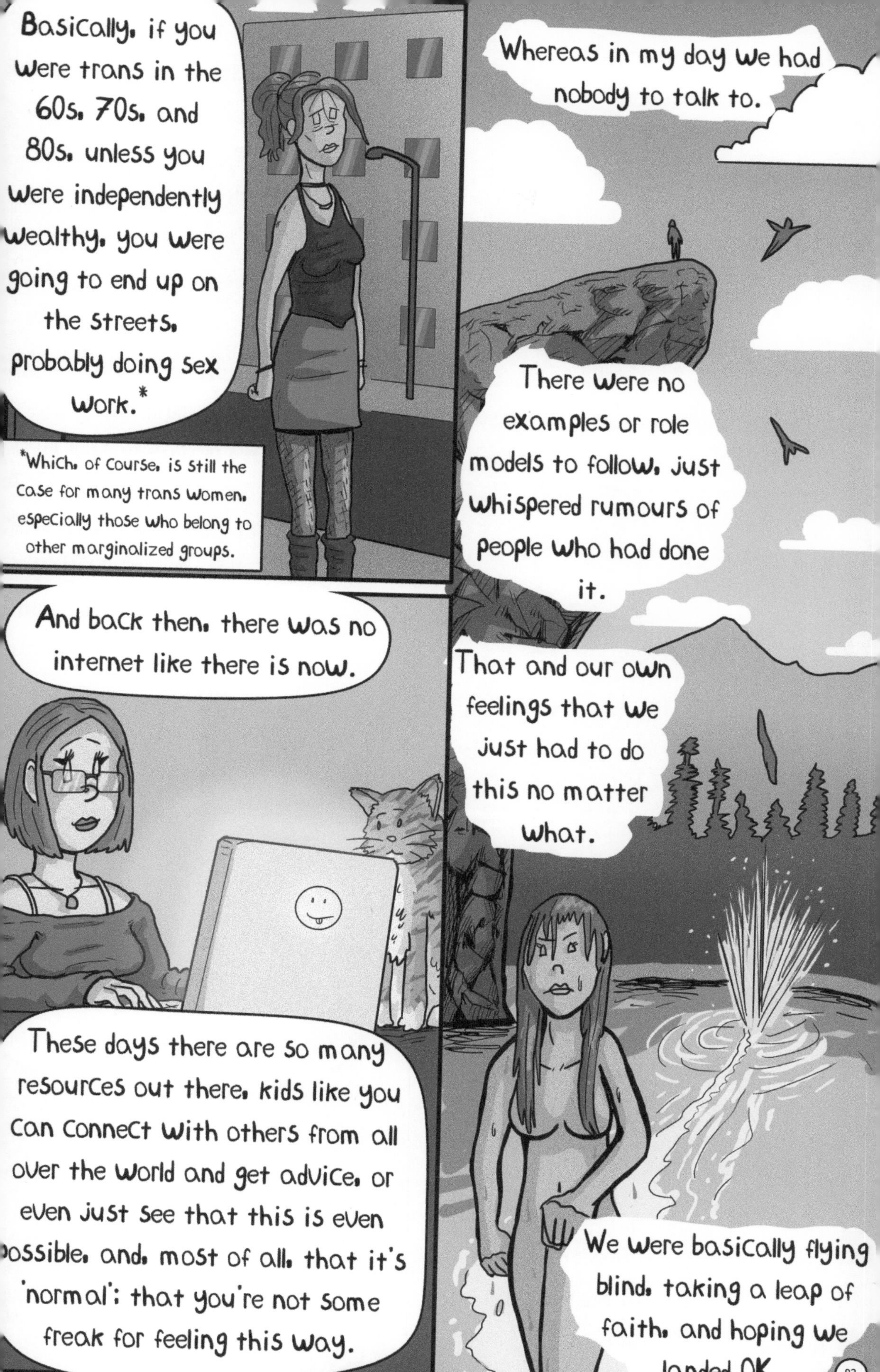

Basically, if you were trans in the 60s, 70s, and 80s, unless you were independently wealthy, you were going to end up on the streets, probably doing sex work.*
*Which, of course, is still the case for many trans women, especially those who belong to other marginalized groups.
Whereas in my day we had nobody to talk to.
There were no examples or role models to follow, just whispered rumours of people who had done it.
And back then, there was no internet like there is now.
That and our own feelings that we just had to do this no matter what.
These days there are so many resources out there, kids like you can connect with others from all over the world and get advice, or even just see that this is even possible, and, most of all, that it's 'normal': that you're not some freak for feeling this way.
We were basically flying blind, taking a leap of faith, and hoping we landed OK.

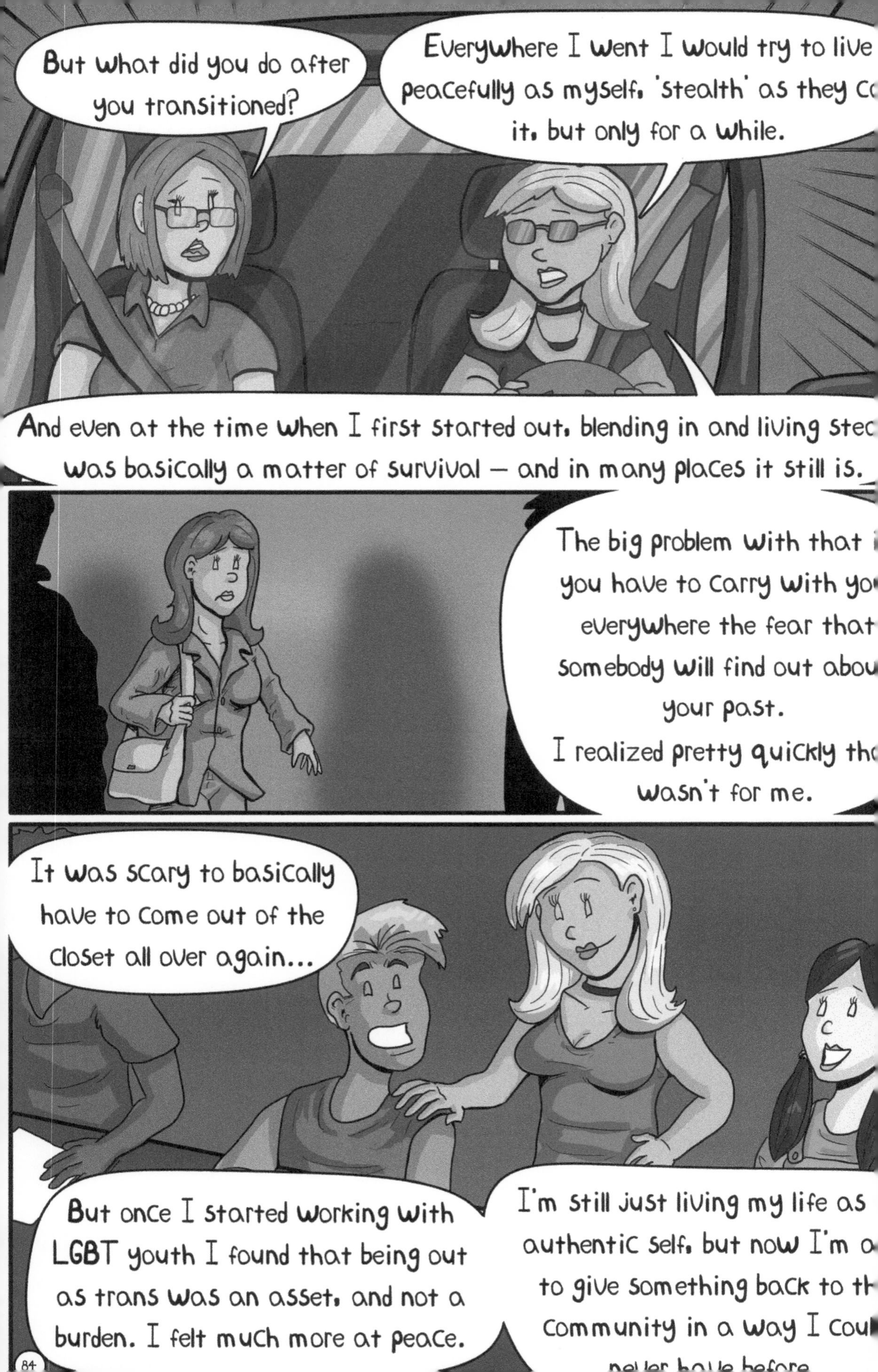
But what did you do after you transitioned?
Everywhere I went I would try to live peacefully as myself, 'stealth' as they c
it, but only for a while.
And even at the time when I first started out, blending in and living stea
was basically a matter of survival – and in many places it still is.
The big problem with that
you have to carry with yo
everywhere the fear that
somebody will find out abou
your past.
I realized pretty quickly th
wasn't for me.
It was scary to basically have to come out of the closet all over again...
But once I started working with LGBT youth I found that being out as trans was an asset, and not a burden. I felt much more at peace.
I'm still just living my life as
authentic self, but now I'm a
to give something back to th
community in a way I coul

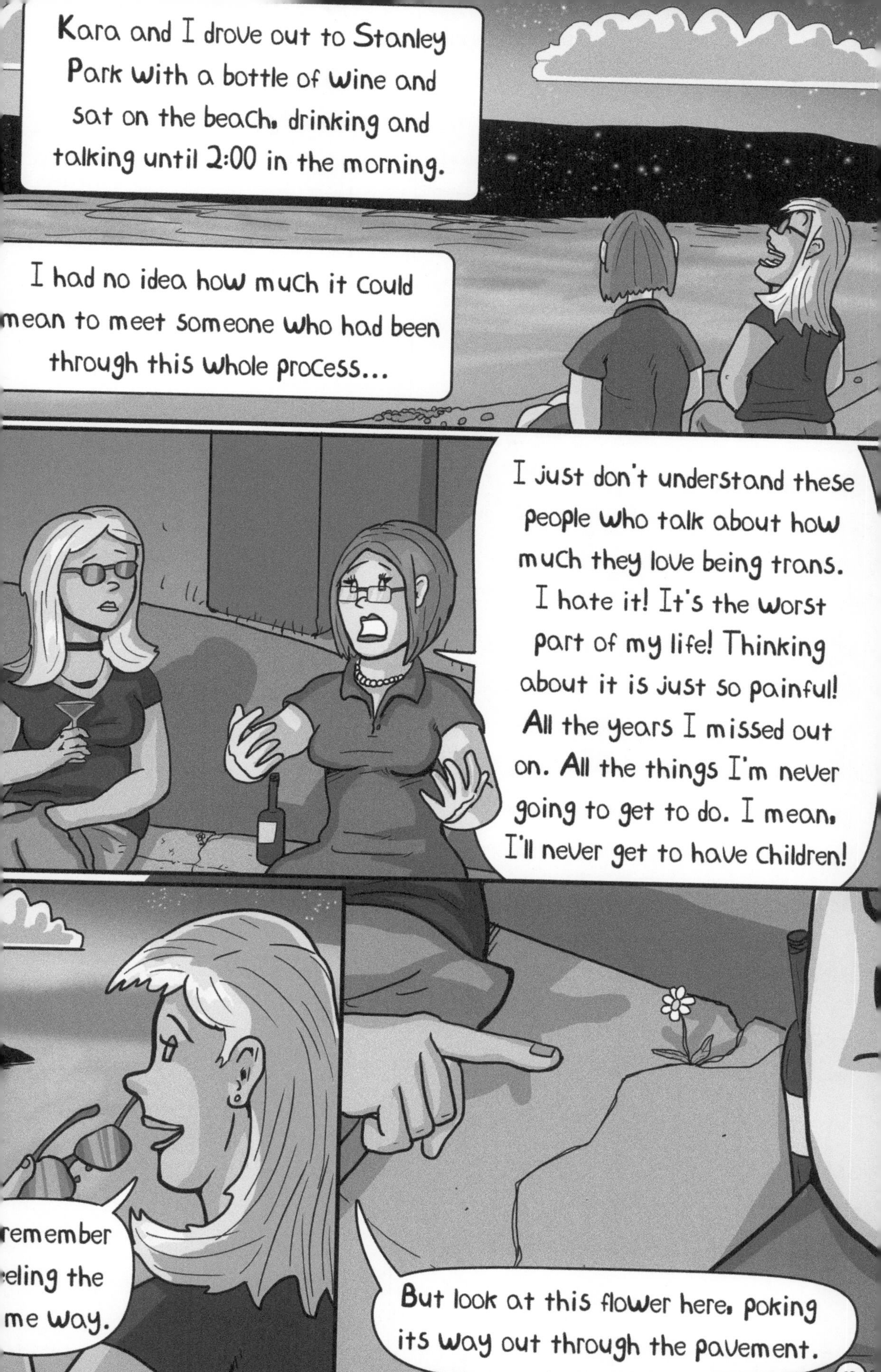

Kara and I drove out to Stanley Park with a bottle of wine and sat on the beach, drinking and talking until 2:00 in the morning.
I had no idea how much it could mean to meet someone who had been through this whole process...
I just don't understand these people who talk about how much they love being trans. I hate it! It's the worst part of my life! Thinking about it is just so painful! All the years I missed out on. All the things I'm never going to get to do. I mean, I'll never get to have children!
remember eeling the me way.
But look at this flower here, poking its way out through the pavement.

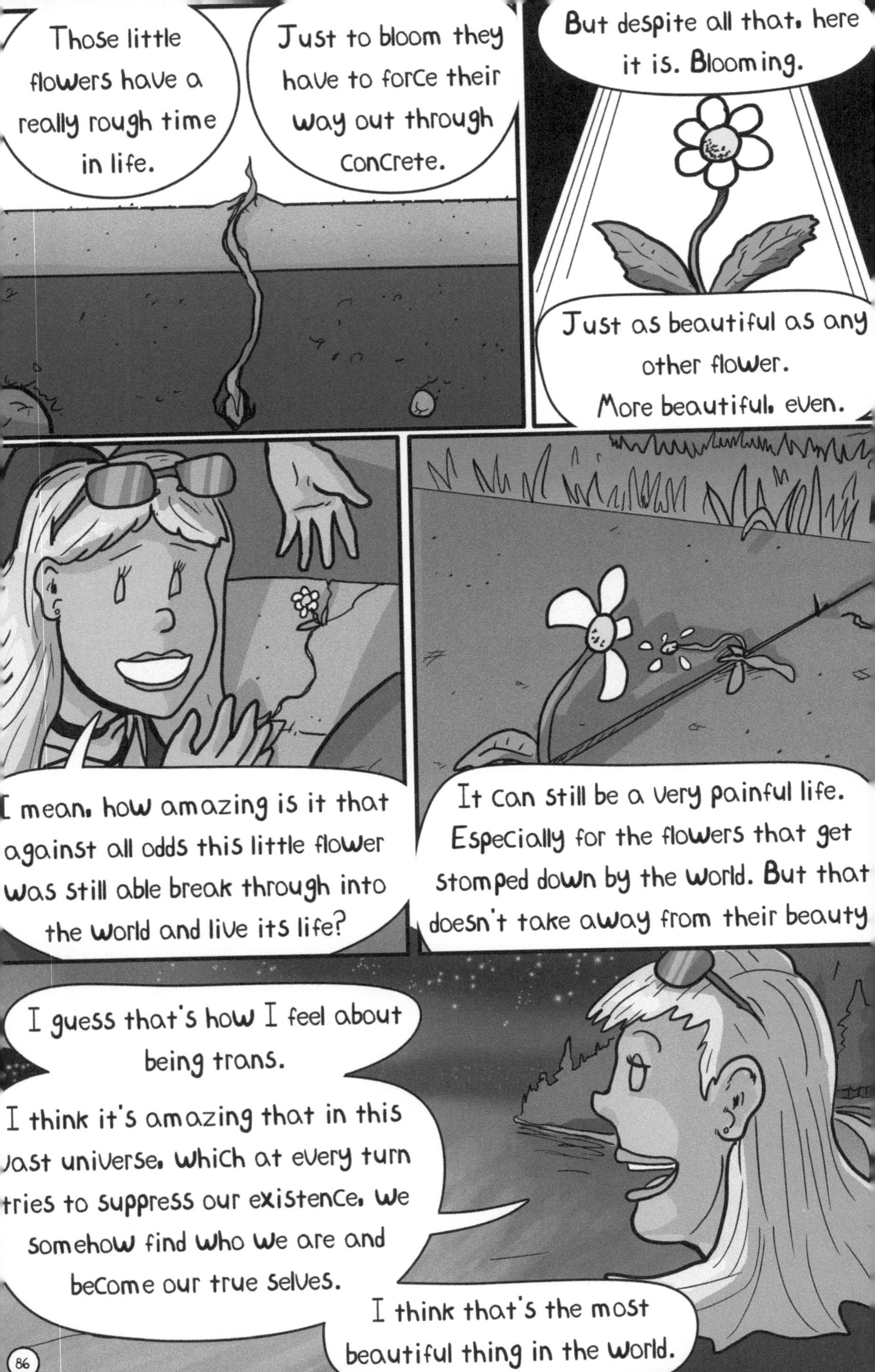
Those little flowers have a really rough time in life.
Just to bloom they have to force their way out through concrete.
But despite all that, here it is. Blooming.
Just as beautiful as any other flower.
More beautiful, even.
I mean, how amazing is it that against all odds this little flower was still able break through into the world and live its life?
It can still be a very painful life. Especially for the flowers that get stomped down by the world. But that doesn't take away from their beauty
I guess that's how I feel about being trans.
I think it's amazing that in this vast universe, which at every turn tries to suppress our existence, we somehow find who we are and become our true selves.
I think that's the most beautiful thing in the world.

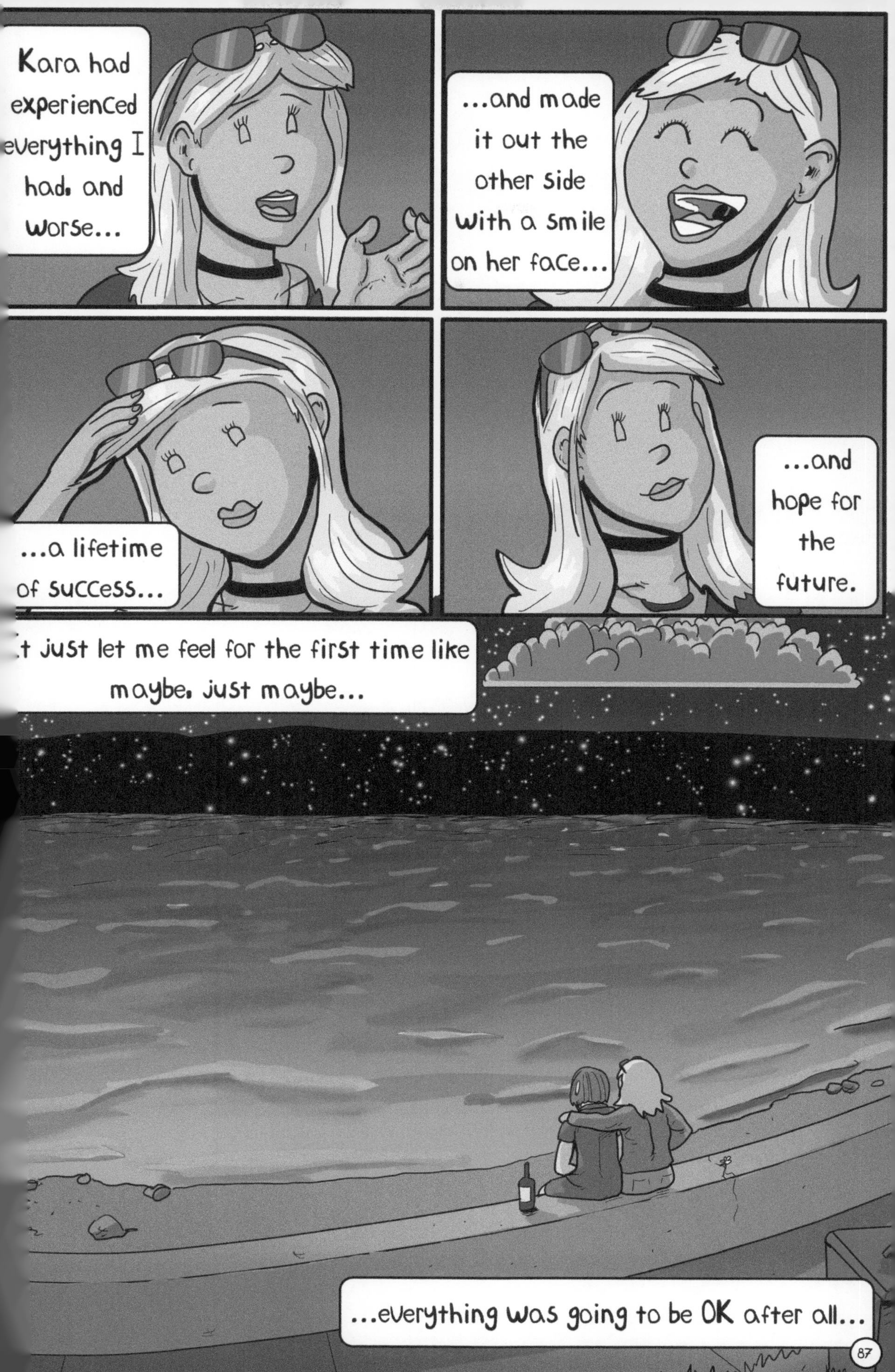
Kara had experienced everything I had, and worse...
...and made it out the other side with a smile on her face...
...a lifetime of success...
...and hope for the future.
It just let me feel for the first time like maybe, just maybe...
...everything was going to be OK after all...

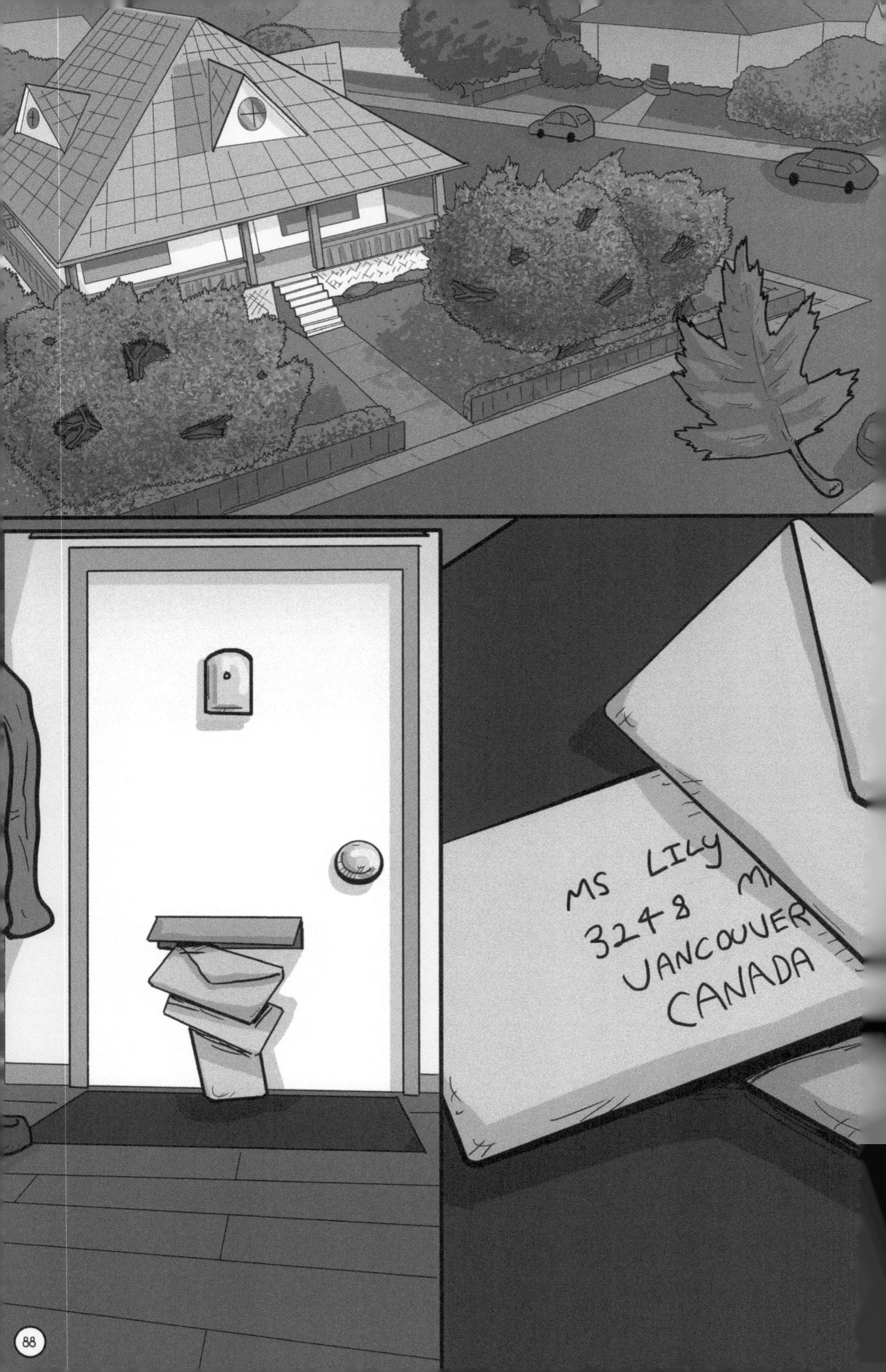
MS LILY
3248 M
VANCOUVER
CANADA

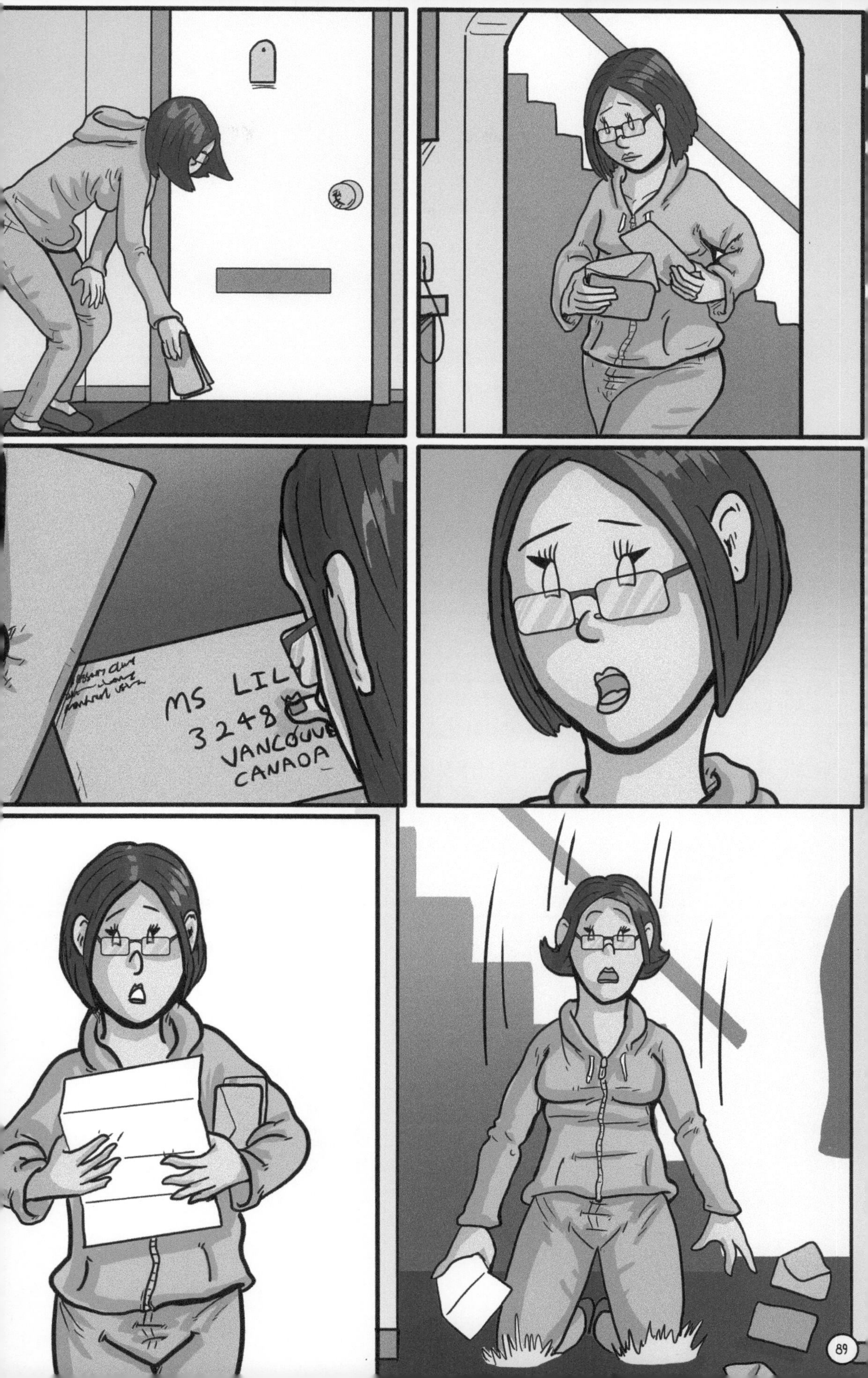
MS LIL
3248
VANCOUVE
CANADA

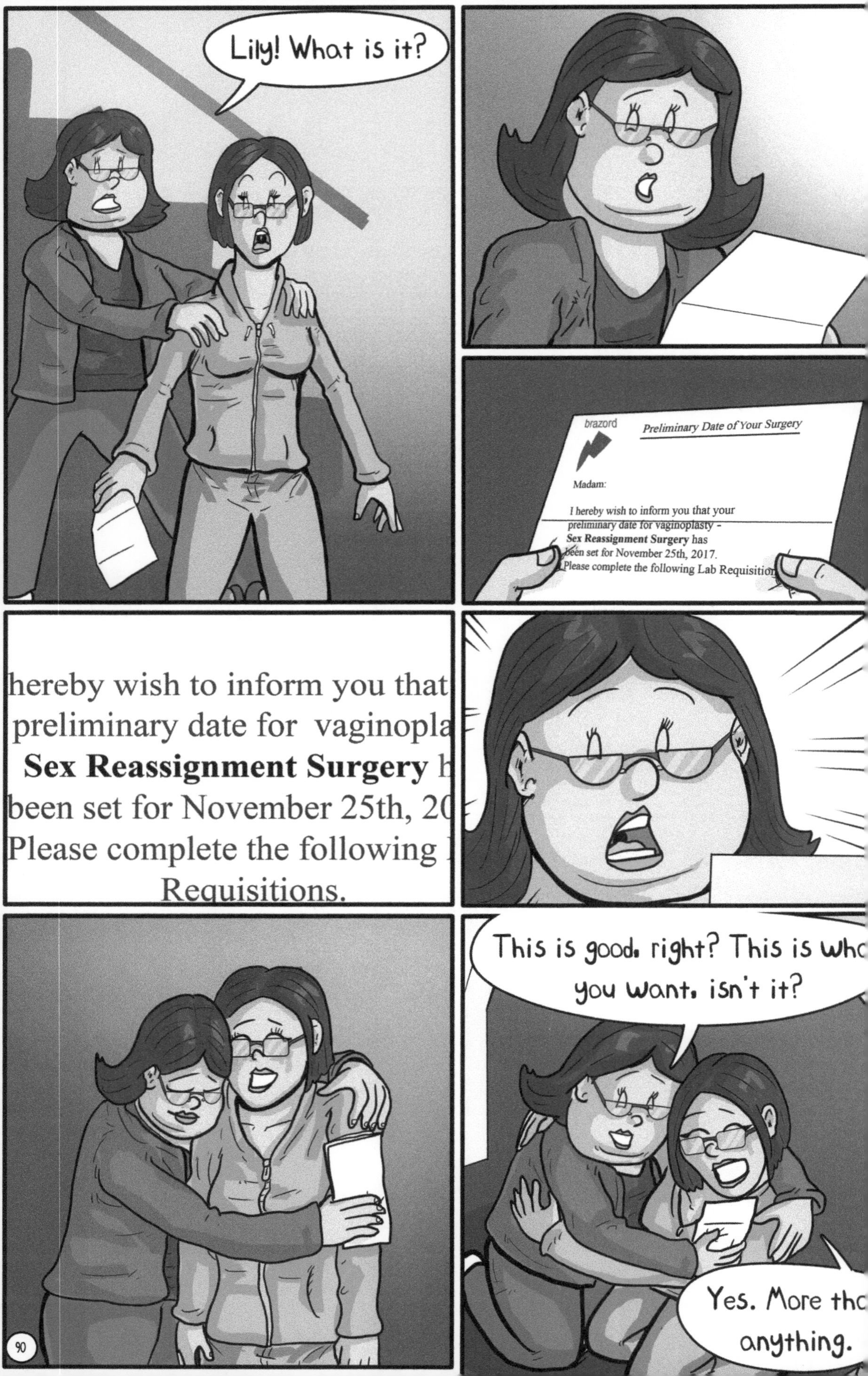

Lily! What is it?
brazord
Preliminary Date of Your Surgery
Madam:
I hereby wish to inform you that your
preliminary date for vaginoplasty -
Sex Reassignment Surgery has
been set for November 25th, 2017.
Please complete the following Lab Requisition
hereby wish to inform you that
preliminary date for vaginopla
Sex Reassignment Surgery h
been set for November 25th, 20
Please complete the following
Requisitions.
This is good, right? This is wha
you want, isn't it?
Yes. More tha
anything.

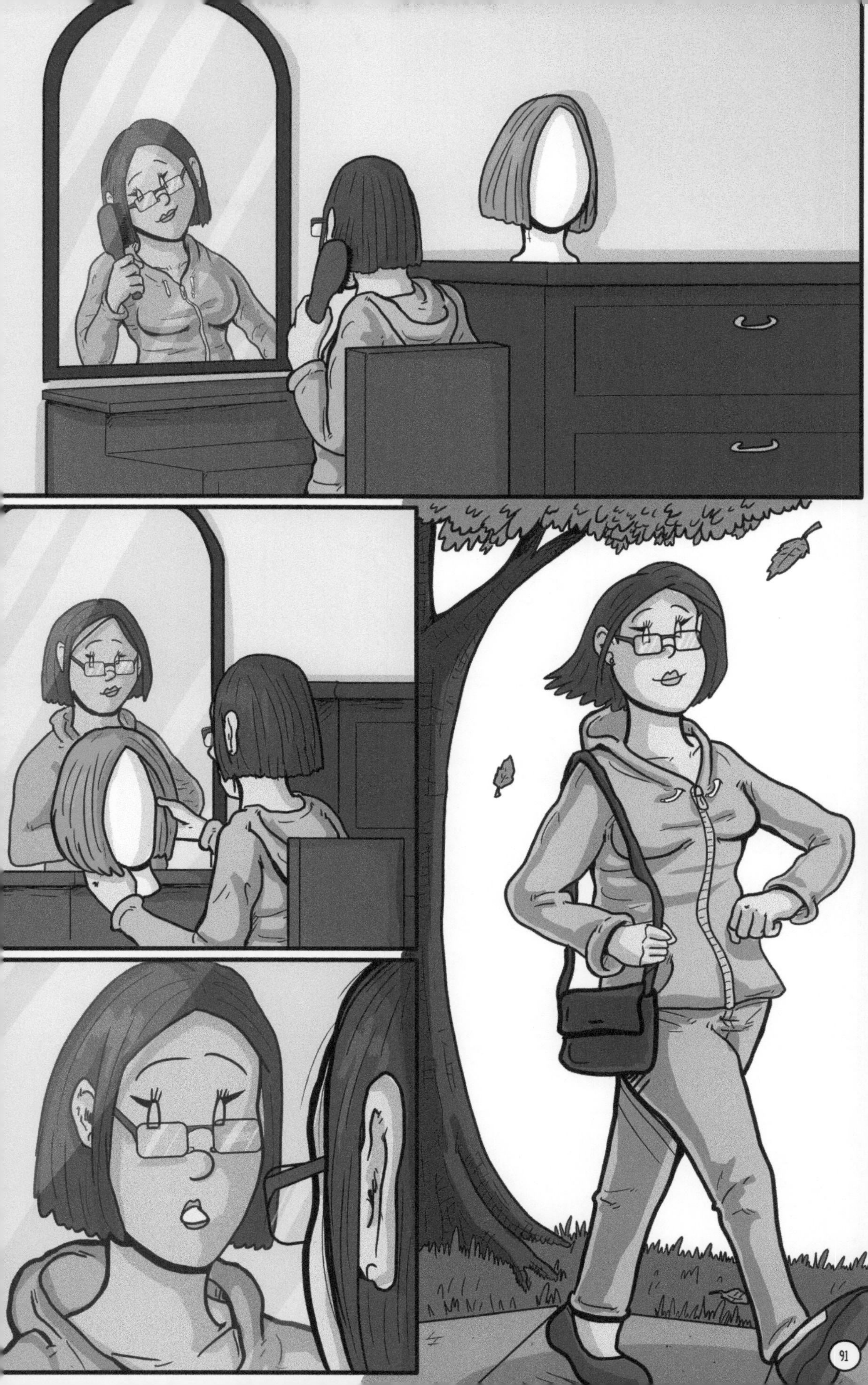

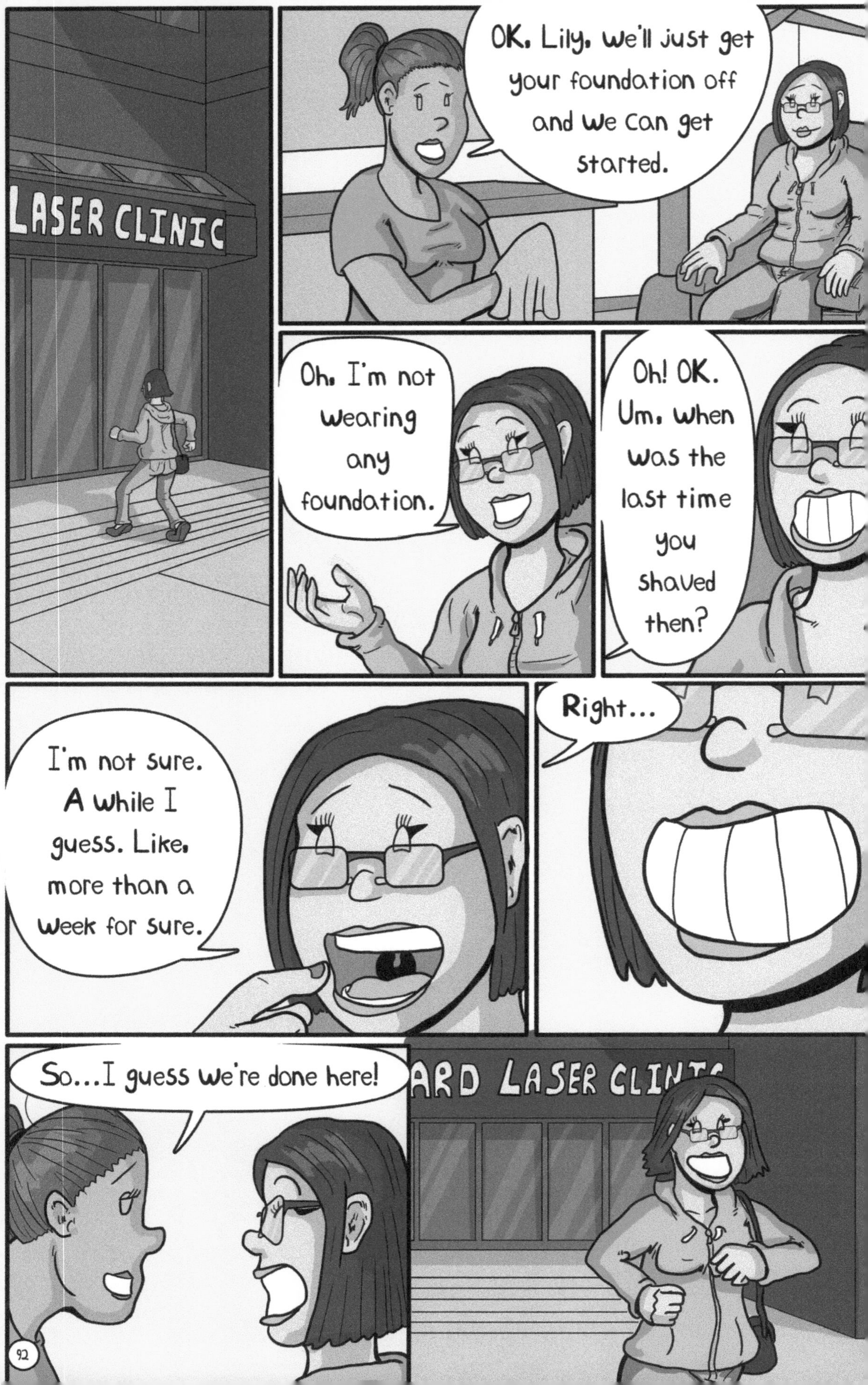
LASER CLINIC
OK, Lily, we'll just get your foundation off and we can get started.
Oh, I'm not wearing any foundation.
Oh! OK. Um, when was the last time you shaved then?
I'm not sure. A while I guess. Like, more than a week for sure.
Right...
So...I guess we're done here!
ARD LASER CLIN

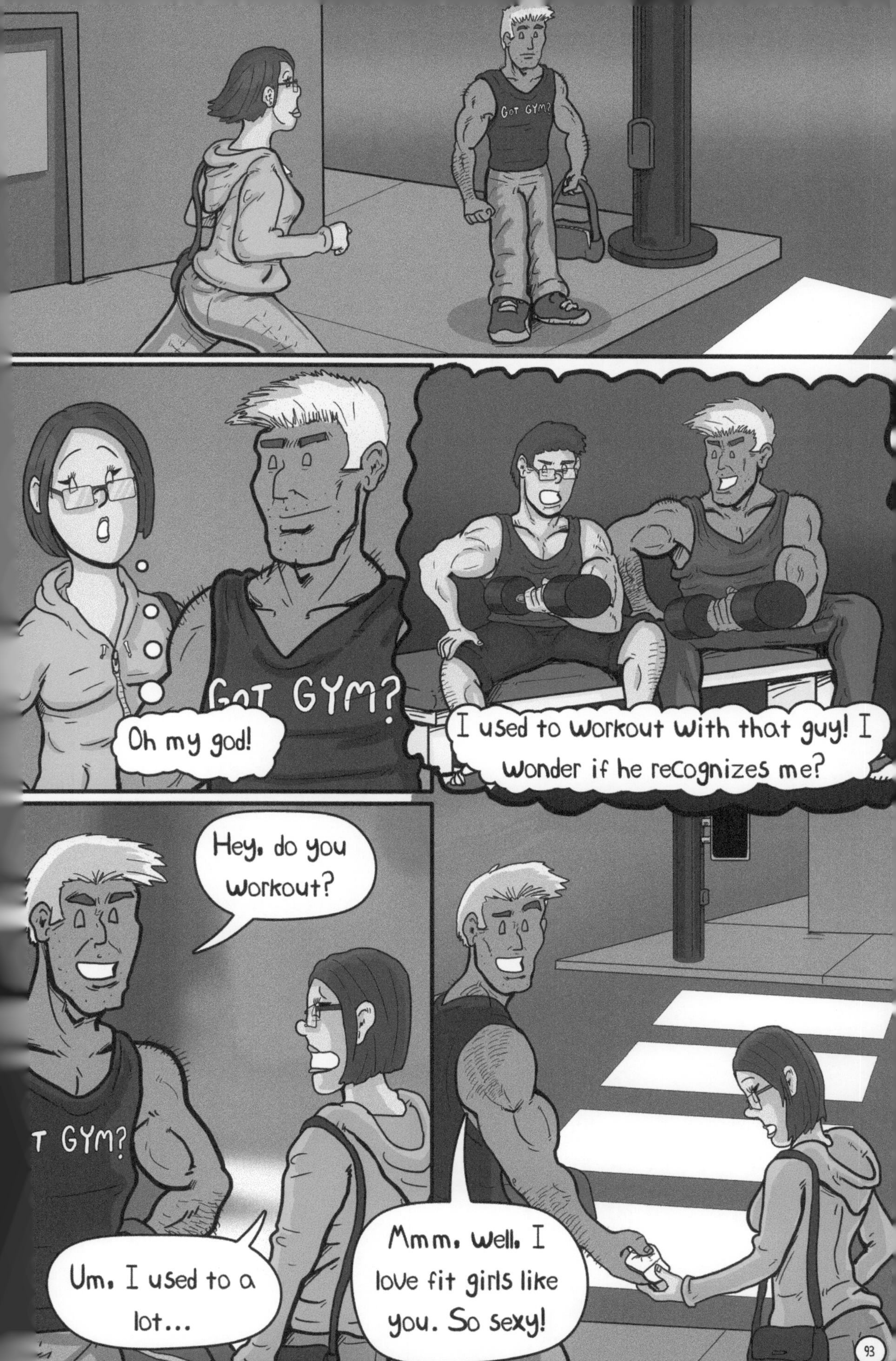
GOT GYM?
GOT GYM?
Oh my god!
I used to workout with that guy! I wonder if he recognizes me?
Hey, do you workout?
T GYM?
Um, I used to a lot...
Mmm, Well, I love fit girls like you. So sexy!

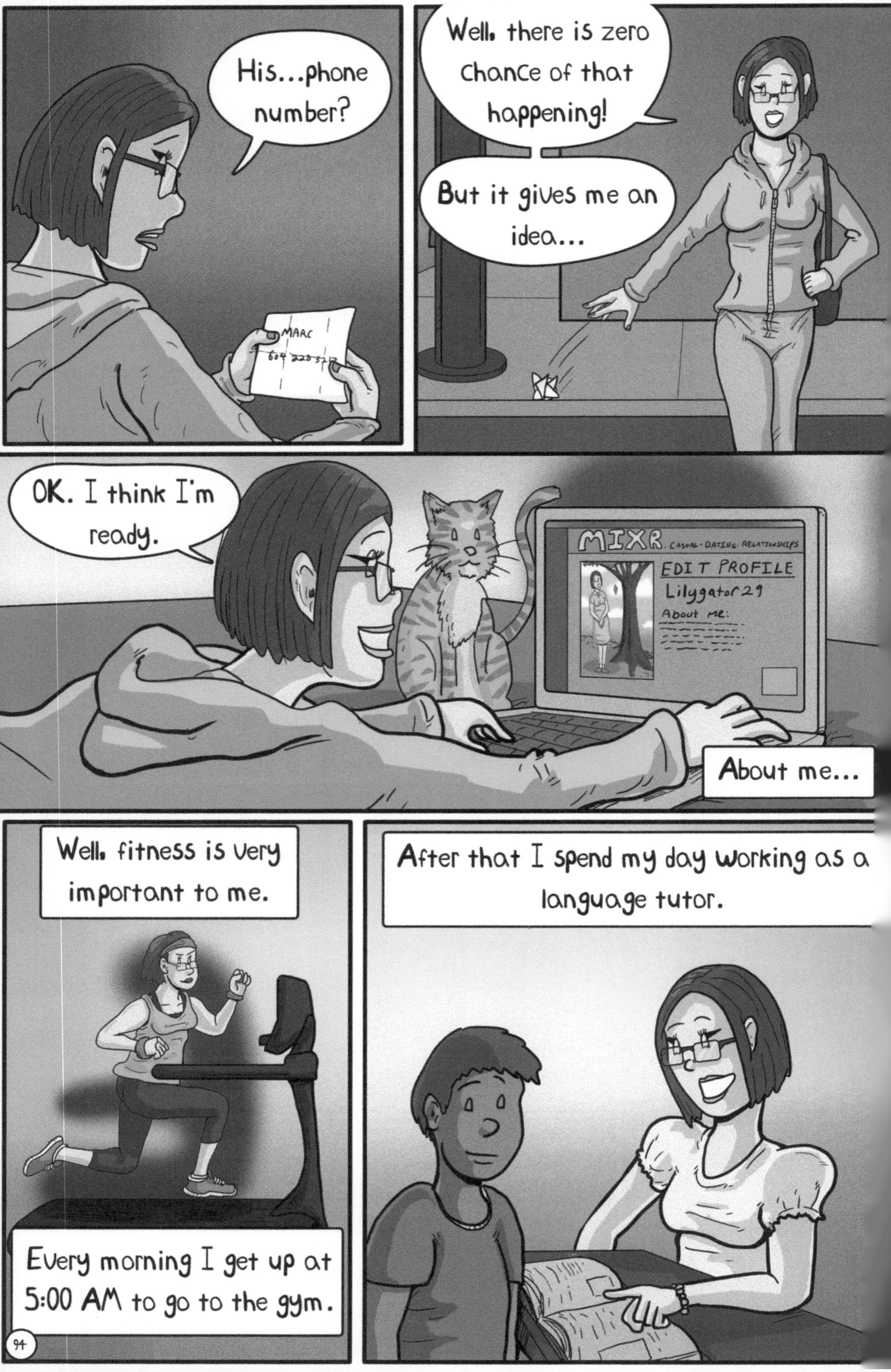

His...phone number?
MARC
Well, there is zero chance of that happening!
But it gives me an idea...
OK. I think I'm ready.
MIXR. CASUAL · DATING · RELATIONSHIPS
EDIT PROFILE
Lilygator29
About me:
About me...
Well, fitness is very important to me.
Every morning I get up at 5:00 AM to go to the gym.
After that I spend my day working as a language tutor.

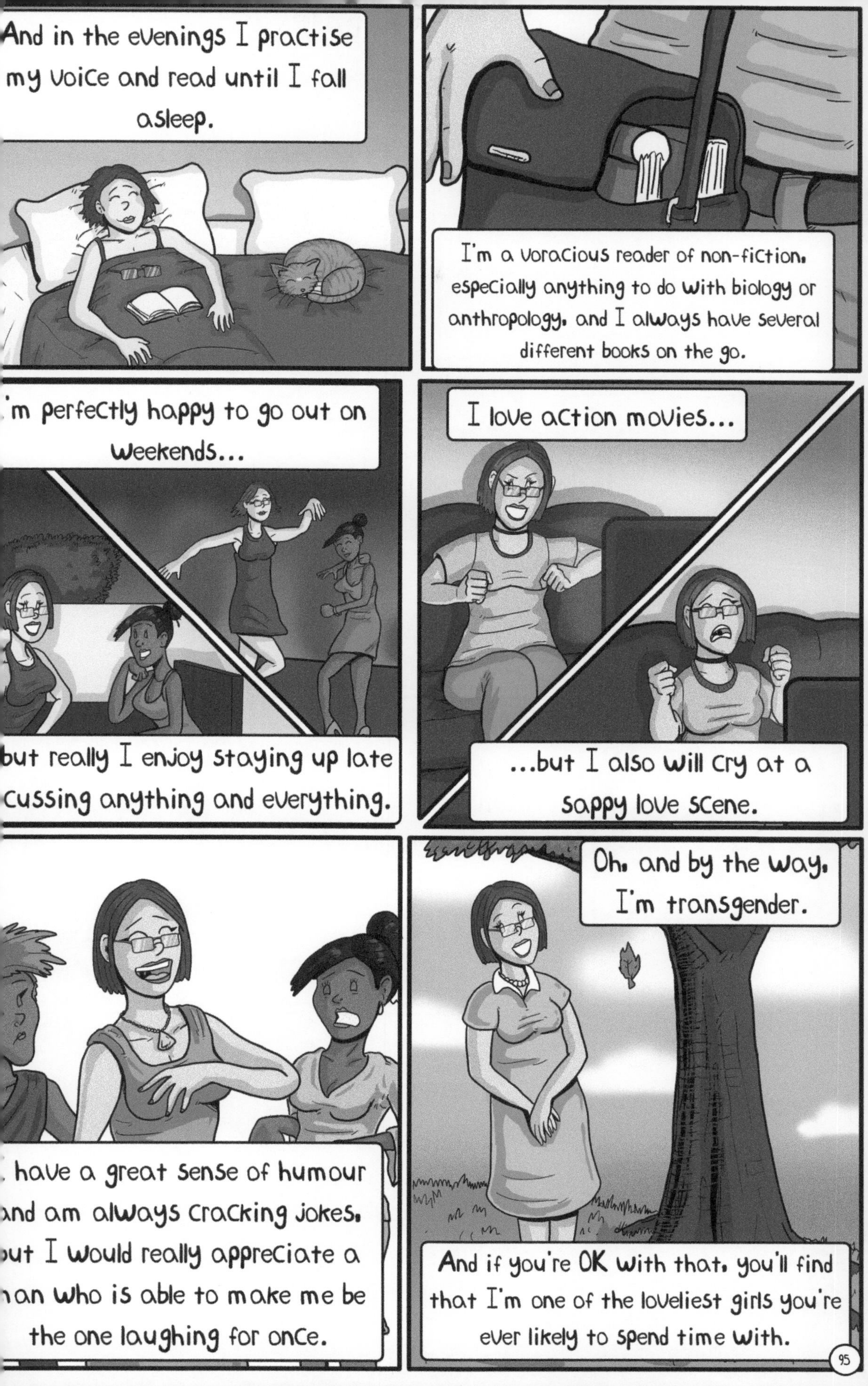
And in the evenings I practise my voice and read until I fall asleep.
I'm a voracious reader of non-fiction, especially anything to do with biology or anthropology, and I always have several different books on the go.
'm perfectly happy to go out on weekends...
but really I enjoy staying up late
cussing anything and everything.
I love action movies...
...but I also will cry at a sappy love scene.
have a great sense of humour
nd am always cracking jokes,
ut I would really appreciate a
nan who is able to make me be
the one laughing for once.
Oh, and by the way, I'm transgender.
And if you're OK with that, you'll find that I'm one of the loveliest girls you're ever likely to spend time with.

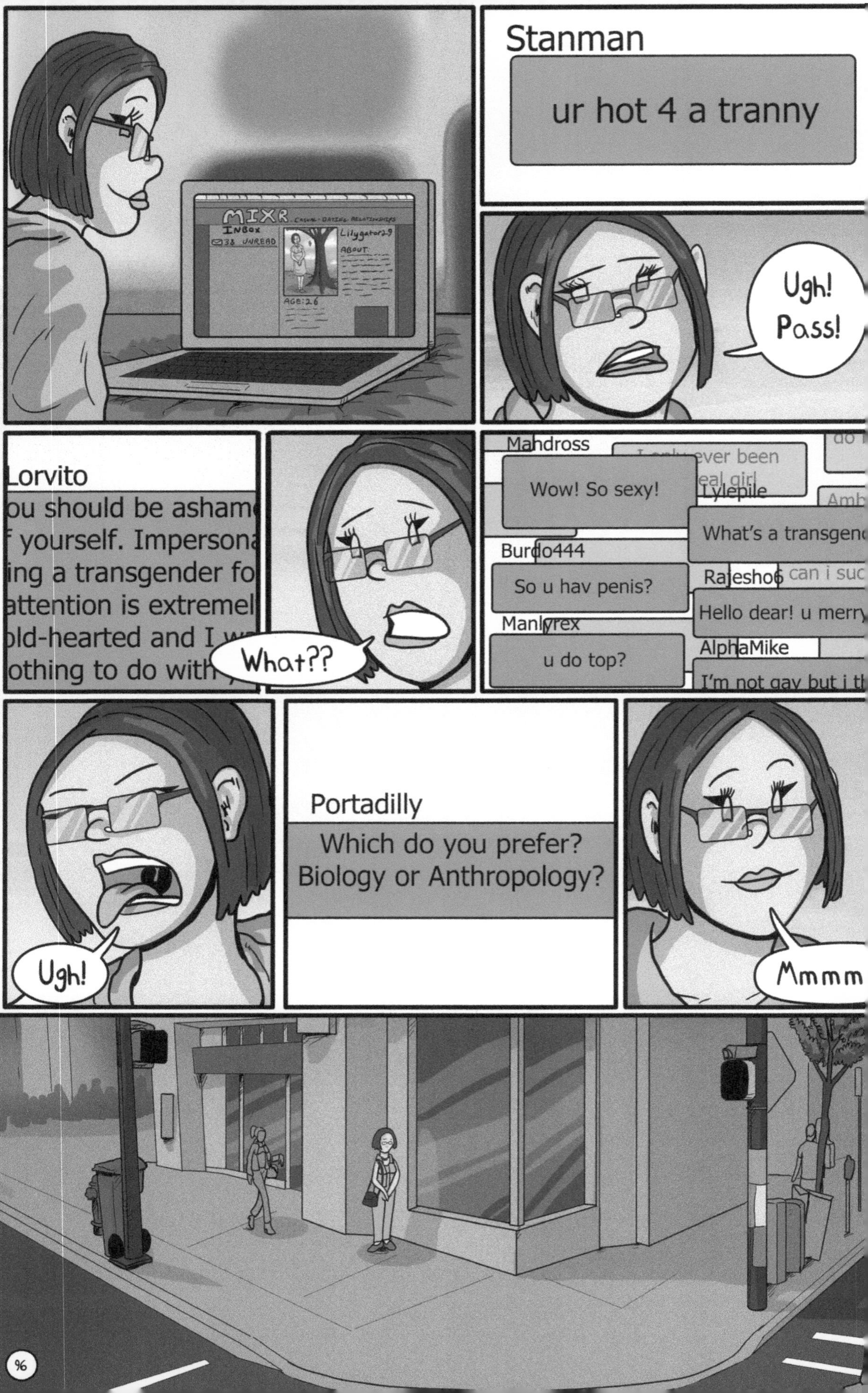
MIXR
INBOX
38 UNREAD
ABOUT
AGE:26
Stanman
ur hot 4 a tranny
Ugh! Pass!
Lorvito
ou should be asham
f yourself. Imperson
ing a transgender fo
attention is extremel
old-hearted and I w
othing to do with
What??
Mahdross
Wow! So sexy!
Lylepile
What's a transgend
Burdo444
So u hav penis?
Rajesho6
can i suc
Hello dear! u merr
Manlyrex
u do top?
AlphaMike
Ugh!
Portadilly
Which do you prefer?
Biology or Anthropology?
Mmmm

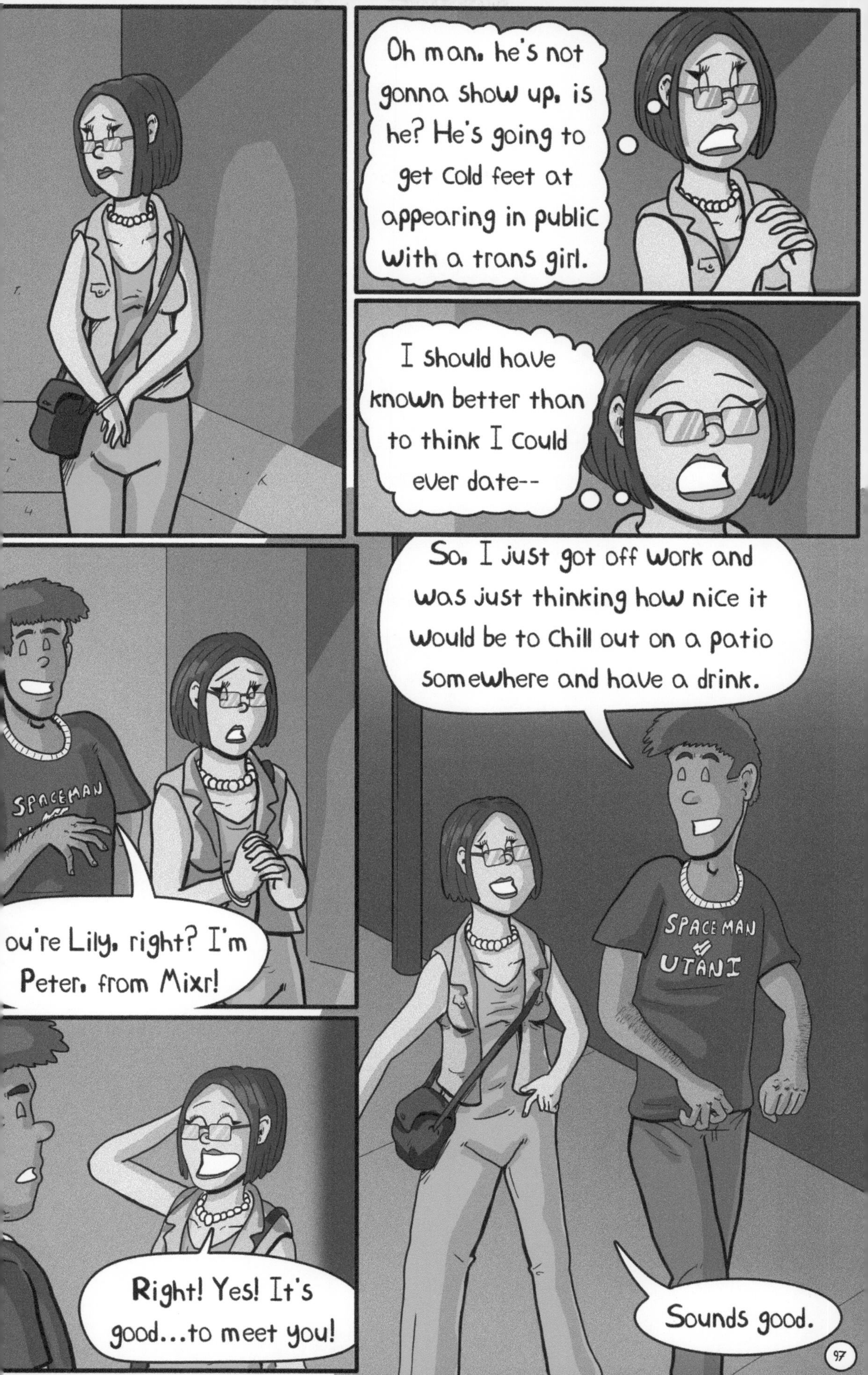

Oh man, he's not gonna show up, is he? He's going to get cold feet at appearing in public with a trans girl.
I should have known better than to think I could ever date--
ou're Lily, right? I'm Peter, from Mixr!
SPACEMAN
Right! Yes! It's good...to meet you!
So, I just got off work and was just thinking how nice it would be to chill out on a patio somewhere and have a drink.
SPACE MAN UTANI
Sounds good.

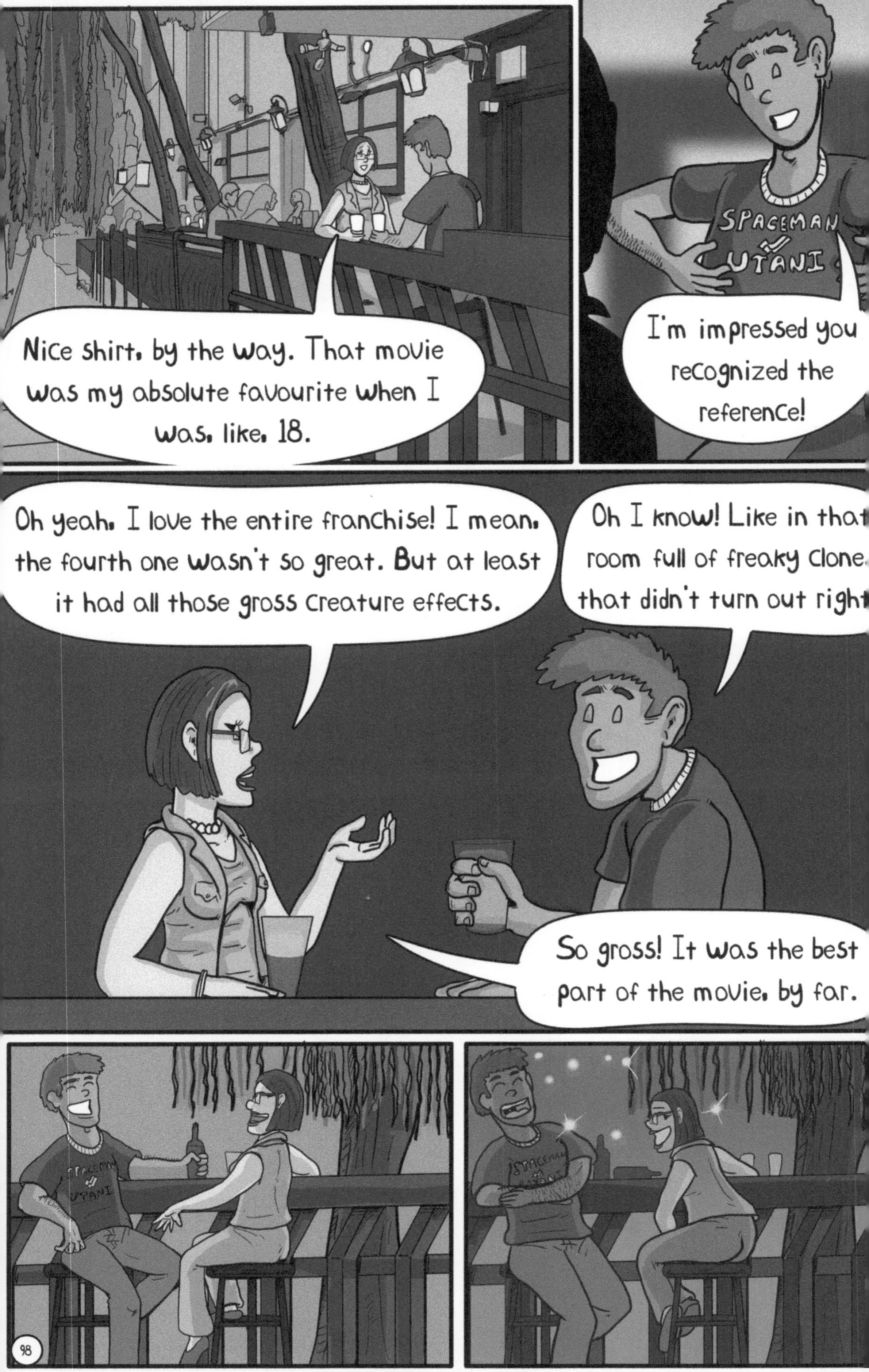
Nice shirt, by the way. That movie was my absolute favourite when I was, like, 18.
SPACEMAN UTANI
I'm impressed you recognized the reference!
Oh yeah, I love the entire franchise! I mean, the fourth one wasn't so great. But at least it had all those gross creature effects.
Oh I know! Like in that room full of freaky clone that didn't turn out right
So gross! It was the best part of the movie, by far.
SPACEMAN UTANI

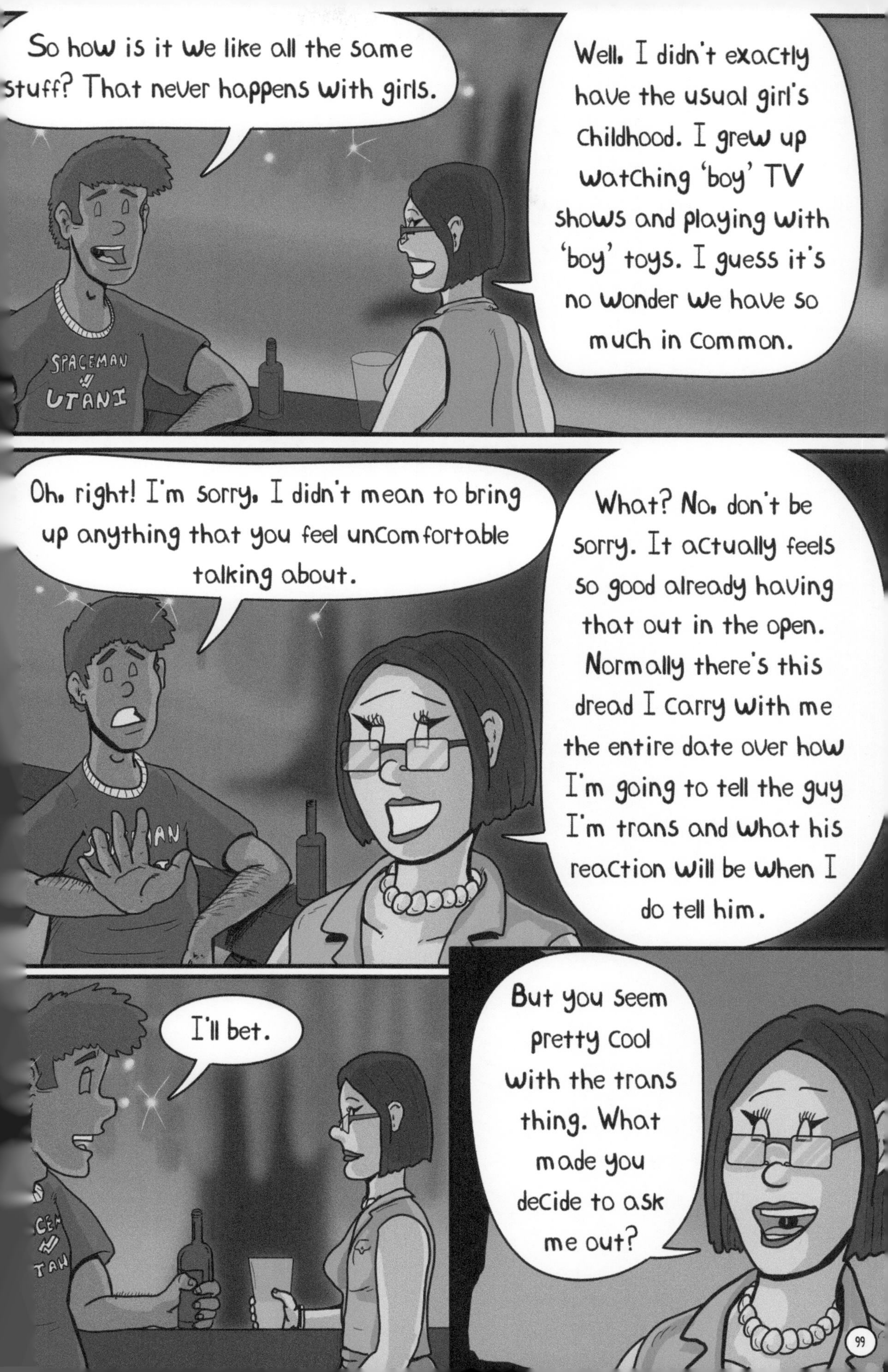

So how is it we like all the same stuff? That never happens with girls.
Well, I didn't exactly have the usual girl's childhood. I grew up watching 'boy' TV shows and playing with 'boy' toys. I guess it's no wonder we have so much in common.
SPACEMAN UTANI
Oh, right! I'm sorry. I didn't mean to bring up anything that you feel uncomfortable talking about.
What? No, don't be sorry. It actually feels so good already having that out in the open. Normally there's this dread I carry with me the entire date over how I'm going to tell the guy I'm trans and what his reaction will be when I do tell him.
I'll bet.
But you seem pretty cool with the trans thing. What made you decide to ask me out?

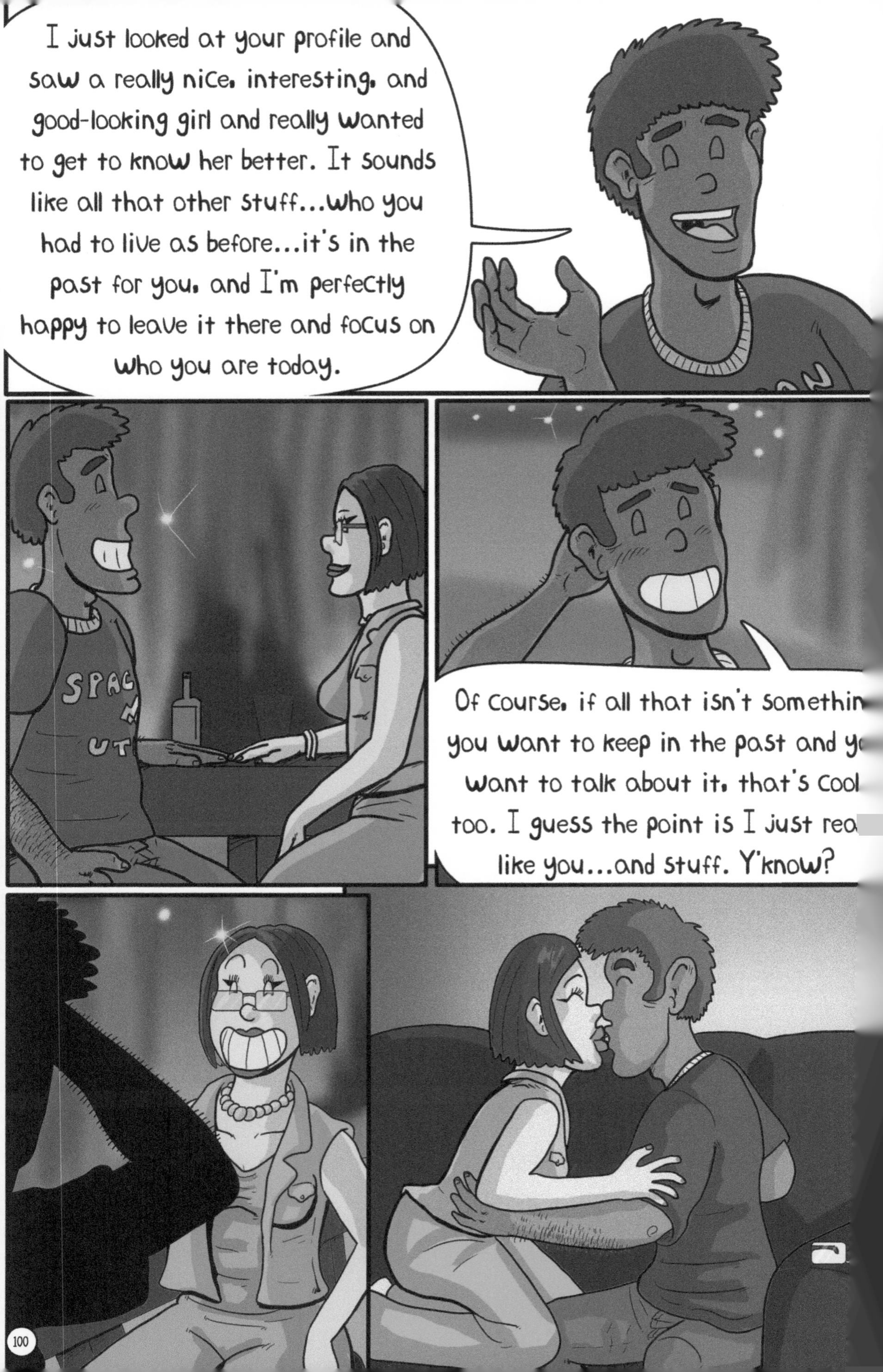
I just looked at your profile and saw a really nice, interesting, and good-looking girl and really wanted to get to know her better. It sounds like all that other stuff...who you had to live as before...it's in the past for you, and I'm perfectly happy to leave it there and focus on who you are today.
Of course, if all that isn't somethin you want to keep in the past and yo want to talk about it, that's cool too. I guess the point is I just rea like you...and stuff. Y'know?

Don't worry about that. I don't really like it being touched.

It's OK. Let's just focus on what's happening here.

Yeah? But what can I do to make sure you have fun, too?

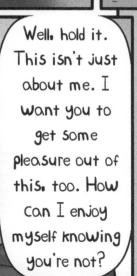

Well, hold it. This isn't just about me. I want you to get some pleasure out of this, too. How can I enjoy myself knowing you're not?

You're making that up! There is no way he said that!

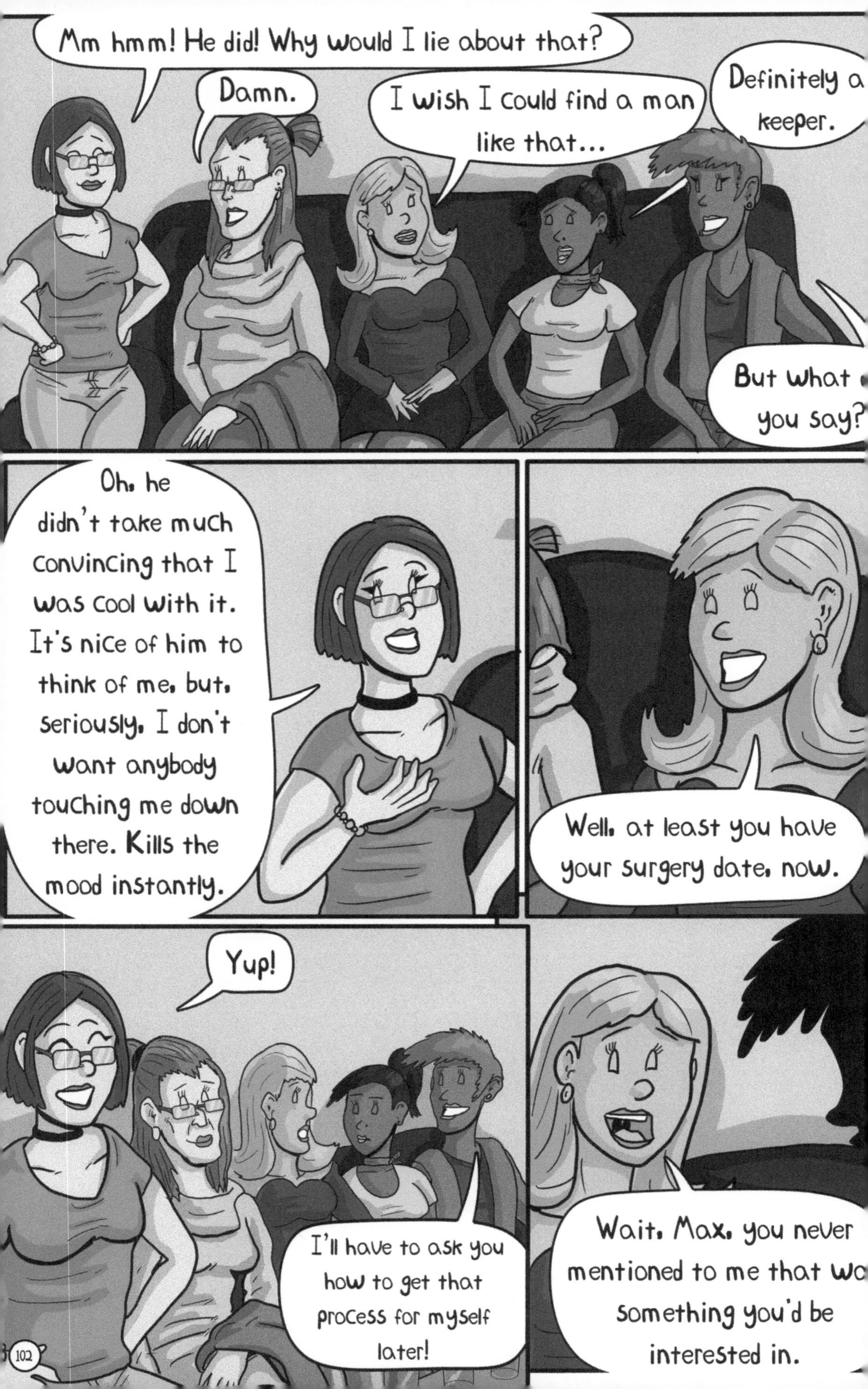
Mm hmm! He did! Why would I lie about that?
Damn.
I wish I could find a man like that...
Definitely a keeper.
But what you say?
Oh, he didn't take much convincing that I was cool with it. It's nice of him to think of me, but, seriously, I don't want anybody touching me down there. Kills the mood instantly.
Well, at least you have your surgery date, now.
Yup!
I'll have to ask you how to get that process for myself later!
Wait, Max, you never mentioned to me that wa something you'd be interested in.

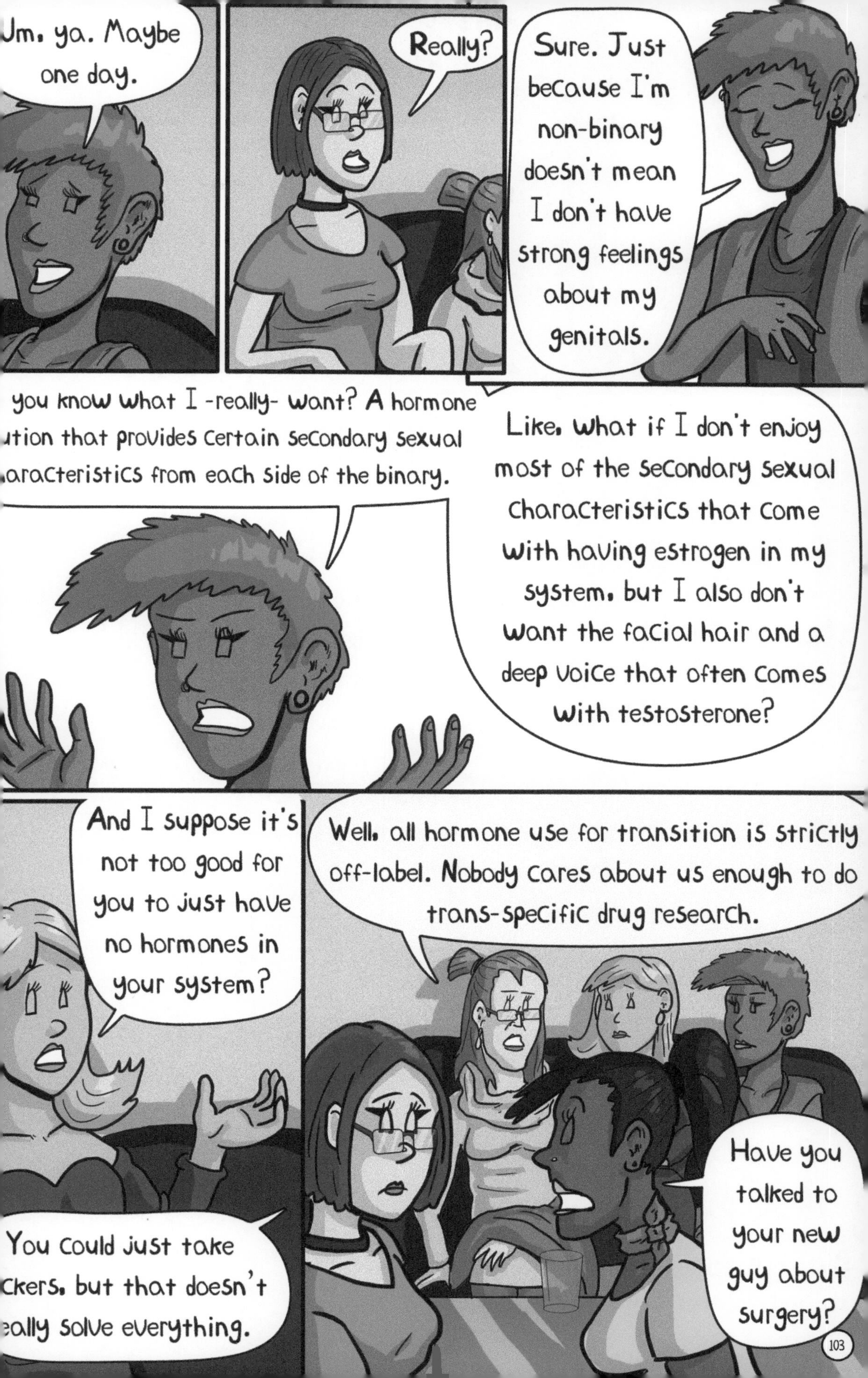

Um, ya. Maybe one day.
Really?
Sure. Just because I'm non-binary doesn't mean I don't have strong feelings about my genitals.
you know what I -really- want? A hormone ution that provides certain secondary sexual aracteristics from each side of the binary.
Like, what if I don't enjoy most of the secondary sexual characteristics that come with having estrogen in my system, but I also don't want the facial hair and a deep voice that often comes with testosterone?
And I suppose it's not too good for you to just have no hormones in your system?
Well, all hormone use for transition is strictly off-label. Nobody cares about us enough to do trans-specific drug research.
You could just take ckers, but that doesn't eally solve everything.
Have you talked to your new guy about surgery?

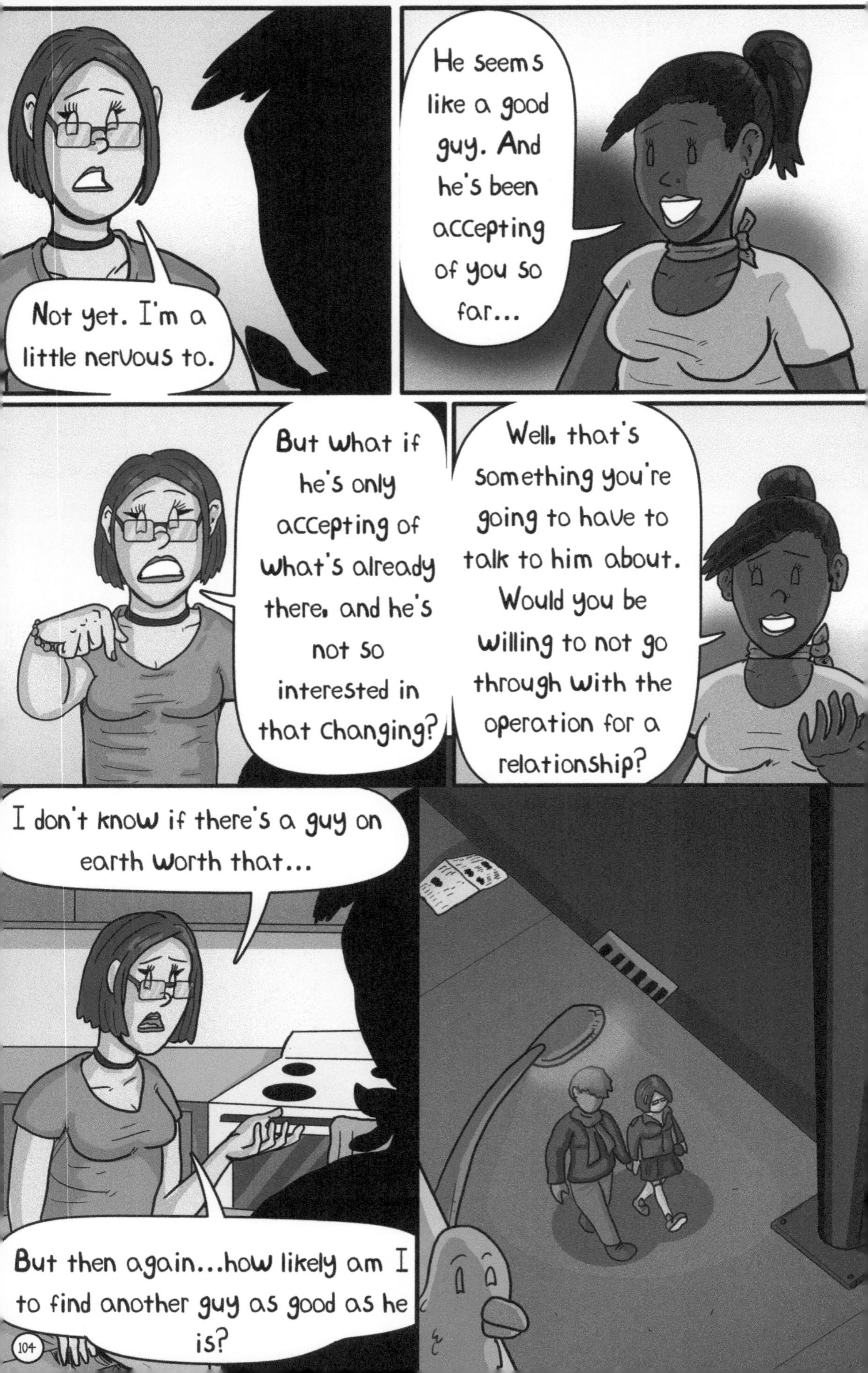
Not yet. I'm a little nervous to.
He seems like a good guy. And he's been accepting of you so far...
But what if he's only accepting of what's already there, and he's not so interested in that changing?
Well, that's something you're going to have to talk to him about. Would you be willing to not go through with the operation for a relationship?
I don't know if there's a guy on earth worth that...
But then again...how likely am I to find another guy as good as he is?

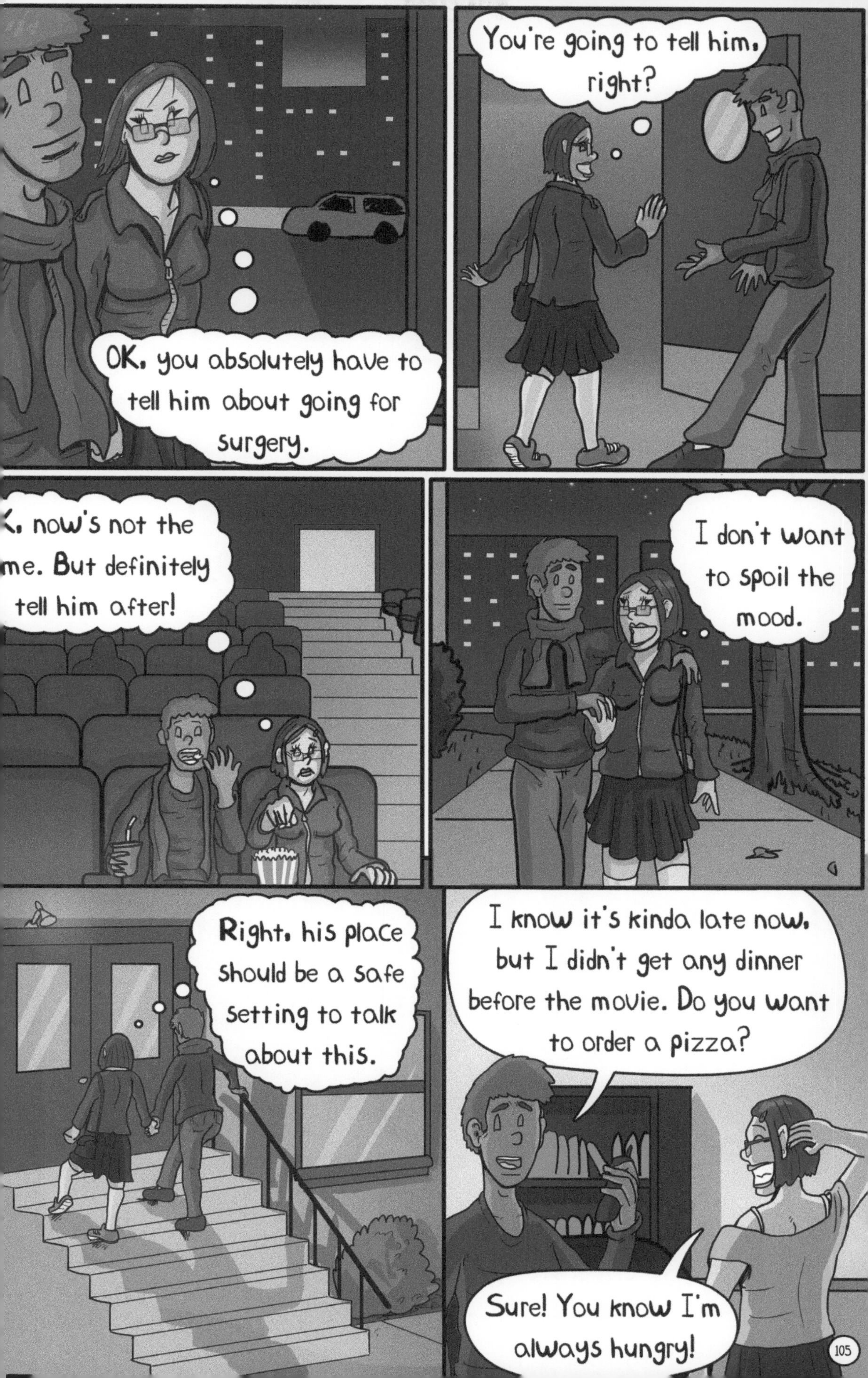
OK, you absolutely have to tell him about going for surgery.
You're going to tell him, right?
K, now's not the
me. But definitely tell him after!
I don't want to spoil the mood.
Right, his place should be a safe setting to talk about this.
I know it's kinda late now, but I didn't get any dinner before the movie. Do you want to order a pizza?
Sure! You know I'm always hungry!

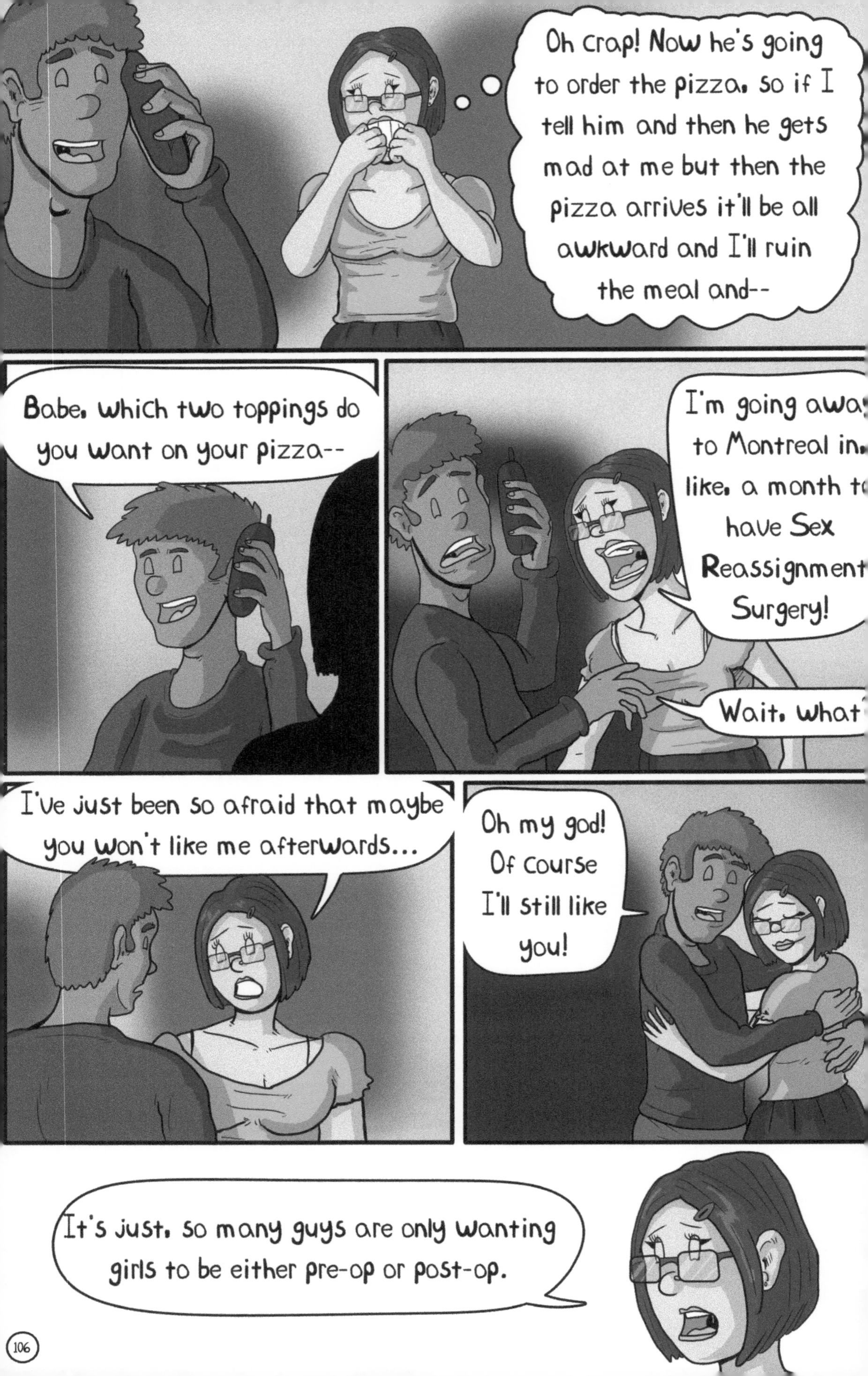
Oh crap! Now he's going to order the pizza, so if I tell him and then he gets mad at me but then the pizza arrives it'll be all awkward and I'll ruin the meal and--
Babe, which two toppings do you want on your pizza--
I'm going away to Montreal in, like, a month to have Sex Reassignment Surgery!
Wait, what
I've just been so afraid that maybe you won't like me afterwards...
Oh my god! Of course I'll still like you!
It's just, so many guys are only wanting girls to be either pre-op or post-op.

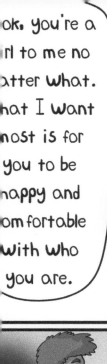

ok, you're a irl to me no atter what. hat I want nost is for you to be happy and omfortable with who you are.

I would still love you just as much if you decided not to do surgery. It's not about what's between your legs. It's about who you are as a person, and I think who you are is pretty great.

Where the hell did a man like you come from and what did I do to deserve having you in my life?

Oh crap, right, the pizza.

Hello? Hello?

Well, I'm going to really miss you while you're gone.

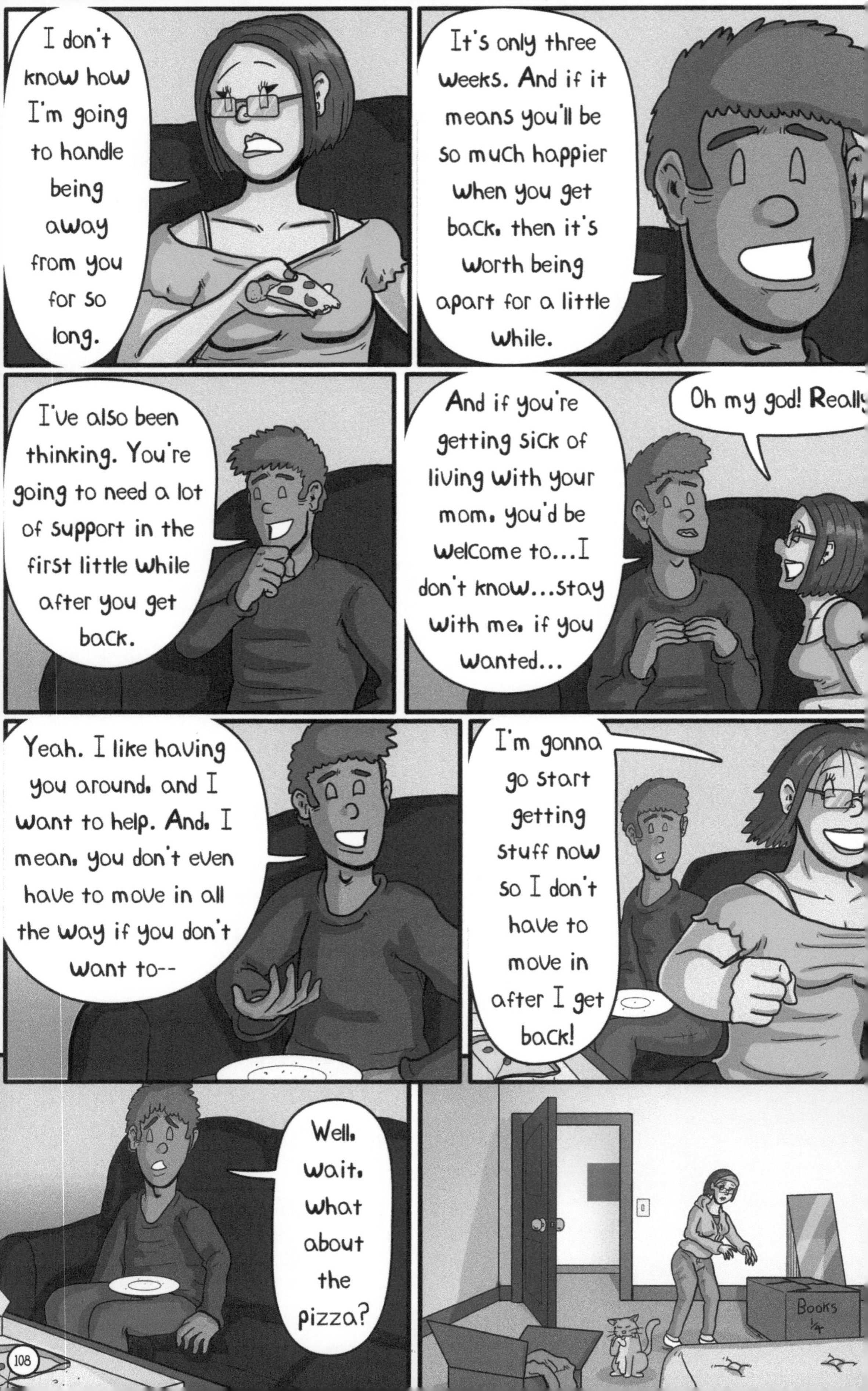
I don't know how I'm going to handle being away from you for so long.
It's only three weeks. And if it means you'll be so much happier when you get back, then it's worth being apart for a little while.
I've also been thinking. You're going to need a lot of support in the first little while after you get back.
And if you're getting sick of living with your mom, you'd be welcome to...I don't know...stay with me, if you wanted...
Oh my god! Really
Yeah. I like having you around, and I want to help. And, I mean, you don't even have to move in all the way if you don't want to--
I'm gonna go start getting stuff now so I don't have to move in after I get back!
Well, wait, what about the pizza?
Books 1/4

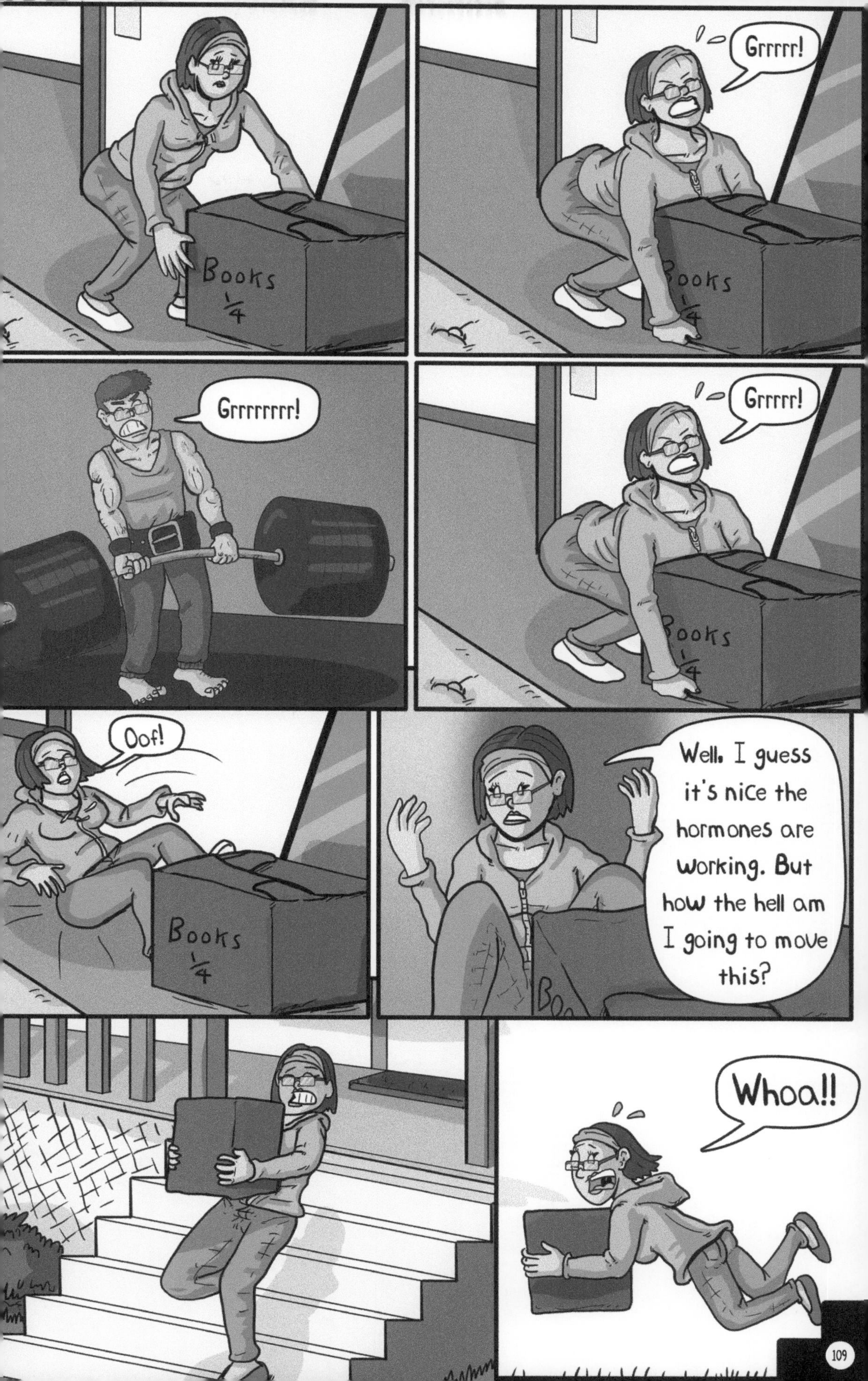
Books
1/4
Grrrrr!
Books
1/4
Grrrrrrrr!
Grrrrr!
Books
1/4
Oof!
Books
1/4
Well. I guess it's nice the hormones are working. But how the hell am I going to move this?
Whoa!!

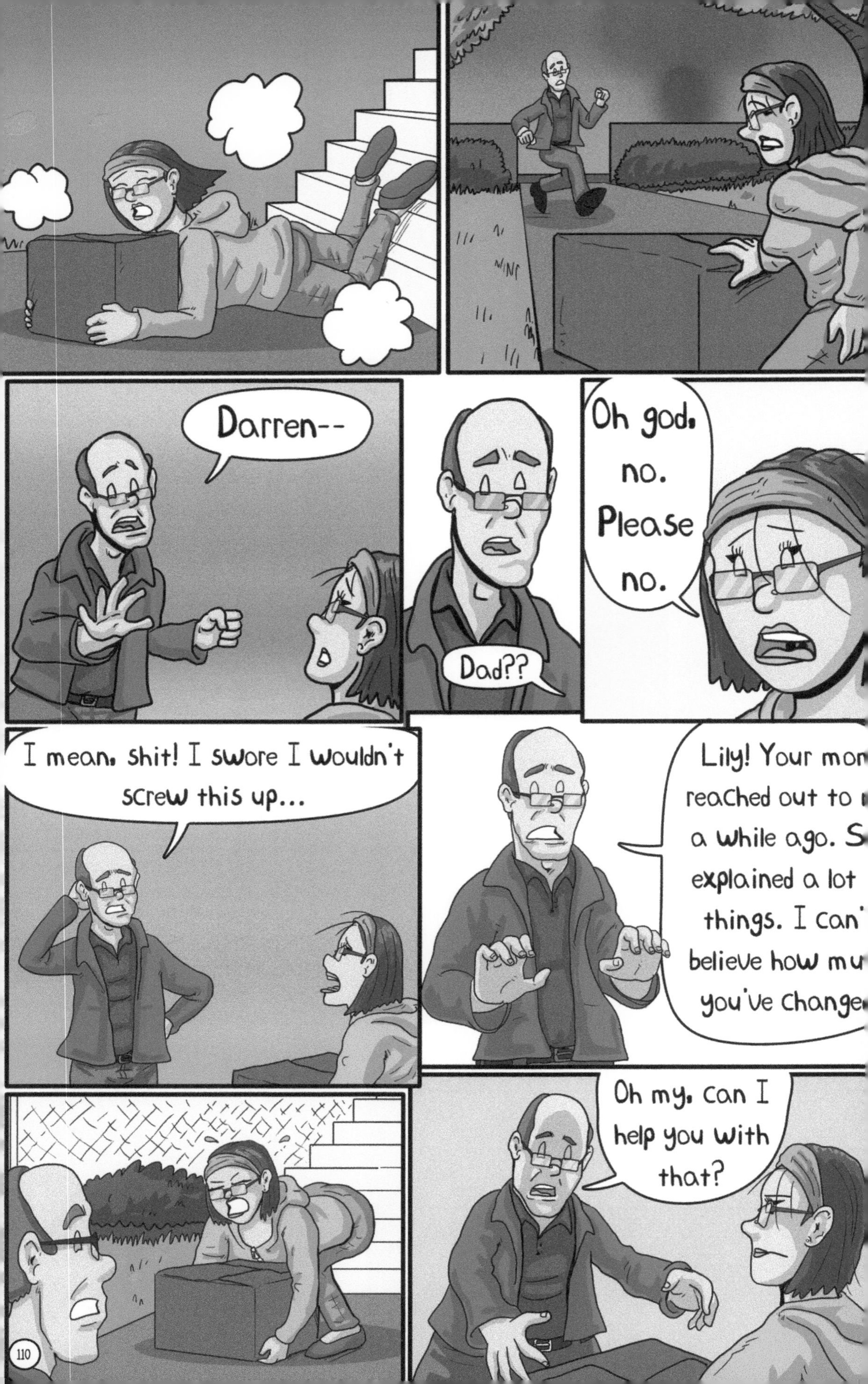
Darren--
Dad??
Oh god, no. Please no.
I mean, shit! I swore I wouldn't screw this up...
Lily! Your mon reached out to a while ago. S explained a lot things. I can' believe how mu you've change
Oh my, can I help you with that?

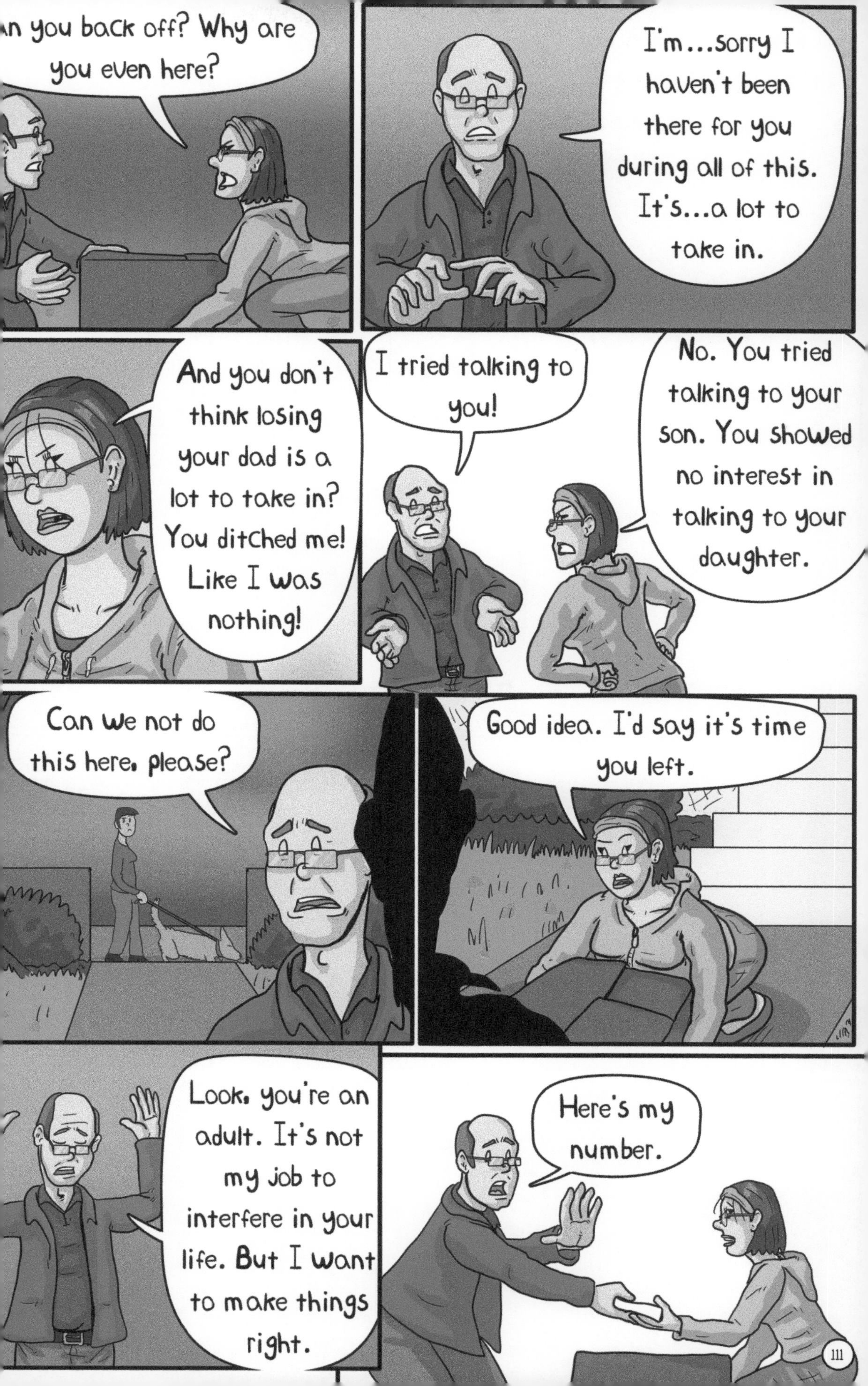
an you back off? Why are you even here?
I'm...sorry I haven't been there for you during all of this. It's...a lot to take in.
And you don't think losing your dad is a lot to take in? You ditched me! Like I was nothing!
I tried talking to you!
No. You tried talking to your son. You showed no interest in talking to your daughter.
Can we not do this here, please?
Good idea. I'd say it's time you left.
Look, you're an adult. It's not my job to interfere in your life. But I want to make things right.
Here's my number.

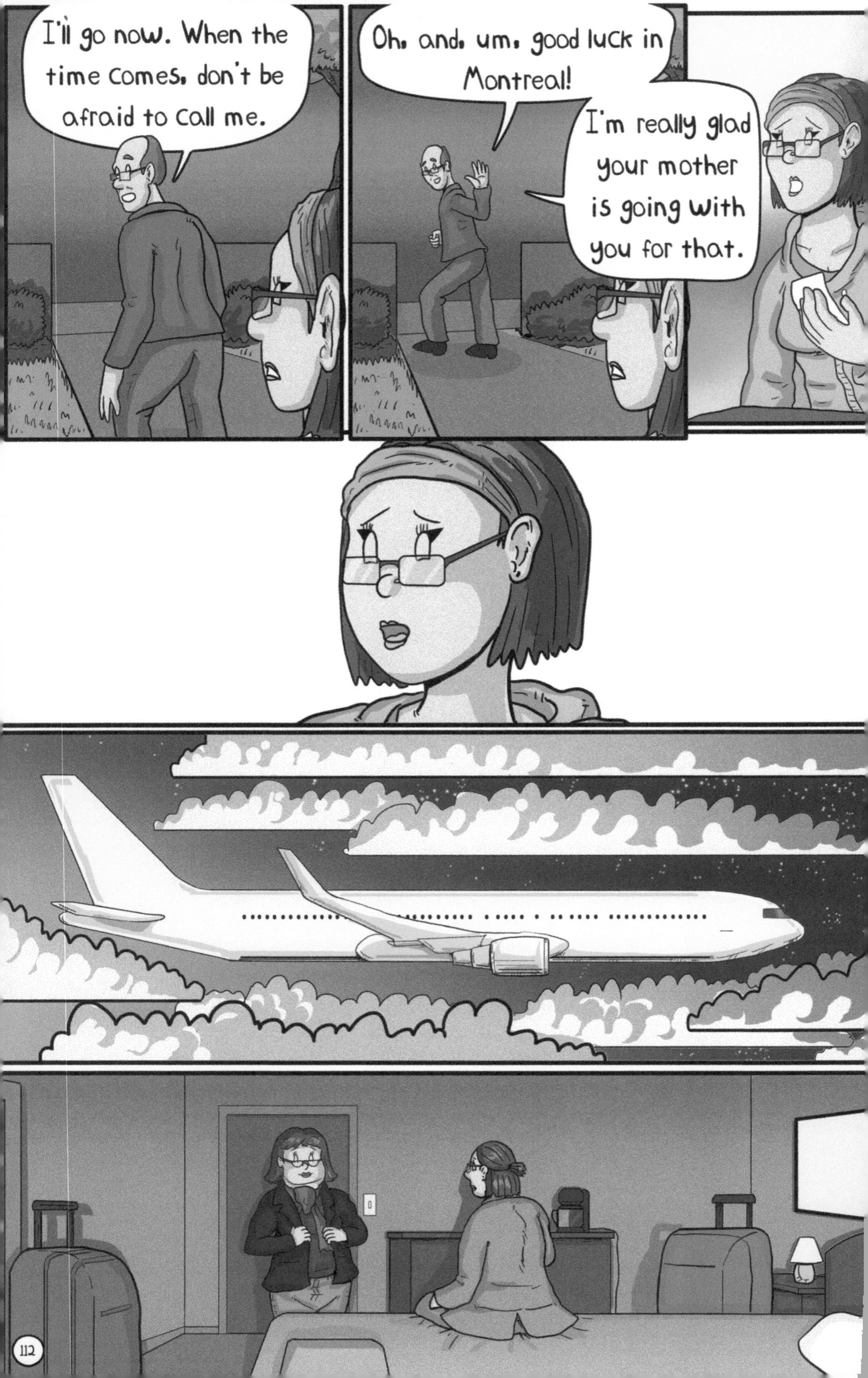
I'll go now. When the time comes, don't be afraid to call me.
Oh, and, um, good luck in Montreal!
I'm really glad your mother is going with you for that.

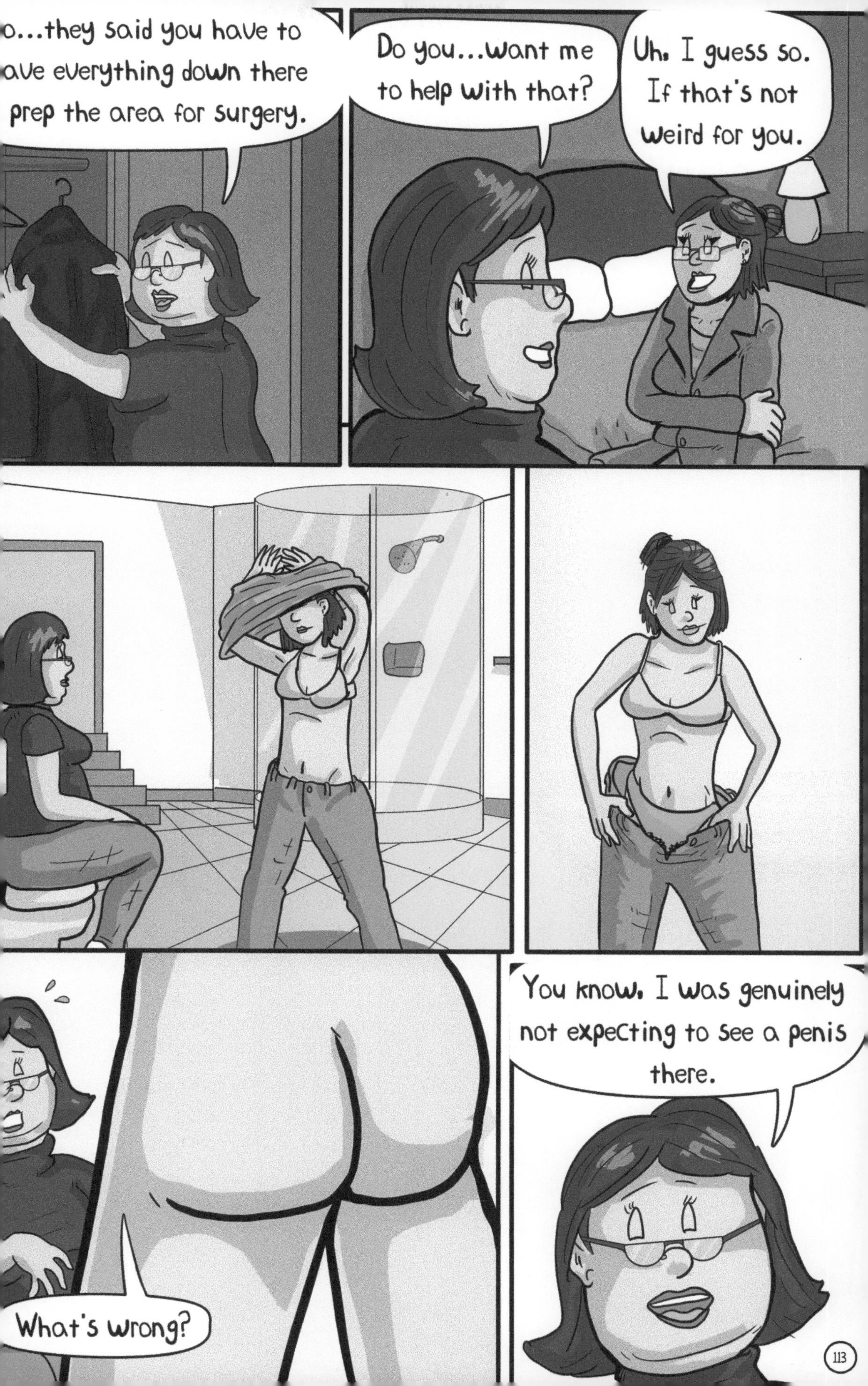
o...they said you have to
ave everything down there
prep the area for surgery.
Do you...want me to help with that?
Uh. I guess so. If that's not weird for you.
What's wrong?
You know. I was genuinely not expecting to see a penis there.

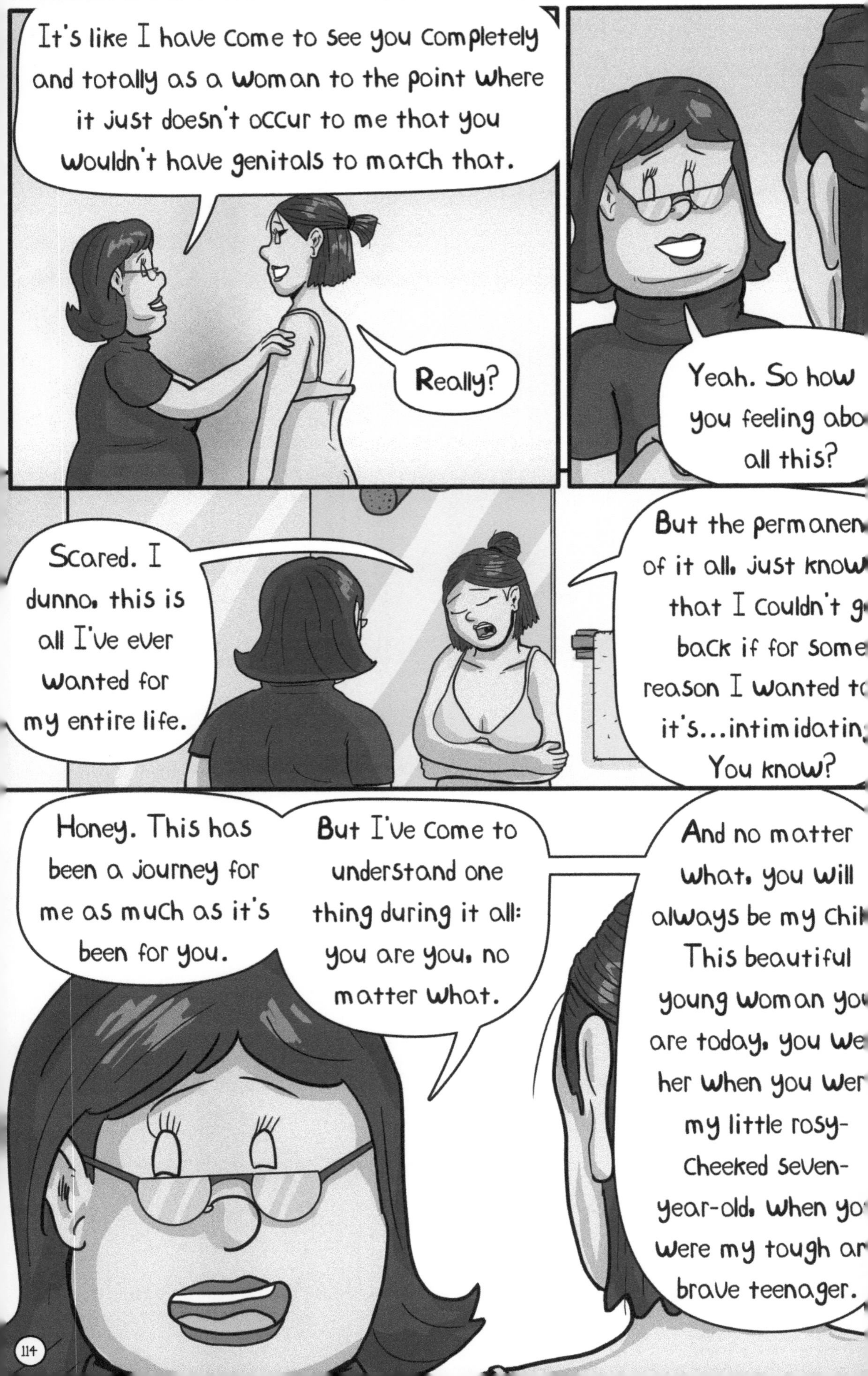

It's like I have come to see you completely and totally as a woman to the point where it just doesn't occur to me that you wouldn't have genitals to match that.
Really?
Yeah. So how you feeling abo all this?
Scared. I dunno, this is all I've ever wanted for my entire life.
But the permanen of it all, just know that I couldn't g back if for some reason I wanted t it's...intimidatin You know?
Honey. This has been a journey for me as much as it's been for you.
But I've come to understand one thing during it all: you are you, no matter what.
And no matter what, you will always be my chil This beautiful young woman yo are today, you we her when you wer my little rosy-cheeked seven-year-old, when yo were my tough ar brave teenager.

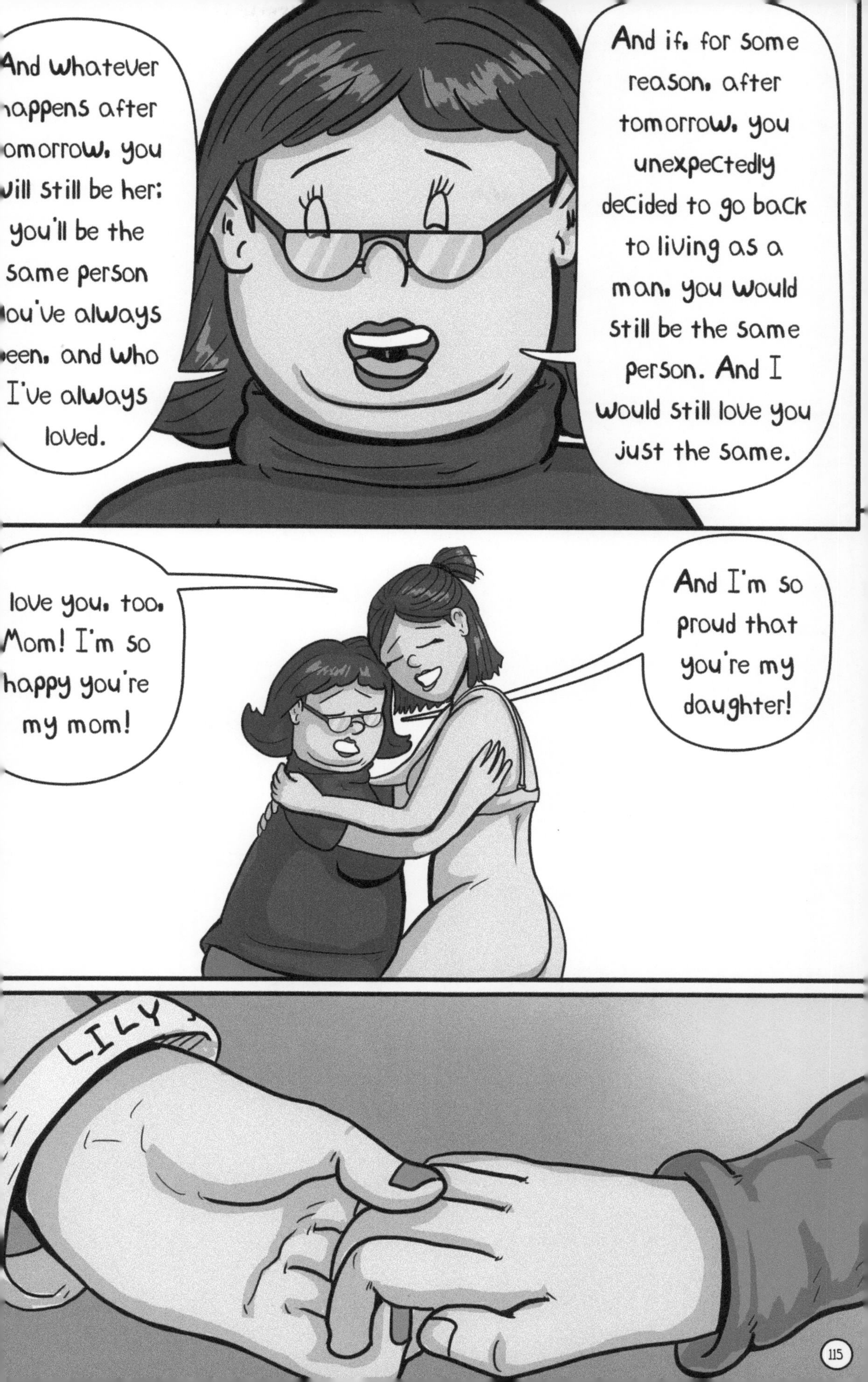
And whatever appens after omorrow, you vill still be her: you'll be the same person ou've always een, and who I've always loved.
And if, for some reason, after tomorrow, you unexpectedly decided to go back to living as a man, you would still be the same person. And I would still love you just the same.
love you, too, Mom! I'm so happy you're my mom!
And I'm so proud that you're my daughter!
LILY

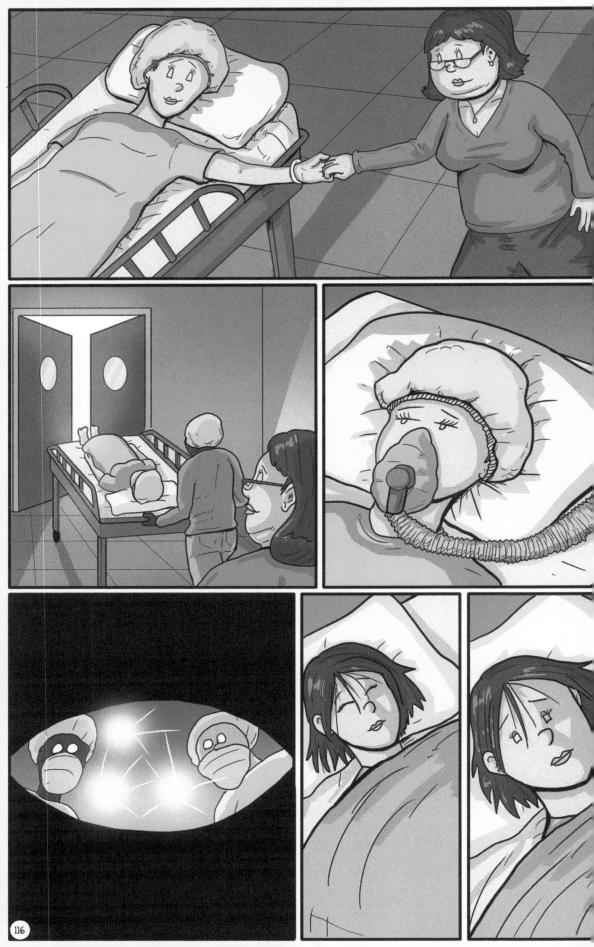

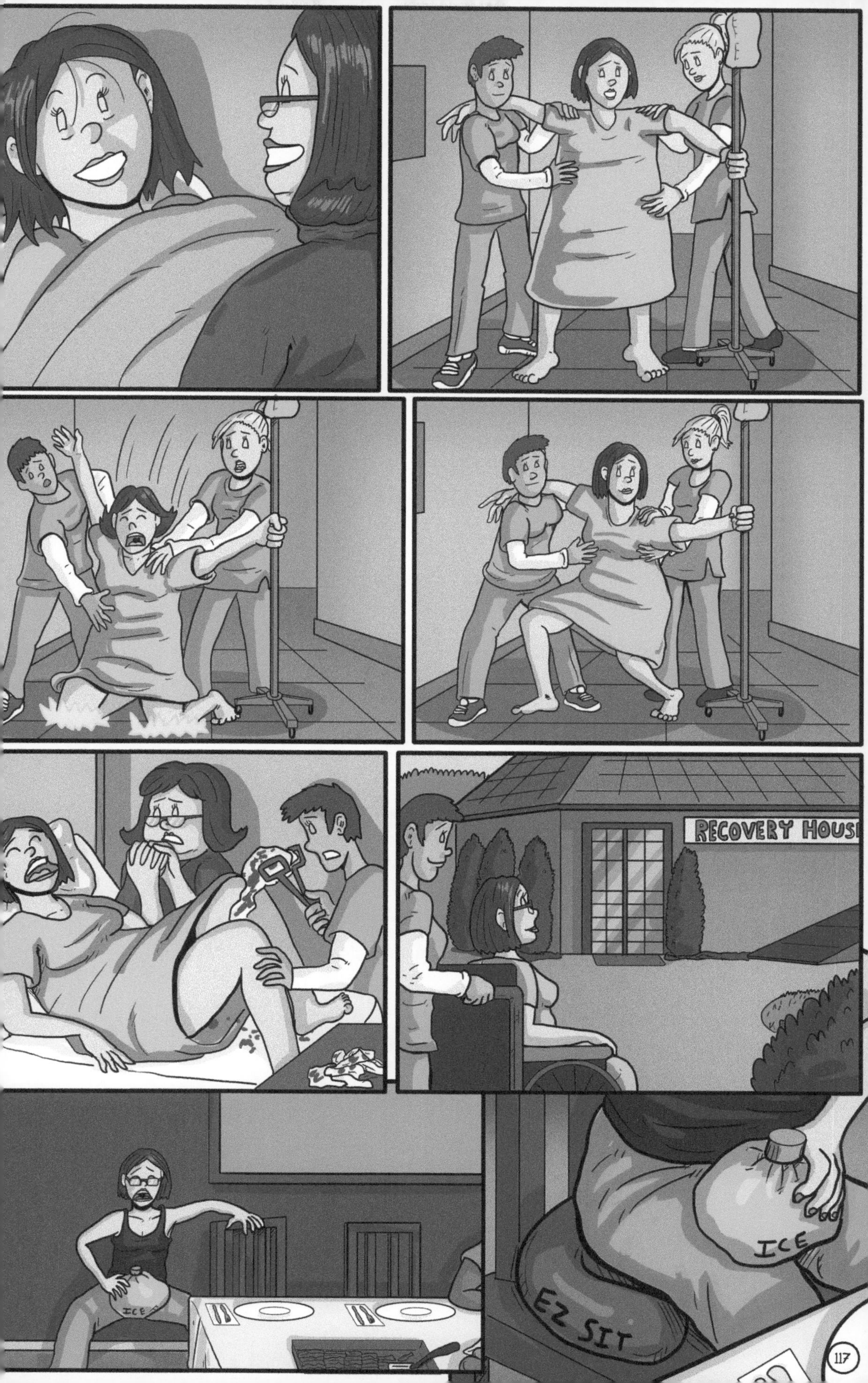
RECOVERY HOUS
ICE
ICE
EZ SIT

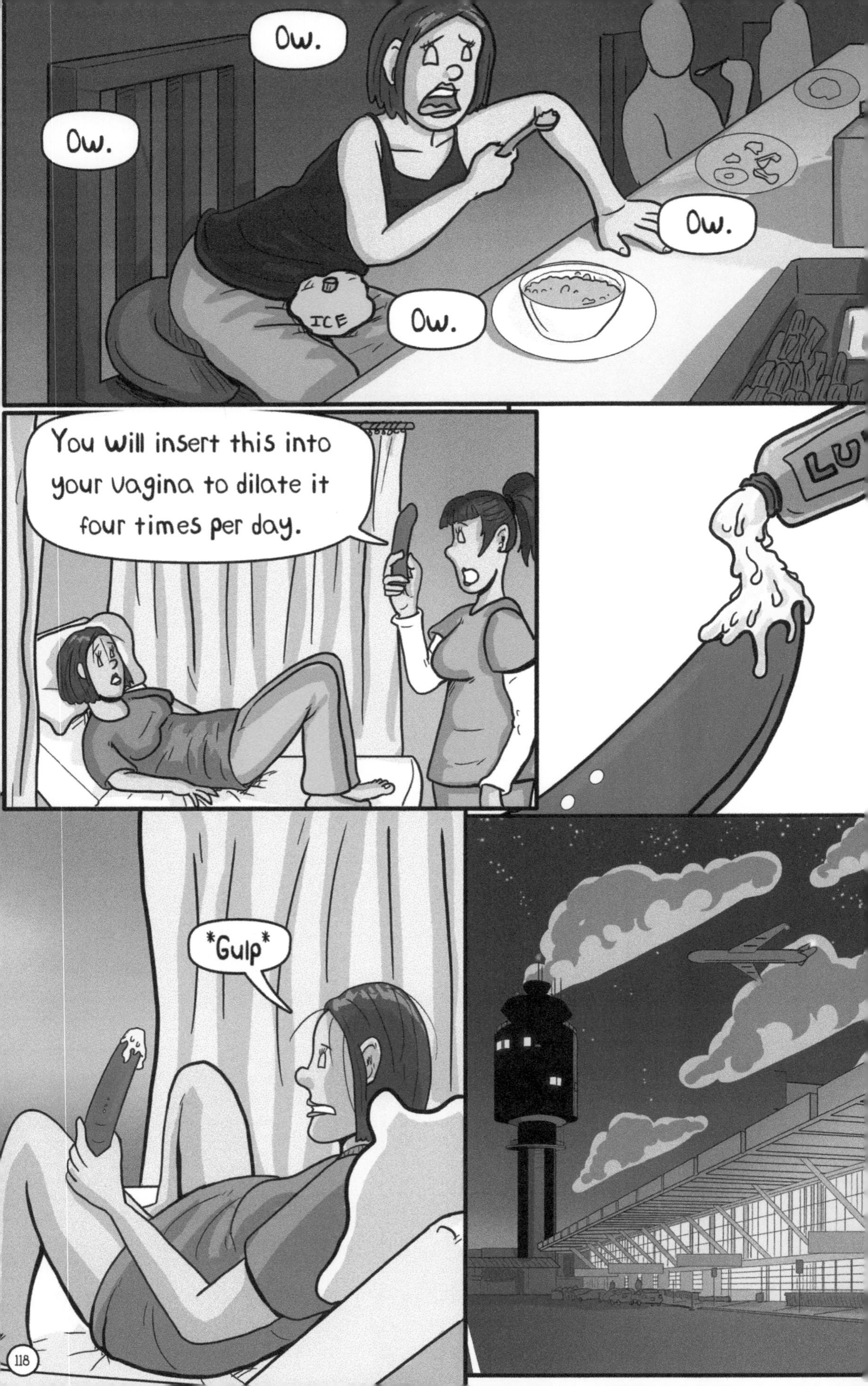
Ow.
Ow.
Ow.
ICE
Ow.
You will insert this into your vagina to dilate it four times per day.
LU
Gulp

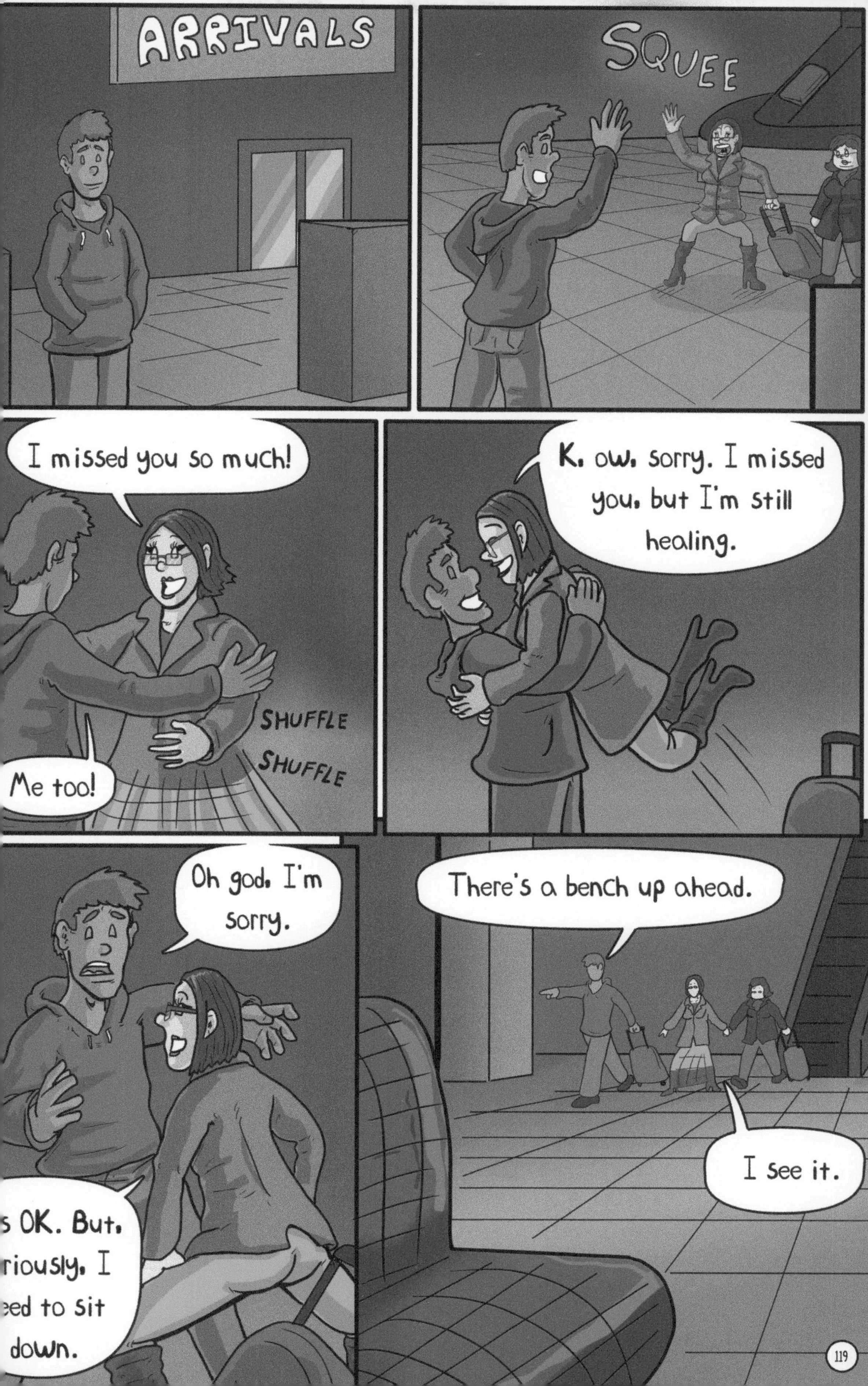
ARRIVALS
SQUEE
I missed you so much!
Me too!
SHUFFLE
SHUFFLE
K, ow, sorry. I missed you, but I'm still healing.
Oh god, I'm sorry.
s OK. But, riously, I eed to sit down.
There's a bench up ahead.
I see it.

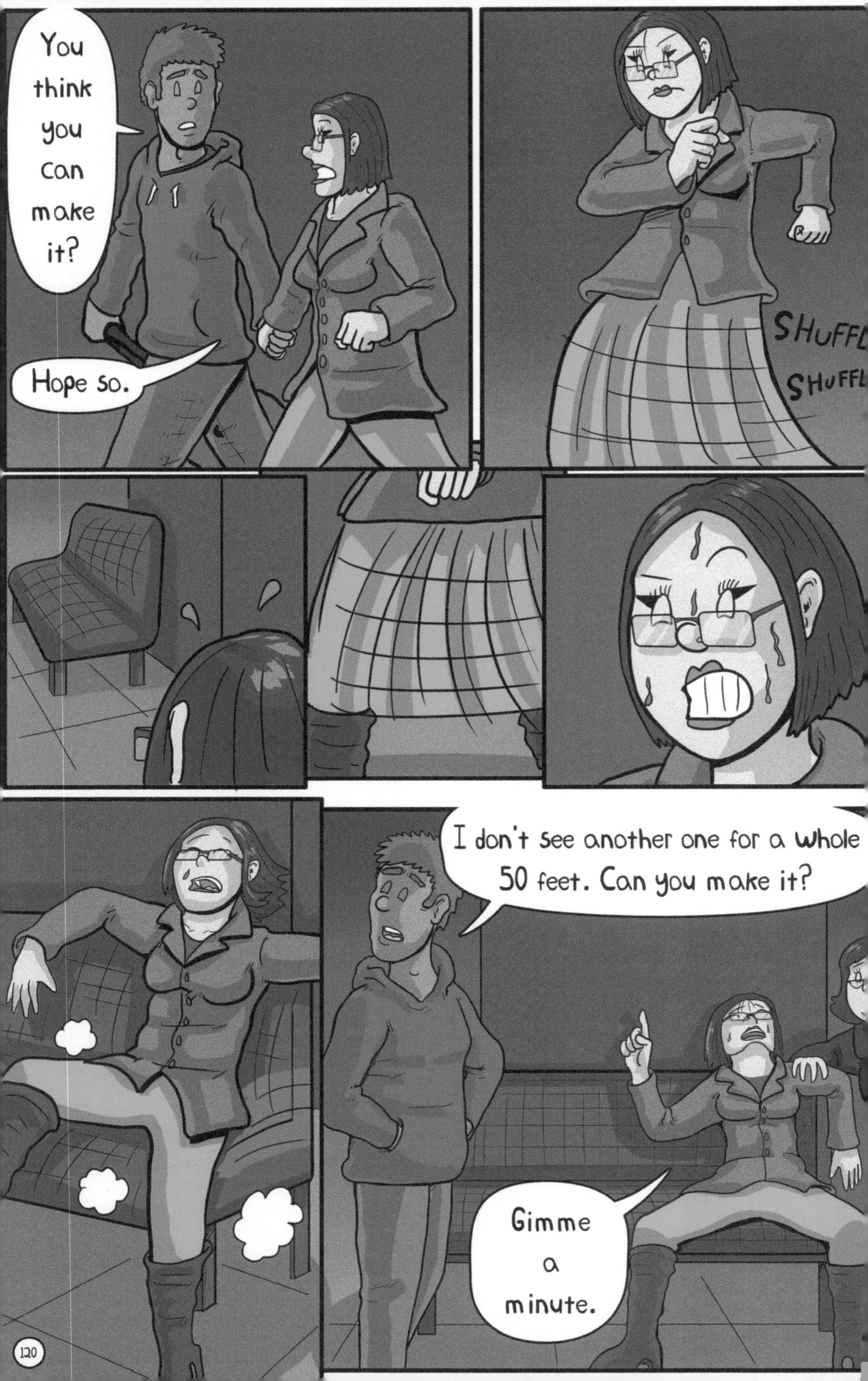
You think you can make it?
Hope so.
SHUFFLE
SHUFFLE
I don't see another one for a whole 50 feet. Can you make it?
Gimme a minute.

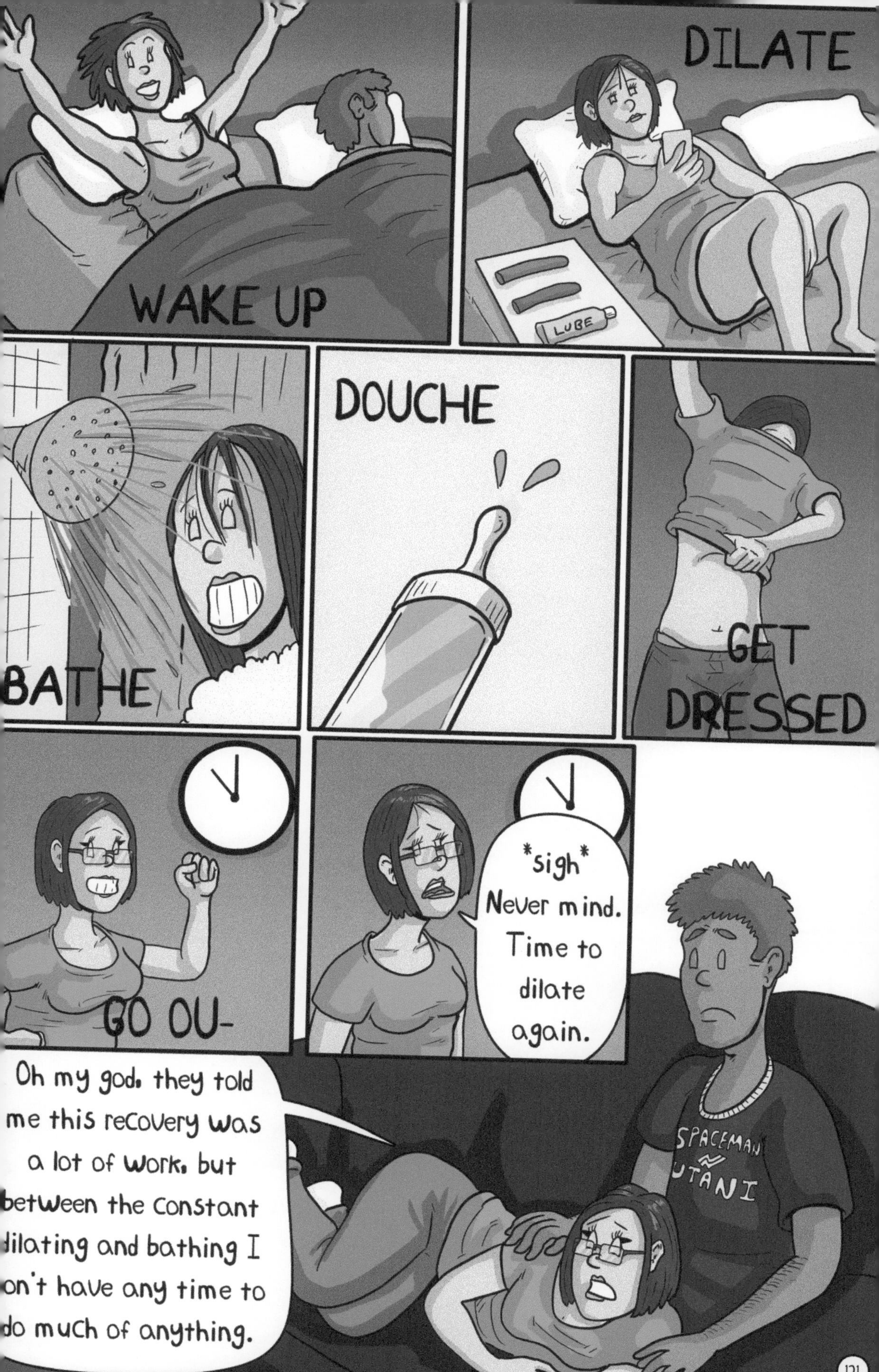
WAKE UP
DILATE
LUBE
BATHE
DOUCHE
GET DRESSED
GO OU-
sigh Never mind. Time to dilate again.
Oh my god. they told me this recovery was a lot of work. but between the constant dilating and bathing I don't have any time to do much of anything.
SPACEMAN UTANI

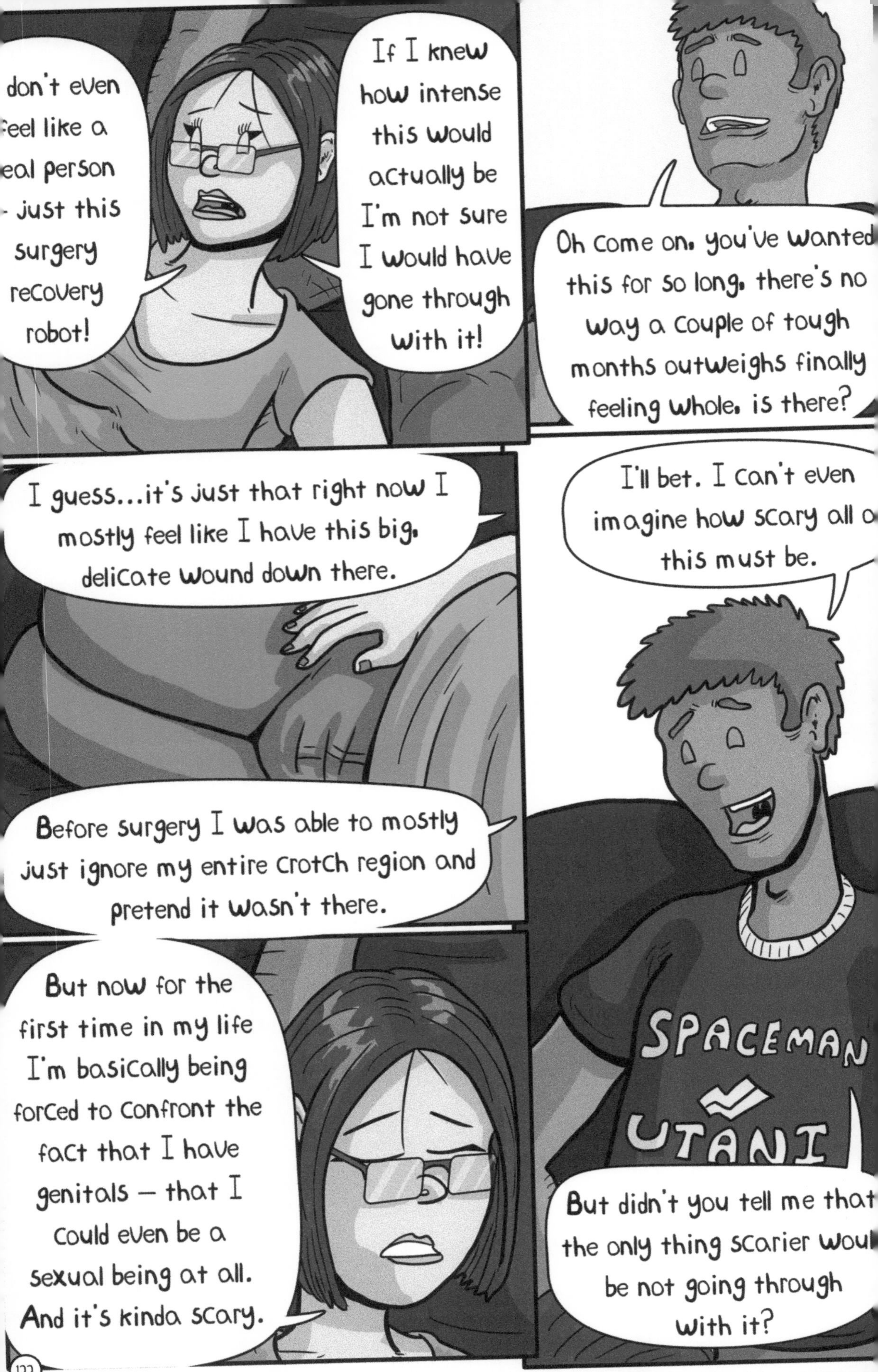
don't even feel like a eal person - just this surgery recovery robot!
If I knew how intense this would actually be I'm not sure I would have gone through with it!
Oh come on. you've wanted this for so long. there's no way a couple of tough months outweighs finally feeling whole. is there?
I guess...it's just that right now I mostly feel like I have this big. delicate wound down there.
I'll bet. I can't even imagine how scary all o this must be.
Before surgery I was able to mostly just ignore my entire crotch region and pretend it wasn't there.
SPACEMAN UTANI
But now for the first time in my life I'm basically being forced to confront the fact that I have genitals – that I could even be a sexual being at all. And it's kinda scary.
But didn't you tell me that the only thing scarier woul be not going through with it?

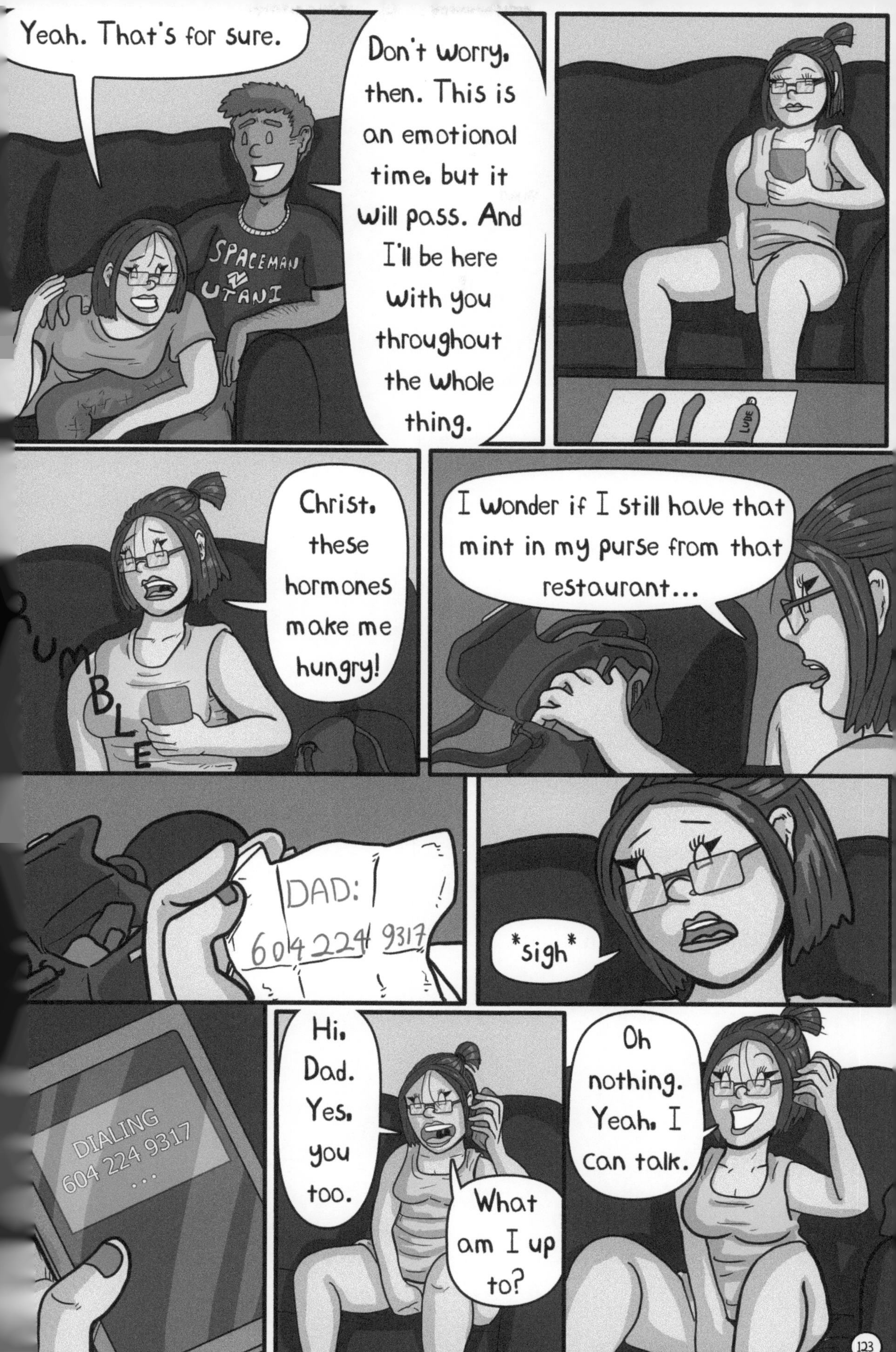

Yeah. That's for sure.
SPACEMAN UTANI
Don't worry, then. This is an emotional time, but it will pass. And I'll be here with you throughout the whole thing.
LUBE
RUMBLE
Christ, these hormones make me hungry!
I wonder if I still have that mint in my purse from that restaurant...
DAD: 604 224 9317
sigh
DIALING 604 224 9317 ...
Hi, Dad. Yes, you too.
What am I up to?
Oh nothing. Yeah, I can talk.

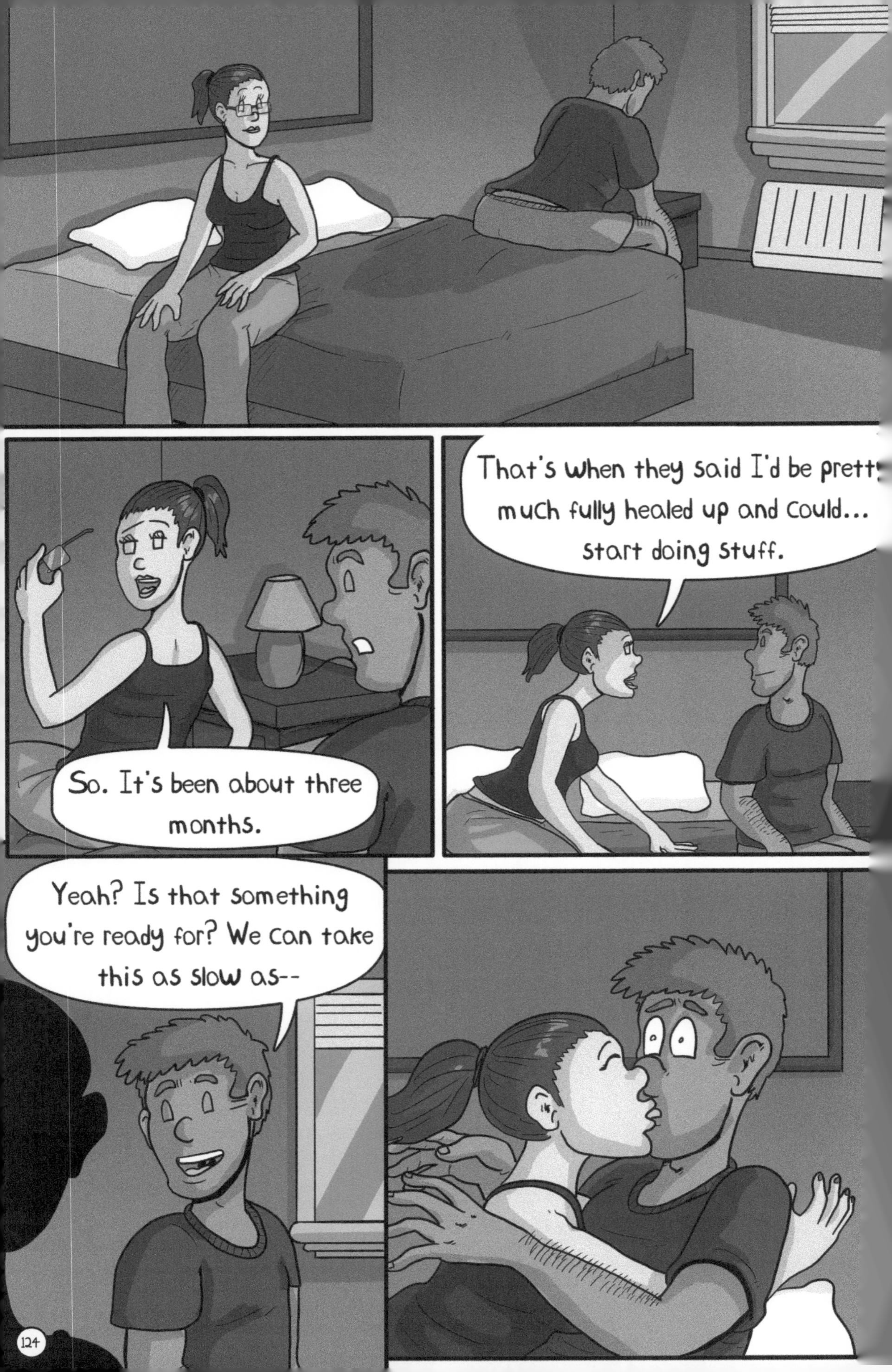
So. It's been about three months.
That's when they said I'd be prett
much fully healed up and could... start doing stuff.
Yeah? Is that something you're ready for? We can take this as slow as--

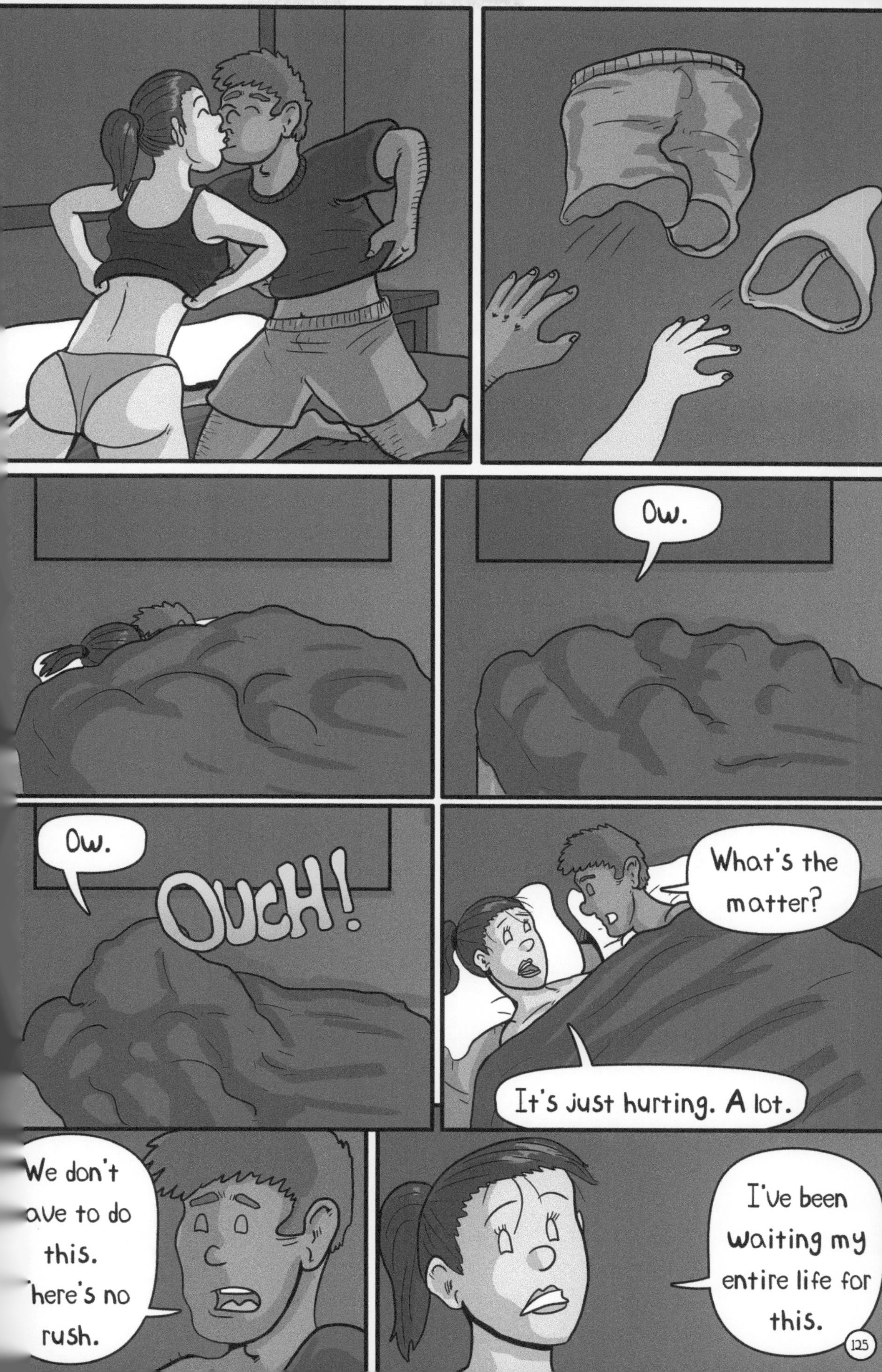
Ow.
Ow.
OUCH!
What's the matter?
It's just hurting. A lot.
We don't
ave to do
this.
here's no
rush.
I've been waiting my entire life for this.

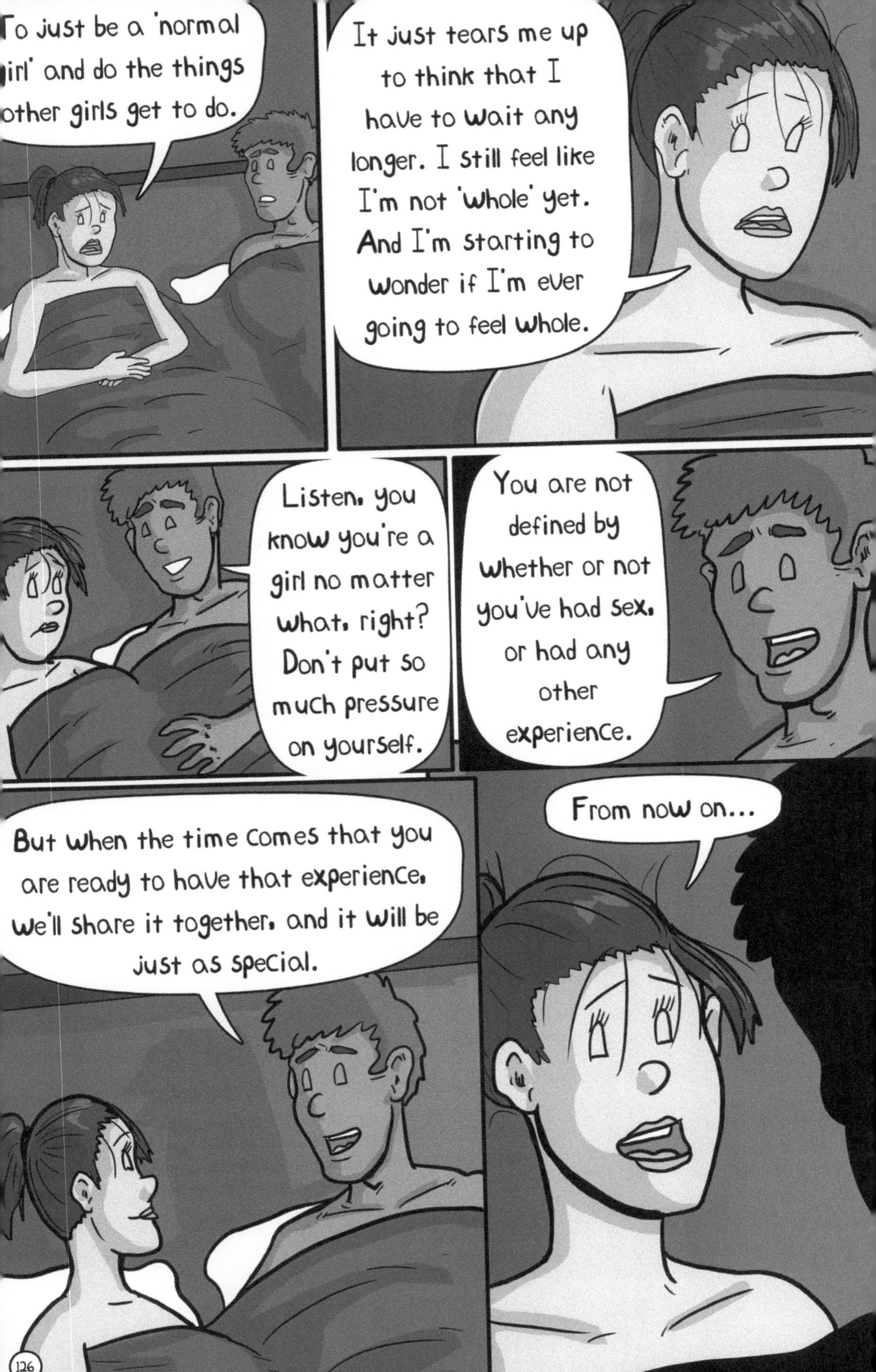

To just be a 'normal girl' and do the things other girls get to do.
It just tears me up to think that I have to wait any longer. I still feel like I'm not 'whole' yet. And I'm starting to wonder if I'm ever going to feel whole.
Listen, you know you're a girl no matter what, right? Don't put so much pressure on yourself.
You are not defined by whether or not you've had sex, or had any other experience.
But when the time comes that you are ready to have that experience, we'll share it together, and it will be just as special.
From now on...

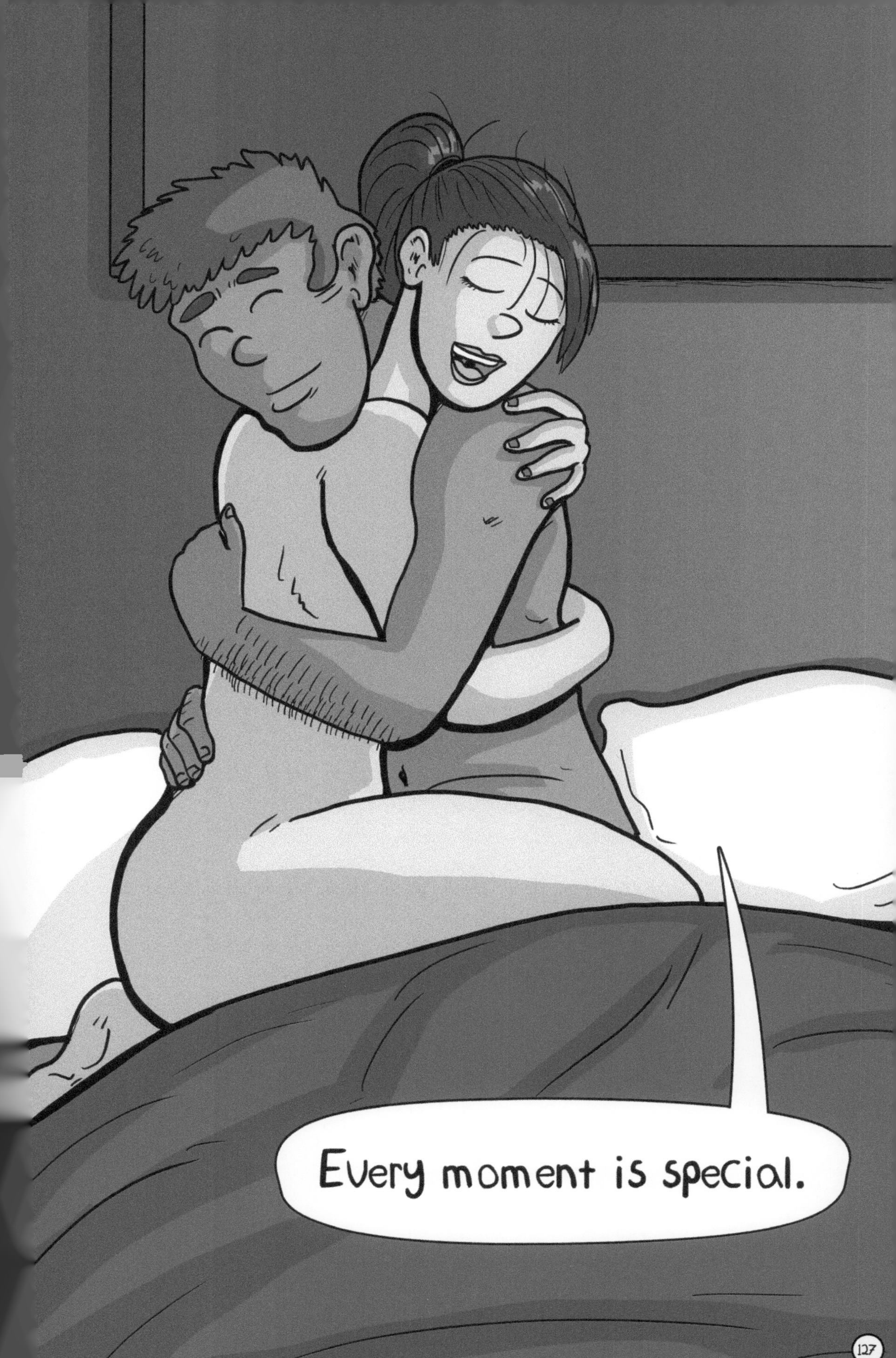
Every moment is special.

First edition published in hardback in Great Britain in 2018
by Jessica Kingsley Publishers
This paperback edition published in Great Britain in 2023
by Jessica Kingsley Publishers
An imprint of Hodder & Stoughton Ltd
An Hachette UK Company

1

A CIP catalogue record for this title is available from the British Library
and the Library of Congress

ISBN 978 1 83997 772 5
eISBN 978 0 85701 303 3

Printed and bound in Great Britain by Ashford Colour Press

Jessica Kingsley Publishers' policy is to use papers that are natural, renewable
and recyclable products and made from wood grown in sustainable forests.
The logging and manufacturing processes are expected to conform to the
environmental regulations of the country of origin.

Jessica Kingsley Publishers
Carmelite House
50 Victoria Embankment
London EC4Y 0DZ

www.jkp.com